HISTORICAL PATTERNS OF INDUSTRIALIZATION

Also available from Longman by Tom Kemp:

Industrialization in Nineteenth-Century Europe (second edition 1985)
Industrialization in the Non-Western World (second edition 1989)
The Climax of Capitalism (1990)

Historical Patterns of Industrialization

Second Edition

Tom Kemp

Longman
London and New York

Longman Group UK Ltd,
Longman House, Burnt Mill,
Harlow, Essex CM20 2JE, England
and Associated Companies throughout the world.

*Published in the United States of America
by Longman Publishing, New York,*

First published 1978
Sixth impression 1989
Second edition 1993

ISBN 0 582 09547 6

British Library Cataloguing in Publication Data
A catalogue record for this book is
available from the British Library

Library of Congress Cataloging-in-Publication Data
Kemp, Tom.
    Historical patterns of industrialization / Tom Kemp. – 2nd ed.
        p.   cm.
    Companion volume to: Industrialization in the non-Western world.
2nd ed. 1989.
    Includes bibliographical references and index.
    ISBN 0–582–09547–6
    1. Industrialization – History.   2. Economic history.   3. Economic
development.   I. Title.
    HD2321.K43   1993
    338.09 – dc20   92–7494
                                                                        CIP

Set by 9B in 10/12 pt Bembo

Printed in Malaysia by PA

Contents

Preface to the First Edition

Like its predecessor, *Industrialization in Nineteenth-Century Europe*, this book is addressed principally to students of economic history and the social sciences. It assumes that it will be read and used as part of a programme of study making use of the books and articles mentioned in the 'Bibliography', but does not take a great deal of prior knowledge for granted. To be useful such a book must be readable and yet must tax the reader's comprehension – and, hopefully, keep him awake. If he has to resort occasionally to a dictionary that is not a bad thing. If some points are not immediately intelligible they may become so as his knowledge of the subject improves, and the aim of this book, among other things, is to improve it.

In some ways this book does not fit in entirely with economic history as it is taught – on a country basis, beginning, and often ending, mainly with Britain since the Industrial Revolution. That is not to say that it may not have some application to such courses, at least as supplementary reading. But it may also help those teachers already moving towards a less conventional teaching programme centred around problems of industrialization, economic growth and development in which economic history is blended with political economy and development economics.

In the previous volume emphasis was laid on Europe as a counter-weight to the insular trend of much economic history. This book is equally conscious of the defects of Eurocentrism and considers the development of non-European areas. Much remains to be done, of course, particularly in the economic history of the advanced countries. It is amazing, for example, how little is said about Britain's economic ties with India and other parts of the Empire in most textbooks of nineteenth-century economic history; there is still not a good study of Indian economic history from an up-to-date standpoint despite an increasing volume of specialized work by Indians and foreigners.

Despite a considerable literature on Japan, there is still not a textbook that can be wholeheartedly recommended. Even for Canada there is only one good modern textbook, and interest in Canadian economic history seems to be at a low ebb. Perhaps the present volume will do something to stimulate interest in these countries' economic history.

A book such as this is bound to be derivative. It depends upon the work of innumerable economic historians and other scholars, upon discussions with colleagues and students over many years. It does not profess to be a work of originality or research, and lengthy references and footnotes would therefore be out of place. The principal books used are acknowledged in the bibliography, though the fact that it is intended for use by students means that it is confined to those available in English (though not necessarily still in print).

This book was written in 1976 and the first weeks of 1977 against the somewhat turbulent background of the Department of Economic and Social History in the University of Hull. Mike Brown was kind enough to read the drafts and to give me the benefit of his experience as a teacher. I am also grateful to the anonymous readers appointed by the publishers for their helpful comments.

T.K.

Preface to the Second Edition

Preface to the First Edition

The steady, if modest, demand for this book since its first publication in 1978 suggests that a revision would be timely, making it possible to review the text from the perspective of the closing decade of the twentieth century. Indeed, the economic life of that century owes possibly more to industrialization than to any other factor. Despite its contemporary references, however, the subject matter of this book was, and remains, primarily historical. But while being the work of an economic historian with students in mind, it aspired to find a wider audience by showing what light a study of economic history might shed on contemporary trends and problems. Practitioners of this discipline are as divided as those of others and it cannot prescribe courses of action as such. My own points of view will become obvious to the reader; there is no attempt at a spurious objectivity or to impose my views on the readers who are hereby invited to work out their own positions. While being firmly based in the past, the book hopefully suggested that economic history might throw some light on the present, whether or not we may think that it has any 'lessons' to convey.

It is worth pointing out to the reader that this volume followed an earlier book, *Industrialization in Nineteenth-Century Europe*, which sought to give a broad picture of the different approaches to industrialization in the main European countries. It was also aiming to get away from the rather insular tendency of economic history in Britain at that time – which has to a considerable extent been overcome since.

The present volume was conceived with the object of moving away from a 'Eurocentred' view to take in the experience of non-European countries but without losing sight of the continued validity of the European models. Probably it did not fully succeed in this laudable objective and continued to be too influenced by European examples.

viii

This revised edition does not attempt to overcome this shortcoming, if it is such, since it would require a much more basic revision than is offered here. However, the reader's attention is drawn to the other companion volume, *Industrialization in the Non-Western World* (second edition 1989) based on six case studies of industrialization outside 'the Western World'. Some of the questions dealt with in the present volume are pursued more fully in its successor, which is more closely concerned with contemporary trends while attempting to show the need to trace each country's problems to its historical roots. One of the serious criticisms of the first edition was that the links were not close enough between the case studies and the thematic chapters. It has not been possible to deal fully with this question within the framework of the original book, indeed it would require a different book.

This edition contains a new chapter on South Africa intended as a very basic introduction to the economic history of that country. There is a considerable body of writing about the economic history of South Africa and it is reasonably well represented in the universities. It does not seem to be particularly well known among students of economic history in Britain or the United States. This chapter may help to explain the sources of apartheid and the reason for its collapse, though it must be stressed that it was written at a time when South Africa stood at an historic crossroads. It is to be hoped also that students in South Africa who read this book will, by comparison with the other countries dealt with, obtain a better idea of the specific characteristics of the process of industrialization in their own country

The addition of a chapter on South Africa is a result of the goadings of Professor Kathleen Monro of the Economic History Division of the University of the Witwatersrand, Johannesburg, but she has absolutely nothing to do with its contents. I can only thank her for her encouragement and confess my lack of experience in the field of South African studies.

An attempt has been made to incorporate, at any rate briefly, into this volume the enormous changes brought about by the collapse of the economies of Eastern Europe and the former Soviet Union. The Soviet model of industrialization had long ago lost its attractive power in most parts of the world. It had become clear, too, that the Soviet Union was not able either to catch up with Western capitalism on its own terms or to project alternative goals or patterns of consumption.

Finally something is said about the spectacular growth of the newly-industrializing Asian countries, apparently undermining some older generalizations. Their 'success' has generated some perhaps exaggerated enthusiasm for the export-orientated model of industrialization.

Some recent titles have been added to the bibliography, which remains selective.

This book is dedicated to my wife of 45 years.

Gravesend, April, 1992

CHAPTER ONE

Presentation

During the past twenty-five years economic history has made great strides as a university discipline in Britain as well as internationally. The sheer weight of writing and research findings published in the field must greatly exceed everything previously available to the student or interested reader. The emphasis on problems of growth and development by economists and politicians, reflecting the imperious demands of a troubled world, has given it more relevance than ever. But when we come to consider the influence and attraction of economic history to those outside the lecture room or library – and indeed to many inside – some sobering reflections are in order.

As the subject has gained more votaries, become more professional and specialized, something of the common touch has been lost. The tendency towards antiquarianism that dogs all historical studies is complemented by the attempt to apply more advanced theoretical and statistical techniques requiring two or three years' study in the field in question. Much of the literature therefore tends to be a battlefield for the specialist, or rather for the various sorts of specialists between whom only slender ties of sympathy and comprehension may exist. This situation is not unique to economic history; growing academism is, perhaps, the price that has to be paid for any growth in learning and expansion of the universities.

Despite their multiplication in numbers, economic historians have not in recent years made a proportionate contribution of general validity to the social sciences. The specialist studies remain disconnected as pieces of research; controversy has often focused upon secondary issues. The need for guidance from the specialist in the field is shown by the alacrity with which theories and explanations of past economic development put forward by those with a power to

1

communicate have been taken up. The best known and most influential of these was undoubtedly the Rostow stage theory, which for some time swept all before it and is now generally discredited*. But one-sided and schematic as it was, it generated enormous interest well outside the ranks of economic historians and resulted in a considerable amount of research being done, deepening our knowledge of the process of industrialization. Nevertheless, the non-specialist understanding of, say, the Industrial Revolution in Britain in neighbouring disciplines such as economics and sociology tends to reflect the influence of outdated stereotypes and concepts including those of Rostow.

Economic historians need to be able to feed into wider circles the results of knowledge and investigations in their discipline. For that, of course, they have to have confidence in its value. Of this there should be no doubt; in fact, such a doubt can come only from someone who is intensely preoccupied by one narrow study or problem, neglecting both the broader sweep of economic development and the interconnections between economic history and other disciplines.

Like *Industrialization in Nineteenth-Century Europe*, the present book is addressed to the teacher and student concerned with introductory courses; it presents an interpretation rather than a detailed description and is intended as an invitation to further study. It may be said that it lacks rigour by the standards of the quantitative history in vogue today or that its theoretical framework is not sufficiently explicit. Without wishing to disarm what may be well-founded criticisms, the aim of this book, like its predecessor, is to stimulate interest and show the contribution that economic history can make to the understanding of the modern world and the problems of our time. This is conspicuously what much of the work published as economic history fails to do. Most of it, although academically impeccable and written at a high level, consists of specialists addressing specialists and fails to score with most students or even with many of their teachers.

There was a time when economic history, and its close cousin, social history, evoked much interest on the part of adult students and readers. It is only necessary to refer, for example, to the influence of writers like Tawney and the Hammonds and, in a somewhat different context to Weber and Sombart. Other names could no doubt be mentioned from the past, and there are worthy successors today –

---

* Rostow stage theory, see Rostow, W. W., *The Stages of Economic Growth*, Cambridge U. P., 1971.

Fernand Braudel or Carlo Cipolla, for example, to avoid invidious choices from among British historians. What distinguishes these historians is their willingness to embark upon informed syntheses, trusting in insight without being deterred by charges of dogma or *a priori* reasoning from making a hypothesis where lack of factual material precludes a definitive statement.

Even before the current interest in problems of growth and development, many leading economists have been aware of the contribution economic history can make to theory. Marx and Engels, for instance, wrote economic history long before it emerged as an academic discipline, as part of their attempt to reveal the laws of human development. Among their disciples Lenin and Rosa Luxemburg made major contributions to the subject, the former in *The Development of Capitalism in Russia*, while the latter's doctoral dissertation (not translated into English) was entitled *The Industrial Development of Poland*. But it is not only the Marxists who have been aware of the value of history in the formulation of economic theory. That high priest of neoclassical orthodoxy, Alfred Marshall, carried out a good deal of research into economic history for his *Industry and Trade* (which can be still read today with profit). Both John Maynard Keynes and Josef Schumpeter, who rank among the leading economists of the first half of the twentieth century, wrote economic history and were appreciative of its contribution. Needless to say, many specialists in other fields, notably economists, have written economic history after the style of Monsieur Jourdain. It is regrettable, therefore, that there should be a tendency among economists today – though it is not the only tendency – to draw a sharp dividing line between analysis and history and to neglect the contribution that economic history can make to a general economic education or to the understanding of contemporary economic problems. However, this is not entirely the fault of specialists in economics; it is also, in part, a consequence of the way in which the subject has developed as an academic discipline, with the emphasis on the historical rather than the economic component. Admittedly, there are contrary tendencies, among which, fortunately, is an emphasis on theoretical analysis and explanation.

It is hoped that the reader of this book will at least feel that economic history is a subject with some vitality, indeed that it has an indispensable contribution to make to the understanding of the problems of the contemporary world. Yet it is disturbing to find that many economic historians appear to have lost confidence in its abililty to make such a contribution. It is not surprising, therefore, that non-economic historians and even many economists tend to neglect the lessons that may be derived from it. On the credit side, whatever one may think about the attempts by the 'new' economic historians to apply econometric methods to historical material or to try to work out whether development would have been different – and by how much – if one or another factor had not been present, they do believe that there are some lessons to be drawn from history. No attempt will be made to encroach on these fields, for venture into which the student has to be equipped with a knowledge of statistical and econometric techniques requiring considerable study and effort to acquire. The student has in any case to have a knowledge of the broader historical trends before he can embark on the study of detailed problems, whatever method he uses. It is not sufficient to deal in detail with the history of one country in a relatively short period, as economic history in Britain has tended to be dominated by the study of the Industrial Revolution. Both the present book and the previous one seek to break out of the conventional and restrictive limits and pose problems in a wider, international context, taking account of as many varied experiences of economic development as possible.

It is a necessary but not a sufficient task of the economic historian to find out what happened and to put it down in readable form. It is also necessary to sift and arrange the facts, to analyse them and bring out their significance. For this it is necessary to have an analytic framework; and, for its study to be worthwhile, it surely has to have some relevance to the understanding of man's activity in the present as well as in the past. For we live in the present, and if history cannot connect with the preoccupations of present-day man it becomes a lifeless thing. And yet it sometimes seems that archaeology has more life in it and generates more enthusiasm than the economic history of the past few centuries, which permits a much more detailed reconstruction of how life was led, its material basis and the social relations it involved. In any case, the present is determined irrevocably by the working out of past historical processes; and this is more true of the economic than of any other aspect. What after all are the overriding problems facing mankind in the last decade of the twentieth century? Nothing less than the material, and therefore economic, conditions for continued existence on this planet, and the social dispensation and political system that shall prevail. Is it possible for the advanced countries to maintain their present standards of living, based as they are upon a growing consumption of wasting resources? And even if it were, can it be done without doing irreparable harm to the environment and indeed to the atmospheric zones surrounding our planet? Then there are the two-thirds of humankind who live well below the tolerable minimum considered necessary for civilized life, most of them in countries formerly part of the colonial empires of a handful of rich countries. Is it possible for them to raise living standards and follow the same path as the highly industrialized countries? In any case, the changed economic environment in the latter since 1970 – growing international monetary chaos, the steep rise in petroleum and raw material prices and high rates of inflation eating away at the value of money – poses new questions for the developed world as well. The countries making up that world have their own structural crises, varying it is true from one to another and differing according to the prevailing social system. In all cases, without a study of history it is unlikely that these problems can be understood let alone tackled with any prospect of success. We can, for example, no longer be confident that industrialization on the existing models, whether drawn from the ex-Soviet Union or from the 'West', can be applied in the underdeveloped countries because there is some doubt about how successful it has been, or can be in the future, in coping with the problems specified above.

It may seem that to approach the history of industrialization in this way transcends the limits of economic history, and in a sense it does; but it shows the sort of questions in today's world upon which study of the past should shed some light. It cannot provide solutions if only because different scholars will come up with different explanations of what happened in the past and will derive different lessons from it. What is required is information and illumination, not definitive answers.

The previous book, which was confined to Europe, saw that continent as having adopted the path of industrialization in the footsteps of the pioneer, and in a series of short, introductory case studies sought to define the distinguishing characteristics of the process in different national and historical contexts. The point was emphasized that the reasons for Britain's priority in industrialization had to be seen in a European context, and it was implied that the very uniqueness of the British case made it unsafe to generalize about. Indeed, the 'late-comers' all, in one way or another, so diverged from Britain that her path can scarcely be considered as a model. Some economic historians – in France but also outside – have suggested that that country was more of a model as far as the continental nations were concerned. They all, unlike Britain, had to contend with a large peasant population, and in the present volume something is said about the way in which the English peasantry disappeared and the consequences of its preservation as a class elsewhere. They all, unlike Britain, saw the state playing a more positive role, although as a later chapter will show this should not be exaggerated, as economic liberalism, rather than state intervention, was almost everywhere the predominant ideological trend during the industrialization process. They all, unlike Britain, passed more rapidly into a phase of industrial and financial concentration with the banks contributing more to the finance of industry; this question, too, will be examined in a later chapter. Central to the Industrial Revolution and the entire industrialization process was a continuous and cumulative development of technology. The great technical breakthroughs were made specifically in Britain; the reason for this and the process of technological advance in general will also be dealt with in a chapter of its own.

The previous volume also stressed the international character of industrialization; its dependence upon the creation of a world market. The tying together of the different regions of each country and the integration of the various nation-states into a world economy were made possible by those immense improvements in the means of transport that took place in the nineteenth century. As much, perhaps, as anything else it was the ability of the nineteenth century to move large masses of people and unprecedented volumes of goods at low cost that distinguished it from the past. This revolution in communications, so basic for modern economies, also calls for closer examination. Industrialization did not take place without sharp breaks and interruptions in social and political life. There were spurts of growth and periods of slow-down; changes of phase if not actually the sharply differentiated stages that some historians, like W. W. Rostow, have been tempted to use as the basis for their picture of development. Such a phase, it seems, appeared in the latter part of the nineteenth century; it formed a kind of transition from the old type of industrialization based upon cotton, coal, iron and steam to one associated with new technologies – those that were to prepare the way for the transformations of the twentieth century. It saw, also, the emergence of a new-style capitalism, better organized and less dependent upon free markets than the old. It saw a reshuffling of positions in the world economy: the rise of the new industrial giants Germany and the United States and the relative decline of Britain. This thesis, too, will be looked at more closely.

While the previous volume considered industrialization as primarily a European phenomenon, the present one looks further afield at the experience of extra-European countries. There is a good reason for this shift of focus. Whatever the differences between continental experiences of industrialization and the contrasts between Britain and the late-developers, they all had a good deal in common. Their civilization and culture derived from a common stem. Their agrarian systems had once had a similar pattern (although the fact that they had changed at different rates, or failed to change very much, had created original characteristics, with Russian serfdom at the one extreme and the individualist farming of England at the other). They had had more or less continuous intercourse with each other for many centuries. Their levels of development varied but were commensurate. It could be said without too much inaccuracy that Eastern Europe and Russia conserved many of the traits that had distinguished the more developed parts of Europe in the Middle Ages. By the latter part of the nineteenth century the whole of the European continent can be said to have been at one stage or another of industrialization. In that sense Europe as a whole was moving in the same direction. But also, by that time industrialization had ceased to be exclusively European in a geographical sense. Europeans had settled North America and planted there a purely capitalist-type social and economic system almost entirely free from feudal leftovers and the attributes of a traditional society. A study of industrialization would, therefore, be incomplete without taking account of these very vigorous transplants in the newly settled countries. Of course, the United States was the most vigorous and impressive of all, but rather than trying to take on in a short space the task of examining this giant, Canada has been chosen to represent a case of industrialization in a country of recent settlement.

However, it is not sufficient to deal only with the experience of European settlement; by the latter part of the nineteenth century industrialization was beginning to make its impress upon the whole world. It did so principally by turning the rest of the world into economic dependencies of those countries in which industrialization was succeeding. One country was notably able to resist the incursions of Western imperialism by adopting the methods of organization and the techniques of the advanced countries and itself moving on the road to industrialization: the case of Japan, 'the spectacular exception to the rule' that industrialization was a European phenomenon, thus requires examination. Her rise to industrial power resulted in military adventurism and imperialism, as the twentieth century knows to its cost. But the period since 1945 has seen Japan achieve even more spectacular economic successes than ever before, to become the second largest industrial power. An attempt will be made to show

how the roots both of aggression and economic growth were to be found in the period when Japan made the transition from being a backward, feudal country to a modern capitalist one.

In the case of South Africa, also part of the British Empire for a long period, it was not until diamonds and gold were discovered that a new dynamic and disruptive factor was introduced into a dependent agrarian economy. Industrialization is a comparatively recent phenomenon and the whole economic history of the country is bound up with the attempt to maintain white supremacy. These examples, among other things, raise the question of how political considerations may delay or distort the industrialization process.

But what of the countries that failed to grow? They include almost all those subject to European colonialism until the mid-twentieth century. Instead of following in the track of the advanced countries, those areas of the world subordinated to imperialism experienced a history of their own: forced into economic dependence, they became the 'under-developed' countries of the twentieth century. A study of industrialization would not, therefore, be complete without examining such a case if only because, in an assessment of industrialization on a worldwide scale, the effect of the unevenness of its geographical spread and the effect it had on areas that remained primary producers and markets for the advanced metropolitan countries must be taken into account. By its size and its lengthy history as a colony of Britain from the time that country began its industrialization, India virtually selects itself for inclusion here. It must be a matter of some amazement and concern that economic historians in Britain have been so reluctant to study the relationship between Indian underdevelopment and the rise of industrial capitalism in Britain. The extent to which the plunder and exploitation of India contributed to capital accumulation and growth in Britain remains an unresolved question. As for India's lack of development, how far that was a consequence of colonial rule must also remain a matter for debate; a case has been stated as a starting point for further study.

Both by taking up particular problems of economic history in a general context and by focusing on the development of particular countries whose experience will be unfamiliar to many readers, it is hoped that the study of the subject can be approached from a different angle to that which is often customary. This method connects historical problems more directly with present-day concerns. It suggests that a study of economic history can shed some light on the contemporary crises in the world economy, whether of the advanced or of the 'developing' countries. Of course, within its narrow compass and in the outline form that has been chosen, this book is intended as an invitation to further study, a handbook or guide rather than something complete in itself. It suggests lines of enquiry for further reading and possibly for research. It emphasizes the need to explain and analyse factual material, to find connecting links, to make comparisons between countries and over time and to create an interest above the acquisition of factual knowledge. It must be seen, therefore, as a starting point from the questions it raises rather than as a recipe book from which answers can be drawn.

CHAPTER TWO
Industrialization in historical perspective

About 200 years ago, unbeknown to those living at the time, a fundamental revolution began in the history of mankind, which was to lead to the development of the world as we know it today. First in Britain, then in a few areas of Europe and North America, a structural transformation, seen in perspective as having been in preparation for centuries, shifted the balance of productive activity from agriculture to industry and opened up boundless possibilities for increasing the productivity of human labour. This process, best described as industrialization, brought into existence those forms of labour and styles of living distinguishing the modern world from the past, the advanced countries from the 'backward' ones.

The central characteristic of industrialization is machine production, the basis for an enormous growth in productivity and thus for economic specialization in all directions. It created a new environment for work, with its own demands and laws – the factory. It brought about the concentration of workers in big industrial units and the growth of towns to house the working population, creating a new urban environment for social living. The new type of town, growing mushroom-like with industrialization, was not an adjunct to a predominantly agrarian society but a new dynamic force for change, the home of the majority of the population in a predominantly industrial society.

Industrialization imposed new forms of the labour process by bringing together many workers under one roof to operate machines driven by power. Workers were incorporated into an articulated system of division of labour in which they performed only one small part of the total labour going into production. Characteristically, the new labour force was 'free' – not bound to the soil or to a single employer, but dependent wholly upon the market. The instruments of production were concentrated in the hands of a small class of industrial capitalists and represented a heavy outlay of capital upon which it was necessary to obtain a profitable return. A new form of industrial discipline had to be elaborated and imposed, one dependent not upon formal coercion but upon the worker's need to earn a living and his fear of losing his job. Formally free, unlike the majority of producers in history before, the new industrial proletariat worked under the threat of economic deprivation. It was wholly dependent upon the labour market, or, what comes to the same thing, on the employers as a class. This new class division summed up the social relations of production of industrial capitalism; it was the source of conflicts and problems of the kind that still dominate modern society.

The social relations characteristic of the capitalist mode of production had existed for centuries before industrialization began, but they were not dominant. In primarily agrarian societies wage-labour was the exception. Most producers tilled the land in some form of dependence and the dominant class lived on a surplus extracted from the direct producers by non-economic coercion. This surplus was used mainly for consumption; the old ruling classes had little conception of investment. Indeed, it was because most of what was produced was consumed and was not used to increase the wealth-producing capacity of society that economic growth was slow or nonexistent. At some time from about the sixteenth century, however, in the more advanced areas of Europe and then particularly in England, hitherto an economic backwater, a change began to take place. Capital was being accumulated and was finding its way into the enlargement of trade and increase in production, particularly in agriculture. There was a significant transformation of the agrarian sector; the breakup of the old feudal relations began and more goods were produced for the market. As a result, relations based on money, the cash nexus, increased in scope. The rise of markets was connected with the growth of towns, themselves based upon trade. The number of landless and semi-landless people in the countryside grew, some, at least, taking up 'industrial' employment, usually in their own homes. In England, where these developments were most advanced, the landed estates to a growing extent were leased out to capitalist farmers. At the same time, wealth was accumulating in the hands of traders and merchants, the typical capitalists of the pre-industrial era.

The distinguishing feature of the merchant is that he buys commodities in one place from one group of people and sells them in another place to different people. He may deal in foreign trade or provide a connecting link between producers and consumers at home. His function does not necessarily involve any major alteration in the commodities in which he deals. Those he employs are concerned with moving and checking consignments, not with altering their form. The merchant is thus found in all societies in which trade is carried on, regardless of how production is organized. Of course he aims to make a profit, to buy cheap and sell dear; but he takes production as he finds it. If he is successful his capital grows by accumulation and he may expand the size of his business. Living in a society whose ruling class is dedicated to conspicuous consumption, he may be tempted to follow their example. The wealthy merchant thus has frequently aspired to pass into the ranks of the landed nobility through the acquisition of an estate or the purchase of offices sold by the crown (as in France). And, after all, the possibilities of accumulation were limited as long as he did not control production itself.

Thus for centuries merchants had flourished, accumulating capital and expanding their essentially trading activities within the framework of a pre-industrial society without changing its foundations. This was to be seen in India and Japan as well as in European countries where it had been taking place for centuries. It was only when capital that was accumulated in trade began to take hold of production that a new disruptive factor was introduced. Even before this happened, however, the presence of a large and growing merchant class, the core of an urban bourgeoisie, introduced a discordant element and began to influence the social and cultural environment, and more directly the economic foundations, in ways that prepared the ground for industrializaton. Indeed, in perspective European history offers examples of false starts along this road associated, as in northern Italy, with the rise of a bourgeois class of this kind. Whatever the reason for these false starts, the example of England demonstrates the requirements for success.

It was not sufficient for the merchants to establish control over production in its existing small-scale, handicraft form. It was not sufficient merely for a wealthy bourgeoisie to coexist with a mainly feudal social structure. The basis of this structure in the rural sector had to be undermined, as was happening in England from the sixteenth century. This was the condition for the growth of the internal market, which in turn would make more and more people wholly or partly dependent both upon buying in the market those goods needed to satisfy their wants and upon selling commodities or working for wages in order to earn the money needed to do so.

Such a growth of the market meant more time spent on the production of manufactured goods as well as on the production of food for sale. Specifically industrial areas come into existence, in which incomes come more from industry than from agriculture, even before industrialization proper began. This growth of industrial production for the market gave the merchant capitalist a strategically key role as the link between producers and consumers – but it did not necessarily mean that they intervened to break up the old forms of production. In general, merchant control over production took the form of the putting-out system. The direct producers fell into dependence upon the owners of capital, who provided the raw materials, owned the finished product and paid them by the piece. A network of middlemen and markets stood between them and the final consumers. But the producers still worked mainly in their own homes or in small workshops, and in some cases continued to own their instruments of production, simple accessories to hand labour. The putting-out system in this form was still essentially an extension of the merchant business of buying and selling. It was only when the capital accumulated in trade found its way into the process of production that it was likely to lead to revolutionary changes in technique and organization.

Merchant control over production, important as it was, was consistent with the maintenance of productive units of the old type – small-scale, using hand labour and decentralized. But the growth of these industries in the countryside, as well as of others requiring large amounts of capital to be carried on at all, prepared the way for decisive changes. The competitive environment and the restless search for profits coupled with the growth of markets overseas as well as at home, opened the way for the penetration of capital into the industrial structure and thus for the transformation of that structure. This might come from the already established merchant-manufacturers, or through what Marx calls 'the really revolutionary way', when the producer becomes a merchant and a capitalist. Certainly in England the early industrial entrepreneurs who established the factories were not usually established merchant-manufacturers or men of great wealth but new men, pressing forward from the middle layers of society, anxious to grasp new opportunities for enrichment. It was these entrepreneurs who proved to be the active agents of change in the industrialization process. They personified the new forces that, having matured over centuries, were now able to effect a fundamental change in economic relations. They initiated a revolution in production, assuming the role of innovators in introducing the new machines and steam power and ensuring the victory of the factory over the small-scale producers.

By the second half of the eighteenth century – the time of the classic Industrial Revolution in Britain – generally favourable conditions existed in many respects. The first generation of factory entrepreneurs was able to insert itself into an existing situation of economic expansion ripe for further growth and favourable to their activities. They, like the innovations they applied, were social products, and industrialization was a broad social process. Nevertheless, they required specific incentives for the investment of capital in the new machines and techniques of production, in the shape of anticipated profits. It was the inability of the existing forms of industry fully to exploit the market situation, the bottlenecks and factor scarcities and the high premiums available to those who could find a way out, that provided the essential stimulus for the pioneering industrial entrepreneurs. They took advantage of opportunities hitherto nonexistent, and in doing so initiated the Industrial Revolution.

For purposes of analysis it is possible to consider the different 'factors' that contributed to the industrialization process and their interaction. In reality the process was a unity, although one runs the risk of making one 'factor' seem the main one, the first cause or motive force (or of overemphasizing a particular factor, as with the famous Weber thesis about the influence of Protestantism on the development of capitalism). For example, the growth of demand cannot be separated from all the previous changes enabling the capitalist mode of production to become established. The growth of demand, or the growth of the market (because only effective demand is in question), was the obverse side of the division of labour in society, the growing dependence of an increasing proportion of the population upon the purchase of commodities in the market, and thus upon having something to sell, if only their labour power. It was the establishment of a complex network of economic interdependence between different sections of the population that created an expanding internal market. It was a market reflecting the unequal distribution of property and income, naturally, but also the relatively large numbers of people, however poor, who had to buy something in order to exist.

In attempting to account for Britain's priority in industrialization emphasis is often laid on the important role of foreign trade. Certainly this was an extremely dynamic sector in the eighteenth century and perhaps was indispensable for economic growth at this time. However, other parts of Europe, including France, enjoyed something of a foreign trade boom, without the same structural transformation of industry. In fact, what distinguished Britain was not so much her success as an exporter but the character of the home market from which the export industries drew their strength. The latter were an aspect of growing division of labour. The existence of a foreign market, including the American colonies, enabled particular industries to expand beyond the limits of the home market and thus to realize the economies of large-scale production. But although some sections of industry were highly dependent on overseas demand, the prosperity of industry as a whole was linked to home demand. It was the flourishing state of the home market that enabled the export-based industries to have such wide linkage effects (as compared with France, for example) favourable to economic growth at home.

The problem in industries faced with growing demand, i.e. anticipating profits from an increase in production, lay in the inflexibility of the old methods of production, their tendency to run into decreasing returns (or increasing costs). Profit opportunities could no longer be seized simply by increasing production from existing units or by adding more of the same type. In coal-mining, for example, as market demand grew – and prices tended to rise – seams had to be worked at greater depths and new technical problems overcome. In industries like textiles an analogous situation existed. It was not sufficient to increase output from the existing spinners and weavers or to recruit more: this tended to raise costs, reduce quality or make supply less dependable. Merchants required larger supplies, more regularly spaced out over the year and more uniform in quality. Producers were called upon to meet particular delivery dates or the sailing time of ships. The existing forms of production were defective and were increasingly felt to be so as conditions became more exacting. Further, to expand profits every producer knew that it was necessary to increase sales, and that this meant selling at a lower price while producing at a lower cost. These were the objectives confronting entrepreneurs in a number of fields but especially in textiles; there was an incentive for each to lower costs first and to strive for a better than average profit and a larger aggregate profit before his competitors caught up.

For these pressures to become effective and for entrepreneurs to respond to the challenge there obviously had to be in existence a capitalist market economy at a relatively mature stage. At the time, this existed in Britain and nowhere else on a national scale.

To get nearer the heart of the problem it is necessary to look at the way in which the technique and organization of production were transformed. The scope for lowering cost per unit of output was limited as long as the producer was confined to the use of the traditional tools of the old complicated crafts. In fact it was the splitting up of such crafts into their component parts and the placing of each simple repetitive task in the hands of a single worker or group of workers that had hitherto been the main way of increasing labour productivity. As late as 1776, when *The Wealth of Nations* was published, Adam Smith correctly saw the division of labour, and not machinery, as the main way to raise productivity. But, of course, as he recognized, once a complicated craft is broken down into a series of repetitive operations the next stage is a device to 'abridge labour', i.e. a machine that takes the tool out of the worker's hands. This was the crucial technological breakthrough coming on a large scale first of all in the spinning of textiles and making it a factory industry in the last two decades of the eighteenth century. The significance of technology for industrial change has been diversely appraised by historians, and an effort will be made in a later chapter to place it in perspective.

Another aspect quite fundamental to the changes so far mentioned was the breaking down of the local and regional self-sufficiency characteristic of the pre-industrial period. In the past the rule of centralized states and empires had been somewhat loosely imposed or effected through local rulers or chieftains. European feudalism demonstrates this in a classic form. The organization of the manor was designed to supply local needs, i.e. consumption, not investment, and trade with the outside world was marginal. Indeed, once market relations began to penetrate it feudalism began to disintegrate. The difficulty and expense of long-distance transport and communications made this localized type of economy inevitable. Until transport could be improved markets were bound to remain local, or at best regional, with a market town serving a limited area. Likewise, from the administrative point of view centralized and uniform government was impossible without rapid transport and communications. The local lord thus conserved considerable discretionary power notwithstanding the will of the central government.

It is clearly no accident that the growth of the market and the rise of capitalism took place side by side with the emergence of the modern state. Thus a Canadian historian writes 'the growth of modern business and the modern state in Canada have occurred in parallel and symbiotically'. The state, first in its dynastic form, then as the nation-state, could become more coherent politically and more centralized only as communications improved. This was precisely the same condition necessary for the expansion of the market, the breaking down of national and regional self-sufficiency and thus the extension of capitalist relations. This process began as part of what, in perspective, appears as the preparation of conditions for industrialization. Moreover, continuous further improvement in transport facilities, leading to a lowering of transport costs, was fundamental to economic growth. This aspect is thus also worthy of more extended examination.

The British experience in industrialization came about as an autonomous and organic process; it could owe nothing to foreign models because there were none. On the other hand, for special reasons, Britain went ahead of other areas of Europe in which many of the conditions for it had been prepared. Once these areas began to industrialize, however, they did so under different conditions. They had to confront a situation in which Britain had secured a comfortable advantage in technology and had seized world maritime, colonial and commercial leadership. The experience of the pioneer industrial country was unique, but the later developing countries were able to operate with a model before their eyes. The British example was duplicated nowhere else; it was a specific and unique case and therefore has probably little relevance to the developing countries of the present day. Entrepreneurs and governments were able to take note in the nineteenth century of what was going on in Britain. The techniques of the Industrial Revolution could be transplanted; managers, workers, enterprise and capital could be imported from Britain. There were techniques and forms of organization to be emulated and mistakes to be avoided.

The exceptional character of Britain's breakthrough into industrialization needs to be stressed, but at the same time it must be seen in its European context. The accumulation of capital necessary for it had been going on in the commercially advanced areas of the Continent and the necessary conditions for industrialization were being assembled. The gap between them and Britain could be measured in decades rather than years; nevertheless, they were not too far behind. The quarter of a century of wars ending in 1815 no doubt contributed to Britain's lead through its disruption of European economic life, enabling her to secure a stranglehold over the world market. Within the next half century, however, the new techniques and forms of financial and business organization rapidly spread and were assimilated in the more favoured parts of Europe – and also in North America, where a particularly favourable environment for capitalist economic growth existed. In the nature of things, therefore, Britain could not long remain the only industrializing country or retain her initial lead. Indeed, if the process was not to come to a halt and provide another example of a false start (of which there were already several), there would have to be a continuous rise in incomes elsewhere, and that could only come about along the same lines as in Britain. That meant shifting resources from less productive to more productive uses; and almost invariably this could be done only by increasing the relative weight of manufacturing industry in the economy.

The idea of Britain as 'the workshop of the world' could at best be a temporary phase. It was never a true description of the situation, since most of the world's population got along without buying anything, or anything very much, produced in Britain. And when it comes down to it Britain's industrial dominance was confined largely to textile products even in the 1850s and 1860s, when her exports were growing most rapidly.

By its very nature industrialization tended to spread, but it could only do so in particular environments already prepared by a period of capitalist development. In such areas acquisitive men came forward able to undertake an entrepreneurial role in mobilizing capital and labour for the application of the new techniques and the revolution-izing of industrial production and mining. They might at first obtain direct help from Britain (or even be Britons), and could certainly take advantage of British experience in establishing their businesses. Although possibilities for profit-making governed their behaviour, they might also be influenced by nationalist aspirations and receive backing from their governments. Without the necessary conditions being present, however, industrialization could not go forward; if they did not exist, or did not exist fully, they could perhaps be created by agrarian reforms and conscious social changes. There had to be supplies of labour, an adequate internal market and at least a basic infrastructure, especially of transport facilities, if the new industrial economy was to advance. Outside Britain, in the course of the nineteenth century, it was possible to identify what was missing if her example was to be followed. It might lie within the powers of entrepreneurs, individually or collectively, or of their governments (especially when they became more susceptible to the pressures from business) to do something about it. The railway in particular provided a powerful instrument for change, breaking up the self-sufficient forms of economy of the old regime and leading the way for the application of capital in more profitable, and productive, ways.

In all industrialization occurring after the British, an element of conscious emulation was present. Nowhere else did it take place as an autonomous and organic process in which even the participants did not know what lay ahead. Thereafter a textile industry could be established from scratch with machinery imported from Britain or built to designs already available. The aim of a textile firm setting up on the Continent might very well be to provide substitutes for imports from Lancashire. Likewise, in the heavy industries, machinery and equipment could be purchased or capital raised abroad with very specific objects in view. The completed unit could embody the latest in technique then available and quickly enter into full production. In the British case, firms were built up from small beginnings and evolved over years or perhaps decades, gradually incorporating new techniques, adapting to market changes and growing through the reinvestment of profits. Although the contrast must not be driven too far – there were continental firms, especially in the older industries, that had a similar growth path to that of the British model – it does sum up, in terms of the individual firm, the basic difference between the pioneer and the late-comer. It makes clear, also, that the latter, generally speaking, had no choice, least of all where, as in heavy industry, a large investment in fixed capital was required from the start.

This meant that in the earlier stages of industrialization, corresponding to those undergone by Britain in the latter part of the eighteenth century, the late-comers were more likely to make use of the joint stock form of enterprise, to depend on bank finance and look to the state for support. This thesis has been worked out in detail by Gerschenkron and is associated with the further claim that the development of the late-comers proceeded by 'spurts'*. There is no intention here to test out this thesis in detail; it suffices to emphasize that there was a basic difference between Britain's industrialization and that of all the later-developing countries, including those on the Continent following most closely in her wake.

Early industrialization took place under conditions that were particularly favourable for the entrepreneurs and unfavourable for the workers. Wage levels were already low, corresponding to what would be expected in pre-industrial countries that had not yet begun their economic growth. The labour market, at least in Britain, was swollen by the agrarian changes dislodging peasants from the land and even more by the rapid growth of population. These conditions were not

* For Gerschenkron's theories see Gershenkron, A., *Economic Backwardness in Historical Perspective*, Pall Mall Press, London, 1966.

precisely repeated in other countries, but generally speaking labour scarcity was never the major limiting factor and wages were related to the low inomes prevailing in predominantly agrarian societies. Moreover, institutional arrangements favoured the property-owners. Where guilds and corporations conserved any vitality they protected the employers or the self-employed, not the wage-earners. The law frowned on, where it did not explicitly forbid, combination by workers in order to bargain over wages. Where it interfered in the wage contract it did so on the employers' side. Legal intervention to regulate health and safety in the workplace only developed slowly. While wages and working conditions in the early factories may not have been worse, and may well have been better, than in other types of industry, the novelty, concentration and size of the factories attracted public notice and invited controversy. Even apart from the reaction of the workers themselves, the new industrial system was contested from the start. In every country, in some form, a controversy over industrialization took place.

Until the nature of industrialization itself became clear this controversy remained veiled behind a discussion of particular aspects: the place of agriculture, factory legislation, the labour question (i.e. the problems resulting from the existence of an urban proletariat) or the tariff. Behind such issues was often to be found a division between the industrializers and the anti-industrializers.

In the forefront of the opposition to industrialization were naturally all those threatened by change: the agrarian interests, the artisans and small craftsmen, the Catholic Church. Conservatives and traditionalists were joined in their opposition by some utopian socialists and populists. They emphasized the virtues of a society based on agriculture and the self-employed craftsman. They feared and distrusted a society dominated by the impersonal forces of the market and giving free rein to the 'insatiable cupidity' of the individual. On the other side, of course, were the political economists who more or less became the ideologists of industrialization in every country. They were joined very largely by scientists and engineers confident of the ability of man to control natural forces and dominate the environment. The case for industrialization was made out in terms of its ability to increase material wealth, on the whole regardless of its distribution. Ideologists like Claude-Henri Saint-Simon advocated a rational society pursuing material goals under the direction of the industrialists and bankers. Whether the active agents of industrialization required an ideology other than that provided by individual possessiveness and acquisition and the assurances that the free market knew best is debatable. Unlike the utopian socialists, the Marxists were industrializers, though it was only in Russia that they became leading protagonists in the ideological debate, on the other side of which were traditionalists in the tsarist administration and the Populist (*Narodniks*) who hoped to see Russia evade the capitalist stage of development and pass directly to some form of agrarian socialism.

The anti-industrializers and traditionalists emphasized the alleged virtues of an agrarian-based society which, in its main outlines, they wished to preserve. They stood for an 'organic' society ruled by authority and order as represented by the ruling class of the old regime, usually backed up by the teachings of the Church. The industrializers found in the political economists the theory of economic development as a law-governed process, one that obeyed its own laws independent of human wishes. The British Classical School, from Adam Smith onwards, and its continental emulators, adopted more or less automatically a rational and materialist calculus, one well-suited to the needs of the newly emerging industrial bourgeoisie with its highly individualist and acquisitive outlook. Marx accepted the view that capitalism led inevitably to industrialization and from the example of Britain deduced that 'the country that is more developed industrially only shows, to the less developed, the image of its own future'*. Unlike the utopians, therefore, the followers of Marx did not seek to put the clock back to the idealized past (of which elements remain in some of his and Engels's early writings) but looked forward towards the future development of industry under the control of the producers themselves in a society without classes. By and large, without much help from theory, the new class of industrial workers, after initial bouts of Luddism (i.e. machine-breaking), also accepted the fact that machine production and the factory system had come to stay. They therefore concentrated on obtaining regulation of working conditions by the state (Marx also regarded the legal limitation of the working day as a triumph for the workers), the recognition of trade union rights and collective bargaining and a larger share of the product, directly through wages, and indirectly through social legislation.

The destructive side of early industrialization has been responsible for many historical controversies, the most prolonged and heated being over the question of whether or not the standard of living of

* This famous, and sometimes disputed, phrase comes from the author's preface to the first edition of *Capital*. It appears on page xvii of the translation published by Allen and Unwin.

the working class fell. Problems of measurement and comparison over time when social conditions were changing rapidly make it almost impossible to draw any definite conclusions. Moreover, it was in the disruption of a way of life and the creation of a new social order and class division that industrialization had its most profound effects. Everywhere, it can be said, conscious intervention has been necessary to control and limit the operation of market forces in order to establish tolerable conditions for the mass of the people. State intervention in the social arena came in the nineteenth century first of all to correct particular abuses or prevent the working class from following the path of revolution. Subsequently it assumed a recognised and permanent character in the shape of the present-day 'welfare state'.

Industrialization has made possible a great increase in the per capita output of material goods and the provision of an enormous range of services arising under a complex system of division of labour. In fact, it has become common to equate industrialization with economic growth, and countries embarking on the path of development have generally assumed that they will have to industrialize. It is doubtful whether the experience of the early industrializing countries is of much relevance to today's developing countries. The growth of the economies of Western Europe and North America in the nineteenth century was the outcome of a long period of preparation; they were already the most advanced parts of the world when their industrialization began. Among other things, this enabled them to create a favourable international division of labour in which a large part of the world became markets and sources of raw material for the advanced countries. The revolt of the dependent countries against this state of affairs is one of the most burning issues in the modern world, but it can only be understood historically. For this reason a chapter will be devoted to the case of India, today the home of almost half the population of the underdeveloped world outside China. For something like two centuries India was ruled as part of Britain's colonial empire: what kind of balance sheet of this experience can be drawn up? Was Britain responsible for Indian's stagnation and poverty, or was it a consequence of traditional structures and cultural patterns? Why did India not follow the example of Japan, the only non-European country to secure a major breakthrough into industrialization in that period?

As a contrast, in what are described as the countries of recent settlement, where Europeans took over a wilderness, economic growth was rapid and successful. The case of the United States is too well known and also too heavily researched and documented to be easily dealt with in a brief survey. But Canada shares the North American continent with the United States; its economic history is much less well known but is well worth examination. Canada, like India, was part of the British Empire for a long period, but the contrast between the two countries in terms of economic development and income levels could hardly be greater. What is the key to this striking difference?

In the case of South Africa, also part of the British Empire for a long period, it was not until diamonds and gold were discovered that a new dynamic and disruptive factor was introduced into a dependent agrarian economy. Industrialization is a comparatively recent phenomenon and the whole economic history of the country is bound up with the attempt to maintain white supremacy. These examples, among other things, raise the question of how political considerations may delay or distort the industrialization process. In the case of Japan, on the other hand, the drive for industrial power was politically motivated, harnessing economic forces to national goals and harmonizing the interests of big capital with those of the state. Unlike the other examples, Japan was one of the most homogeneous countries in the world. This factor may have contributed to her economic success.

While it is doubtful whether the developing countries of the present day can learn much directly from the experience of Britain and the other European countries, they may at least discover something about the reason for their own lack of development. Today, as is frequently pointed out, the gap between Europe and North America and most of the rest of the world is much wider than it was two centuries ago. Unfortunately for them it is now much more difficult – perhaps impossible – for this gap to be bridged than it was for continental Europe to catch up with Britain. The historical conditions that brought these countries into dependence on a world market dominated by a few advanced countries condemned them to be primary producers, disintegrated their internal structures and raised severe barriers to economic growth. Political independence and a quarter of a century of international conferences, discussion, debate, foreign aid, plans and proposals have done little or nothing to raise the living standards or improve the future prospects of the millions of people in the 'developing' countries. Whether or not industrialization, or industrialization alone, can provide a solution remains questionable. The demographic pressures alone suggest that, without control of the birth rate, income levels will be held back for an indefinite period.

And, as the example of India shows, neither the forces of the market nor planning as at present practised are likely to break the impasse without fundamental social changes, especially in the agrarian sector.

While many concerned with the future of the poorer parts of the world believe that a rise in incomes is conditional upon industralization, its critics in the advanced countries have not been silenced and have won increasing support. New arguments have been found in ecology ('the study of how plants, animals and their biological and physical environment interact and how they influence one another')★: the rapid exhaustion of the raw materials upon which industrialization in its present geographical spheres has depended, especially sources of energy, and the pollution of the environment bringing with it a threat to plant and animal life and thus to man himself. In particular, there are well-grounded fears that uncontrolled chemical emissions into the atmosphere may damage the ozone layer and cause climatic changes of a devastating kind. Whatever the basis for the apocalyptic fears expressed by some scientists and economists, it is certain that new questions will be raised with increasing urgency about the future of industrialism. This is in addition to the perennial sources of contestation arising from the class divisions and industrial relations of modern capitalist society. The alienating character of labour itself under the conditions it requires, the competitive and dehumanizing nature of social relations governed by the market, the bureaucratic and impersonal nature of organization both in private business and in politics are all burning subjects of debate which arise from the industrialization process of the past 200 years.

Technology now marches forward towards greater mechanization and the automation of production. It also makes possible, through the harnessing of the atom, the destruction of all human life on this planet. The contradiction between the enormous potentials of technology, making possible the conquest of space and shrinking the world in the age of jet travel and satellite communication, and the apparently insoluble economic problems both of the poor countries of the world and the crisis-ridden rich ones is apparent to all. Economic history may help to explain the origins of this contradiction, but as an academic discipline it cannot be expected to offer solutions.

What can be said is that man's achievements in the field of science and technology are frequently blamed for the consequences of particu-

---

★ The definition of ecology is to be found in Bennett, C. F., *Man's and Earth's Ecosystems*, Wiley, London, 1975.

lar social arrangements. In this connection the proposals for a return to some idealized pre-industrial past or for putting industrialization into reverse gear would seem to be impossible, not to say reactionary, utopias. It is not in turning one's back on the acquisitions of the past that progress can be made in the future. If we see modern industrialization as the embodiment of human knowledge in production, the real argument is not at all for or against it and its results: it is surely about how it can best be directed and its benefits best distributed. This means taking account of, and consciously counteracting, its negative sides such as the threat to the environment, the reckless consumption of non-renewable resources, the over-emphasis upon material values and the condemnation of the majority of people to uninteresting work which drains their physical and nervous energies leaving them passive spectators of their TV sets.

CHAPTER THREE

The peasantry and economic growth

The peasantry has more often been a victim than a beneficiary of economic growth and it is not difficult to see why. The class of small cultivators making up the great majority of the population in a pre-industrial society becomes an obstacle in the way of a more effective use of the land required for economic growth. In most places in which growth has taken place only a minority of the cultivators have been able to gain from industrialization by turning over to production for the market; much of the remainder have simply stagnated or been turned into a landless proletariat, urban as well as rural.

Where the peasantry itself became a factor in history by making a revolution of its own, this tended to hold up the pace of change and thus the rise in per capita incomes in the society as a whole. The classic case was France after 1789. On the other hand, peasant revolutions of this kind have been rare. Eventually, unless protected and supported by the government, as in Denmark, the process of differentiation within the peasantry and the syphoning off of people from the land has gone ahead, leaving only privileged pockets to enjoy the benefits of growing wealth. This adaptation of the peasantry to capitalism has taken place with varying degrees of success in Western Europe within the past century. In other continents the unrestructured peasantry still remains the most numerous class; its size and poverty measure the economic backwardness of the area.

The wresting of a living from nature by the cultivation of the soil, this basic economic task of mankind, has been the *raison d'être* of the peasantry since settled agriculture began. There have been alternatives: the slavery of antiquity or the plantations of the southern United States, the cultivation of latifundia or large estates with serf labour or wage-labour. But serfs also cultivate land that they hold and thus are rightly considered as peasants even where they also perform compulsory labour services. In some cases slaves may also have plots of their own. The point is that other forms of agricultural organization require an outlet, a market, for the surplus they produce and thus also generally presume a development of trade and a stable government. Not until the capitalist era did these conditions become universal and assume a certain permanency. Otherwise, rational forms of agrarian organization producing for the market or the state existed only exceptionally or were bound up with states and empires whose disappearance was their death-knell. Generally speaking, therefore, it was the small cultivators, living in small communities, producing for the family's needs and handing over the surplus in some form to an overlord or the state, that endured as the cell form of agriculture almost everywhere.

If the role of the peasant in history has been largely passive, despite periodical revolts, it has also been indispensable. This applies to the classic model of European feudalism, where the cultivators were dependants of an overlord in a manorial-type organization, and to the Asiatic forms, in which the surplus was extracted by the state rather than by a landowning class. Historically, therefore, an enormous variety of forms of social and political organization has rested upon the material foundations of the village community. In turn, the village community, connecting the peasant households to each other and to the land, has been one of the most enduring forms of social and economic organization. This holds true whether its members were serfs, freemen or semi-free men and in whatever form the surplus was extracted – in labour services, kind or money. For thousands of years, therefore, the peasant has been the beast of burden: the civilizations of the past were erected on his and her labour.

Peasant agriculture assumes diverse forms and is best distinguished in its essentials by comparison with capitalist agriculture of the type that emerged in England in the eighteenth century and thus is the most familiar in this country. In capitalist agriculture the basic unit is a farm, rented or owned by an entrepreneur who cultivates it not for subsistence but in order to produce a surplus for sale in the market. Where necessary he employs wage-labour and becomes an employer. He makes the major decisions about the crops to plant and the animals to raise without reference to his neighbours. He views the land principally as an instrument of production. His outlook is that of the individualist seeking to raise his net income in money terms. He may, of course, retain some characteristics of the peasant, just as the peasant may acquire some of those of the capitalist farmer, but there is a basic distinction.

In a period from before the Middle Ages until some time within the past two centuries, peasant societies have been subject to the overlordship of a landowning class in Europe. It thus becomes difficult to distinguish the attributes of peasant society from the consequences of its subordination, the object of which was to ensure that the surplus product could be appropriated by the dominant class. This latter and all-important factor determined the status of the peasantry. It was either formally in a state of serfdom or in a form of dependence that greatly limited its freedom, for example by specifying the conditions on which the peasant could dispose of the land he tilled (e.g. pass it on to his heirs or leave it). Although he held land, he did not have unencumbered disposal of it in the sense of the Roman law of property. When the Roman law was reintroduced it operated generally against the peasant and in favour of the lord. Normally, therefore, in return for the land he held and the lord's protection he paid a variety of dues in money or kind even where labour services had been given up. The whole question was whether as the old tenures changed the lords or the peasantry came out on top.

If the peasant was thus behoven to his feudal lord, who skimmed off the surplus over and above the bare needs of his family, he was also part of a village community, which determined the way in which the land could be used. The open-field husbandry characteristic of much of Europe until the nineteenth or even the twentieth century was hostile to individualism. It had been worked out by practice over a long period of time in the interests of community survival, not individual advancement. Peasant society had its own rules and its own outlook, to which its members naturally adapted. It was not against individual moveable property or inequality as such, but it tended to keep possessive individualism within acceptable limits. Those limits were set by the need to deal collectively with the forces of nature and those of the hardly less hostile outside world. The village community tended, therefore, to have a corporate consciousness in opposition to the pressures of the lord and the state. The differences in the course of agrarian change in the various parts of Europe were determined in considerable part by the relative weights of the overlord and the village community. There is no reason to believe that things were different in many parts of Asia and perhaps in other parts of the world.

This meant, of course, that the position of the peasantry and of the state and overlords upon which it was dependent reflected and was moulded by an enormous variety of influences. Some were political, issuing from the state and influencing the legal status of the peasantry and its relationship to the land. Others were economic, dependent upon developments outside the villages such as the growth of trade and markets, the use of money and the extent of its penetration. The rate of growth of population, population movements and the incidence of epidemics could also greatly influence the picture. In some places the state began to emerge as a dominating influence, and the policy it pursued towards land tenure could be instrumental in determining the nature and extent of agrarian change.

A change of overlord or ruler did not in itself matter much unless it was associated with important departures in policy. Such departures were made in Europe as the absolute monarchies embarked upon a more conscious policy of state-building. More fundamental ones came as a result of the French Revolution and the Napoleonic occupation of Europe. A major change of policy in India followed the extension of British rule and the land settlements carried out to extract land tax for the benefit of the new rulers. States could throw their weight on the side of the lords against the peasants, assist the peasantry as a counterweight to seigneurial power or try to hold the ring.

The major change economically was associated with the growth of markets and the penetration of the exchange economy into the countryside. These were powerful dissolvents of the old customary and traditional relationships, but they worked themselves out in different and sometimes contradictory forms. Thus in some places the nobility resumed estate farming and made use of their powers over the peasantry to reimpose serfdom or to establish it for the first time in order to obtain a labour force. This gearing of the state to the market could mean retrogression as far as the peasantry was concerned. On the other hand, the impact of market forces could dissolve the old village structure and lead rapidly to a capitalist type of agriculture, or could accelerate the differentiation of the peasantry, with an enterprising section turning over to farming for the market.

What emerged in the long run would depend upon when, how and under what conditions the old traditional relationships were dissolved and what took the place of the feudal tenures. Wherever the peasantry had a say, where there was a clear-cut peasant revolution, it tried to conserve those parts of the old system that appeared to serve its interests. Where change came from above it was more likely to benefit the rural ruling class, except where the state was trying to build a more centralized nation in opposition to it. In some places an energetic and enterprising class of rural entrepreneurs emerged from the old nobility. Where it was already functionless and parasitic it was most likely to decline or remain as a passive class of rent-receivers. As the pace of change along these lines accelerated the fate of the peasantry itself was in question. Could it survive at all, and if so in what form?

The long and enormously varied history of the peasantry makes generalizations about material levels of living or status impossible. There are peasants in West Germany as well as in India or Indonesia, but they have little in common with respect to income or to their weight in society. Only in relation to time and place can we categorize the peasantry as free or unfree, owners or non-owners, subsistence producers or prosperous capitalist entrepreneurs. Further, in many peasant societies wide differences exist among the cultivators them- selves. Typically, the more exchange relations have developed, the greater the number of families owning more than the average amount of land or leasing it from others, possessing draught animals, employ- ing hired labour and selling their surplus produce in the market. At the bottom there may exist also a landless or semi-landless sub-class unable to support their families without working for wages. In India this situation is complicated by the caste system and the presence of outcastes. In many places the villages have contained a pauperized mass of underemployed, a reservoir of cheap labour for agriculture and industry. In between the rural 'bourgeoisie' and those wholly or partly available for wage-labour stands the 'middle peasant'. His position, defined in relation to those above or below, can be presumed to be mainly self-supporting when his obligations in taxes and dues have been met. He does not usually employ wage-labour or work for others, but in so far as there is insufficient work on the land for all members of the family, especially during the slack seasons, the middle peasants may also turn to a cottage industry and thus be drawn into the exchange economy.

In other words, the further market forces have penetrated into the village, the more marked the differentiation with the peasantry is likely to be. This is confirmed before our eyes in countries where the 'green revolution', associated with high-yield seeds and new methods of cropping, is going on. Requiring capital and the ability to cope with market forces, such changes have favoured the richer peasants and hastened the constitution of a rural proletariat where one did not exist before.

The classic case of a peasantry succumbing to the forces of developing capitalism and disappearing altogether as a class is to be found in England. It can hardly be disputed, furthermore, that the elimination of the peasantry proved to be part of the process enabling that country to industrialize ahead of all others. Forces undermining the position of the peasantry in the feudal system as it operated in England began to appear very early, probably from the fourteenth century. Into this process entered a number of factors, some mainly economic, others social and political; most of them were weighted against the peasantry. The changes that took place in other European countries modified or undermined feudalism in different ways. In the east the peasantry tended to be reduced to serfdom; in the west the lords failed to master the new forces generated from growing trade and their position weakened. The response of the English nobility was more favourable for their subsequent survival and the strengthening of their position.

From an early stage in England landowners began to consider the estate as an economic enterprise to be managed to maximize returns. Thus the demesne was frequently leased out to tenant farmers because they could then produce a surplus for sale in the market and afford to pay a higher rent. The growth of the wool trade and the London grain market were key factors in this development, which also began to bring about differentiation within the peasantry and to undermine the village community.

The nobility and gentry thus came to see in income from rents, rather than in the surplus extracted from the land-holding peasantry of the open fields, the main value of their estates. They developed an interest in extending the area available for leasing to capitalist farmers and reducing that used by the customary tenants. Hence as early as the thirteenth century the lords are extending their demesnes at the expense of the commons, necessary for the economy of the peasant village, and later favouring enclosure, i.e. the abolition of the open fields. In this way contractual rents became a steadily increasing proportion of the income of the landowning class.

At the same time this class was able to maintain its political and juridical powers as against the crown. It was thus able to use the law to enforce changes in its interest. New landowning families came onto the scene in the sixteenth century as a result of the Wars of the Roses, the dissolution of the monasteries and the sale or disposal of crown lands. In this period of rising prices landowners had a further incentive to raise their rent rolls by substituting tenant farmers for peasants. Various pressures could be exercised on the peasantry up to and including outright eviction. But economic forces undermined the position of the lower strata of the rural population and favoured the

31

better-off peasant and the capitalist farmer. Where enclosure took place the peasants lost land, while the lord's position was consolidated; there followed a process of attrition, which was complex and followed different patterns in various parts of the country.

What is certain is that a combination of enclosure, even when, as in the eighteenth century, the legal rights of landholders were respected, and of impersonal economic forces, steadily undermined and destroyed the social and economic foundations of peasant England. The village community, undermined by the growth of trade and money economy from an early date, had little vitality to resist. The restructuring of the agrarian economy could therefore be carried out from above, to the detriment and final destruction of the peasantry as a class.

The final act came with the enclosures of the eighteenth century carried out partly by arrangement but predominantly by means of private Acts of Parliament obtained by the landowners. Before this happened a number of factors unfavourable to the peasants had been developing from the middle of the seventeenth century. Peasants who had previously held their own by selling in the market now faced declining prices and lower incomes at the very time when local rates and the land tax were being raised. The growth of trade and of opportunities for making money in the towns drew off some of the sons of the better-off peasants and tempted them to sell out to the ready and waiting landowners, now able and anxious in many cases to round out their estate and lease the land thus acquired to tenant farmers. The landowners able to do this were mostly those who held large estates and the newer proprietors enriched in trade, the professions or state service.

In the relative balance of forces being established everything favoured the landlord against the peasantry, except for those able to take advantage of the growing commercial opportunities or to become capitalist farmers themselves. Most disadvantaged of all were those inhabitants of the peasant village who had only a small amount of land or no title that a lawyer would recognize and whose existence had been bound up with the common lands and the practice of husbandry in the open fields. For the former the best option seemed to be to sell their land or to resign themselves to enclosure, against which they could do nothing as individuals. For the latter there was nothing that the law could protect and the village community, which might have been able to protect them, had disintegrated as a living force long before.

As enclosure was carried out in one village after another in the eighteenth century it only completed the destruction of a class which had begun perhaps five centuries before and which bore witness to the relatively advanced character of the economy in England. The substitution of tenant farmers, small capitalist entrepreneurs, for peasant cultivators, by increasing the productivity of the soil, made it possible to feed a growing population already (by mid-century) moving out of agriculture or combining agriculture with industrial labour under the putting-out system. Favourable conditions had been created, therefore, for the recruitment of a labour force for industry and for the accumulation of capital in the hands of those who would use it for investment. Agriculture became purely capitalist, and landowners derived their income from contractual rents and not from feudal dues and services as was still the rule on the Continent. Enclosure was not the whole of this process, but it was an indispensable and necessary part of it. It was not in itself the driving force for the disappearance of the peasantry, but an instrument of other deep-rooted economic and social forces which had already undermined the peasant community, sapped its vitality and made part of the peasantry itself an accomplice, unconsciously, of the disappearance of the class of small cultivators of the soil we call peasants.

Nothing comparable with this took place outside a few continental areas. Enclosure in itself could not reproduce conditions that were in various ways unique to England. It was not merely, therefore, that other countries did not have an enclosure movement; it was rather that their whole agrarian history took different paths in response to a complex of specific social and economic conditions, as a few examples will show.

In the absence of powerful external stimuli the peasant village continued on its way as a largely self-sufficient unit, feeding itself and providing, under coercion, a surplus for the ruling class. Where members of this class were drawn away from their estates – to court, for example – and tended to become absentee landlords, they were interested only in drawing an income through the exaction of the feudal dues and services. The bargaining power of the village community might improve, at least to the extent that the obvious badges of servitude – compulsory labour services – were removed, but the subjection of the peasantry, though resented, did not remain in doubt. Once a pattern of this kind was established, on essentially a feudal model, the entry of new landowners from the bourgeoisie was unlikely to alter the picture substantially. The incentive to acquire an estate was to 'live nobly' from the surplus traditionally extracted from the peasantry and to enjoy the prestige which went with landownership.

Lack of powerful economic pressures from trade and the growth of urban markets thus tended to consolidate the peasantry, enabling the village community to retain a certain coherence despite differentiation in the peasant ranks and inhibiting the landowners from initiating major changes. It is true that this pattern did begin to change in some areas in the seventeenth and eighteenth centuries, and in those places, sometimes in conscious emulation of England, a similar process began. Landlords began to organize their estates more rationally, some enclosures took place, new crops and methods of cultivation were introduced, and differentiation within the peasantry became more marked.

This was the case in France, for example, before, the French Revolution. What is notable, however, is the strength of the forces of traditionalism opposed to the development of agrarian individualism, the reluctance of the state to support agrarian changes in the interests of the landlords likely to antagonize the peasantry, and thus the partial and slow nature of change in the rural areas. The peasantry was still by far the most numerous class, while the continued existence, and to some extent the aggravation, of feudal exactions by a largely parasitic landowning class gave it a solidarity in crisis despite conflicts of interest within its ranks. The fundamental issues between the pretensions of the nobility and the aspirations of the peasantry were resolved from below, by the action of the peasantry itself, from the summer of 1789 onwards. From the beginning of the refusal, on the part of a large part of the peasantry, any longer to fulfil their obligations to the total legal abolition of these obligatons without counterpart or compensation took some three or four years. As a result, peasants with a title to their holdings acquired them as unencumbered private property and large quantities of noble and Church land, requisitioned by the state, were put on sale and changed hands. This agrarian and social revolution destroyed what remained of feudalism, abolished the privileges of the nobility and confirmed the hold of the peasantry on a large part of the cultivated land.

This agrarian revolution from below was not desired by the revolutionary bougeoisie, at least not in the form in which it took place. It was the result of action by the peasantry whose support became vital if the revolution was to survive. The interests of the peasantry were tied to the new institutions with which France was endowed. At the same time, the Revolution did not give land to those who did not possess it or could not afford to buy that confiscated from the Church or the *emigrés* and put up for sale. Nor did it expropriate noble estates as such, but only the feudal privileges that went with them. It wanted, on the other hand, to further the cause of agrarian individualism as against the collective practices of the village community, but it could not do this against the will of the peasants. In the main, and for some time to come, the peasantry remained addicted to the old customary methods connected with the open fields and the use of commons and other village lands. Moreover, the practice of divisible inheritance tended to break up peasant holdings into smaller parcels as the generations turned over. These factors operated against the rapid restructuring of agrarian relations on fully capitalist lines. Consequently, surplus population moved out of the village slowly: many men held land or had the hope of obtaining a patch by inheritance, marriage or on a lease or share-cropping basis.

Although differentiation continued, only where markets existed and transport facilities were available was there a strong incentive to improve production methods and increase the surplus available for sale. And the peasantry was held back by the small size of many holdings as well as by lack of capital, ignorance of improved methods of cultivation or the generally inhibiting climate of the peasant village. Change was most rapid where landowners took the initiative or where there were large farms on something like the English model.

The contrast between England and France is striking. The disappearance of the peasantry must be rated as a powerful contributory factor in the economic growth of the former, just as the survival and consolidation of the peasantry by the Revolution of 1789 can only be regarded as a retardative factor in the case of the latter. This is not necessarily to pass a judgement on which type of development was most desirable; it merely states what seems to be an observed economic fact.

France set a model for other West European countries, especially those invaded, occupied and subject to French laws. In other places a revolution from below was not necessary and change from above could have the same effect. The nobility could therefore withdraw from the scene as an active force in agriculture and land management and become simply rent-receivers, while most or much of the land passed into the hands of peasant proprietors. Subject as they would then be to the influence of market forces, demographic pressures and political change, the inevitable process of differentiation followed. The first half of the nineteenth century was thus one of considerable discontent and distress on the part of the European peasantry. Until 1815 there were the ravages of war and the effects of French occupation. The peasantry was pushing for its emancipation and at the same time was increasing in size as the result of population growth. This led in turn, in places, to the breaking up of holdings into smaller parcels. The food demands of the steadily growing urban population offered the better-off peasants opportunities for further enrichment by producing for the market. Overall, the vagaries of the harvest imposed themselves as remorselessly as ever, perhaps even more than in the past, as the potato-growers found in the 1840s. In this decade the agrarian crisis reached a climax resulting in food shortages, the peasant outbreaks during the revolutions of 1848 and large-scale emigration from some regions.

In the post-1848 period a certain stabilization occurred in the peasant agriculture of Europe, partly as a result of the changes imposed in the course of the revolutions, partly because agriculture shared in the general prosperity. Emancipation was completed in Central Europe and was extended into the tsarist empire by the edict of 1861. Governments of the old regime learned that, once some concessions had been made to the peasantry, enabling all or part of it to become full owners of land, they became a largely conservative force. It was therefore possible at the same time to maintain the big estates and create conditions favourable to capitalist farming without destroying or uprooting the peasantry. Of course, the governments were not able to impose a complete historical standstill – economic forces themselves saw to that. Ownership tended to become more concentrated; the landless or semi-landless were squeezed out of the rural areas into the towns; and the bigger and more efficient producers were favoured by the new techniques and methods of cultivation that were becoming available. Nevertheless, throughout Europe the peasantry survived, and the slowness with which economic forces did their work was later to impose difficulties for Marxist theorists, asking whether the laws of capitalist development applied to agriculture at all.

The natural conservatism of the peasantry was exploited by state and Church alike in a period of increasing challenge from disruptive forces emanating from the urban bourgeoisie and proletariat. But as the bourgeoisie itself obtained power, or a share of it, so it looked to the small property-owners in the countryside as a basis for its rule. Universal suffrage, when exercised by the rural masses, proved to be no danger. In 1849 the peasantry voted *en masse* for the candidate of order, Louis Napoleon Bonaparte, and the lesson was not lost on the more keen-sighted defenders of the established order.

It is doubtful whether the peasantry would have fared as well as it did or could have survived as a major force into the mid-twentieth century in the advanced countries of Europe without the support of the state in various ways. True, with one or two exceptions, such as Denmark, governments did little positively for the peasantry to enable it to adapt to the exigencies of the market economy. What happened in most of Europe, however, was that, when the old structure of agriculture was threatened by the influx of cheap food from other continents in the last quarter of the century, governments stepped in and set up protective barriers, thus keeping in existence high-cost producers, whether peasants or estate-farmers. Usually it was the big landlowners, even in 'democratic' France, who were in the vanguard of the demand for protection in the 1870s and 1880s and they operated in close alliance with the industrialists. Undoubtedly, however, there was fear of the social consequences of allowing the peasantry to be forced out of existence by the pressure of cheap imports. The ruling class could not contemplate with equanimity the creation of a disgruntled rural mass and an influx of uprooted people into the towns where they would simply overstock the labour market and become a breeding ground for discontent. Moreover, in a period of increased military preparedness and conscript armies, the peasantry was the main source of recruitment for the army. Nationalists and conservatives of every sort laid stress on the virtues of rural life and contrasted the healthy, loyal peasantry with the proletariat infected with the virus of socialism. Hence, instead of the agricultural depression completing the destruction of the peasantry, the counter-measures taken by the goverments gave it a new lease of life.

This is again a case where political intervention counteracted the tendency of market forces, and one of very great social significance. This intervention could not, of course, prevent the operation of market forces altogether. Indeed, the railways, and the resulting spread of education and of urban influences into the countryside, steadily undermined the old rural structures, placing them on a more capitalist basis. And as this happened, however slowly, the contrast between the prosperous capitalist peasant orientated towards the market and other strata became more marked. The upshot, however, was that the relative decline of agriculture was slowed down. Behind tariff walls high-cost producers were kept in existence – much of the benefit going, it is true, to the landowners and large farmers, not the peasantry. The peasantry was shielded from market forces, but not altogether. When prices fell or the peasants slipped into debt, however, they found the conservatives often ready with a more appealing argument than the radicals. Their plight, the former said, was the fault of urban bankers, the foreigners, the Jews, the socialist agitators and trade unions demanding higher wages. Thus, to a large extent, and especially in Western Europe, the peasantry remained a stabilizing factor and a reserve for the political conservatives. Only where the agrarian revolution was still the central problem, as in Russia and much of Eastern Europe, was this not true.

The conservation of a peasantry – a result of the combination of the slower and more belated operation of market forces with the deliberate intervention of government – thus distinguished the continent of Europe, and much of the world, from Britain. This tended to underline the uniqueness of the British case and to suggest that it could not be a model, as Marx and others had perhaps expected.

A price had to be paid for the preservation of a large class of small cultivators, though one that cannot easily be put into figures. Prices of foodstuffs were kept up for consumers; the market for industrial goods was more limited than it might have been; industrialization and proletarianization were both slowed down. Countries with a large peasantry, more or less artificially kept in being, participated less fully than Britain in the international division of labour. Growth of per capita income was slowed down. Even in wartime their military–economic effort was held back by the need to retain resources of manpower on the land which might have been available for the forces or industrial use (this applies to France during 1914–18 and to Germany in both wars). But, of course, the retention of a peasantry had a strong strategic purpose: it was intended to provide soldiers and food for a siege ecomony. Even Adam Smith agreed that 'defence is more important than opulence' and could thus provide a motive for keeping in existence a peasantry larger than would be justified on purely economic grounds. Whether consciously or not, European countries preferred what they believed was greater military security to a higher standard of living.

There is, of course, another argument. Rural life has always had its adherents, and it may be claimed that even for many of the peasantry it compared not unfavourably with the conditions of life and work of the urban workers. On the other hand, Marx spoke, with some justification, of 'the idiocy of rural life'. Certainly it was by no means idyllic, whichever aspect one takes. Comparisons, however, are enormously difficult even for the same country at a particular time if we consider housing, sanitation, education, working conditions, incomes, prospects for old age and so on. Who would be brave enough to claim that the peasant or the worker comes out best? And yet millions of peasants voted with their feet every decade for the attractions of town life, whatever they were, or perhaps against the disabilities of rural life. It is noticeable that, where the movement was to the towns, young women were often in the lead. The village, with its oppressive patriarchal family relations, could be a prison for its female drudges who hoped to find emancipation in a freer, more anonymous environment. The peasantry, too, was the great reservoir for emigration from country to country in Europe and to other continents. Settlers in North America, for example, intended to get away from the grip of the landlord and sought to realize their desire for independence in the form of the family farm bound to no lord and employing no labour, but closely geared to market demand and treating the land itself as a marketable asset. Here families moved, or the young men led the way. Population pressure, land-hunger, rural poverty, lack of opportunity, limitations on enterprise – whatever the reason for this mass phenomenon, it implies a criticism of and a vote against the old rural order, an escape valve for Europe's peasant masses. Yet it only skimmed off part of the population increase and did nothing to solve the basic problems of the rural sector which remained acute, particularly in the poorer areas.

Thus, although the peasantry declined as a proportion of the population in industrializing countries, in some countries (e.g. France) it increased in absolute numbers during the nineteenth century. It remained until the 1930s a large and important segment of the population in the Western European countries. The depression of that decade, by causing heavy unemployment in the towns, halted the rural exodus and even reversed it. Various movements of the Right had some success in their cry for a return to the land. The peasants themselves were stirred into political action, mainly by movements of the Right or those linked with the Church. As in the past, the peasantry remained a reserve of European conservatism. It also provided a reserve for the new economic upsurge that began after the Second World War.

One of the reasons why the continental countries were able to grow more rapidly than Britain was that a still substantial peasantry could be called upon to provide a labour force for industrial expansion. The post-war period has thus seen a striking reduction in the size of the peasantry, carried out without major upheaval, under conditions of economic boom. Those left behind either have been able to share in this growth by more capital-intensive methods and production for the market or, where less favoured, have been carrying on a protracted rearguard action in an attempt to hang on to threatened positions. Despite pockets of peasant poverty and discontent (discontent with the working of the market system which keeps down or reduces incomes) the European peasantry has survived as a relatively prosperous minority in many places. Economic growth had not only widened the market for high quality and specialized food and other products, it has also offered jobs for members of the peasant family not fully employed in agriculture.

The disappearance of the peasantry in England was therefore not reproduced in a straightforward fashion in the countries of continental Europe. Nowhere else completed, it has proved to be a complex and protracted process, a tendency rather than an accomplished fact. The survival of the peasantry as a substantial section of the nation into the twentieth century and its continued viability even today has had considerable social and economic importance. Tied up with the peasant village were many traders and artisans who also survived, though they met increasing competition from large-scale urban industry and modern capitalist distributive chains at an accelerated pace at least from the early 1920s. Of considerable importance, too, is the effect of a rural upbringing, in the peasant household, on many of those who left the countryside and earned a living in industry or the tertiary sector. The peasant outlook or mentality associated with close family ties, a certain attitude towards money and property and the unconscious preservation of old ways and habits has certainly passed over into part of the urban population in countries conserving a large peasantry. Here again the accelerated breakup of peasant influences has been a characteristic of the past few decades.

If the peasantry has been slow in disappearing and still survives as the predominant element in the agrarian sector in Western Europe, one of the most advanced economic areas in the world, it is not surprising that it has retained its numerical superiority on a worldwide scale. Of course, in those parts of the world referred to as 'underdeveloped' the situation of the peasantry corresponds more closely with that of its counterpart in pre-industrial Europe than with the prosperous, landowning, capital-intensive peasantry of the prosperous parts of that continent today. But even in a country like India the term 'peasant' conceals a great variety of conditions. A prosperous grain-grower in the Punjab does not differ essentially from a West German peasant. But there is no longer anything comparable, except in the poorest areas of southern Europe, to the vast semi-landless and pauperized masses in India and countries like it who are brought under the umbrella of 'the peasantry' at the present day. The problem here is one of missing prerequisites for a spontaneous process of growth through the operation of market forces, coupled with unremitting demographic pressures.

In these countries the peasantry, if it can be so called, increased in numbers without any comparable growth in the demand for labour in the few industrialized areas. Where the existing land system retains 'feudal' attributes there is an enormous disparity between the rich and powerful landowning class and the rural masses of landless or semi-landless families. Where capitalist agriculture has made serious inroads it brings forward a minority of prosperous farmers, turns some of the peasants into full- or part-time labourers and renders the rest superfluous. A seemingly insoluble problem is thus created of growing rural overpopulation and poverty without any corresponding growth of demand for labour in industry. Industrial growth is indeed inhibited by the poverty of the mass of the population, part of which becomes completely pauperized. Only a fraction of the population, perhaps 10 of 15 per cent, is able to consume sophisticated factory-made products. The existence of masses of cheap labour is no necessary spur to industry. The towns become overcrowded with people forced off the land but unable to do more than eke out a precarious existence in the urban suburbs. Thus the experience of Europe, far less of England, cannot be reproduced through the mechanism of the market or 'reforms' from above in the context of these so-called 'underdeveloped' areas. The ultimate alternative would seem to be a thoroughgoing agrarian revolution, changing the agrarian relations of production, if a complete social breakdown is not to be avoided; apocalyptic as it sounds, this choice may not be far off.

CHAPTER FOUR
Technology and industrialization

A convincing explanation of the industrialization process might be worked out presenting it as a function of technological advance. Indeed, Professor David Landes begins his account of the Industrial Revolution in Britain by referring to 'a series of inventions' which 'transformed the manufacture of cotton in England and gave rise to a new mode of production – the factory system'*. He then speaks of the abundance of innovations and improvements that 'constitute the Industrial Revolution' by yielding an unprecedented increase in productivity and a substantial rise in real income per head. It is true that he goes on to discuss how these technical developments came to take place and is led into a discussion of the peculiarities of the English social structure and market situations. It would, however, have been equally possible to *begin* with the social developments, which produced a receptiveness to change not previously witnessed and material incentives to encourage men to apply themselves to working out changes in methods of production and organization in order to lower costs and increase the profits on investment.

Professor Musson, however, after a review of theories and explanations of the relationship between technology and economic growth, says 'technological change was a long-continued response to gradual expansion of markets'†. He is wary of ascribing any revolutionary effect to technical changes taking place in the eighteenth century and becomes preoccupied with 'the motives of individual inventors'. He recognizes a connection between the growth of scientific knowledge

---

* Landes, D. S., *The Unbound Prometheus*, Cambridge U. P., 1969, p. 41.

† Musson, A. E., from the editor's introduction to *Science, Technology and Economic Growth in the Eighteenth Century*, Methuen, 1972, pp. 45, 68.

and the technological aspects of early industrialism and speaks of 'fruitful collaboration' between scientists, technologists and industrialists, suggesting a sociological explanation of the acceleration of technical change. He concludes his survey safely: 'In the end', he writes, 'one has to recognise the existence of a multiplicity of interacting factors – economic, social, political and psychological, as well as scientific and technical – among which there is not much possibility of indicating preponderance.'

Professor Usher is mainly interested in the process of invention, seen as 'a substantial synthesis of old knowledge with new acts of insight'*. However, he stresses that invention is a social process, influenced by the economic and cultural environment. Inventions are not isolated achievements; they require a long period of improvement, trial and error as well as additional modifications before they can become a practical success. Technical change takes place in a whole society when inventions are taken up and applied, with the investment of capital and the expectation of gain. This brings in the market, because it must be possible to sell the goods and services made available by technical change if such change is to continue. In a capitalist economy the adoption of new techniques depends upon the decisions of entrepreneurs seeking profits. They may accept losses in the short run, however, if they expect to raise their profits later. In this sense, technical change is a response to markets.

But something more is involved when we consider the process of industrialization, namely a discontinuity, a change in the production function. Lilley points out that in Europe technological change had been going on since the Middle Ages, but it seems an exaggeration for him to claim that 'the real break in technological continuity came at the beginning of the Middle Ages, not in the eighteenth century'†. True, much, even most, of the technological innovations of the early stages of industrialization would have been feasible much earlier, but that is not really the point. They were not used earlier, and when they were, not separately and discretely, but as a series in the way Landes describes; they could not be assimilated into the existing structure of industry, but brought about basic changes in it, the factory being the characteristic new productive unit (not 'mode of production') required. If the Middle Ages inaugurated anything new, it is probably because, at about this time, development in Europe

* Usher, A. P. from an article reprinted in Rosenberg, N. (ed.), *The Economics of Technological Change*, Penguin, 1971, pp. 43–71.

† See Lilley, S. 'Technological progress in the industrial revolution' in *Fontana Economic History of Europe*, Collins, 1973, Vol. 3, pp. 187–253.

began to move on different lines to that in other parts of the world, which up to then had been on a par with or in advance of it. The conditions began to be prepared, though it took several centuries for them to mature, for a society receptive to and welcoming change, with dynamic classes and élites confident that man could, through science, extend his knowledge of and control over nature. From this followed the Renaissance, the discoveries, the new Christian doctrines of the Reformation, the breakdown of feudalism, the rise of national states and the extension of capitalist relations.

It was the appearance, in Europe and nowhere else, of a specific cultural, intellectual, social and economic environment allowing far greater, if not complete, expression to individual possessiveness and acquisition that made possible an acceleration of technological change. An expansive economy and a society no longer so rigid or so tradition-bound were necessary for the wide application of new techniques. They were social products, just as the existing ways of doing things were. But they were also powerful means for transforming production relations and increasing the productivity of human labour.

It was the capacity massively to increase production and productivity that distinguished the industrializing society, and this was made possible by technology. Of course, this does not explain why the technology was made use of – for that it is necessary to show how the other 'prerequisites' for growth had been assembled. In this preparation technology was constantly present, but as a means rather than as an active force. It was incorporated in the existing instruments of production and ways of producing inherited from the past and slowly improved over the course of long centuries. Indeed, the speeding up of technological change preceded industrialization and by the late seventeenth or early eighteenth century had raised the level of the more advanced parts of Europe above that of the rest of the world in terms of the productivity of labour and in the proportion of the population working outside agriculture. However, except for a few large-scale enterprises, some of which were initiated or subsidized by the state, most production was in small-scale units, in small workshops or the homes of the workers using traditional tools or simple machines still dependent upon the skill and dexterity of the user. Even when Adam Smith was writing *The Wealth of Nations* in the 1770s, it was still the breaking up of complicated processes into their component parts – the division of labour – and not the substitution of machinery for human hands that constituted the basis for raising productivity.

It is the existence of an industry organized on capitalist lines by entrepreneurs employing wage-labour and producing commodities for sale in the market that provides the immediate setting for the technological changes of the Industrial Revolution. But with this type of society went a growing interest in and respect for science and scientists. The rational, materialist outlook of the new generations of businessmen was akin to that of the scientist. It is not surprising, therefore, that historians have been able to trace many direct links between industrial innovation and science. But if a growing interest in science took place at the same time as entrepreneurs were looking for ways of improving production methods, the scientist and the businessman still lived in different worlds. Science was patronized by the state and by more enlightened members of the leisured classes more than by industry, but it lacked formal organization or an established position in education. Its official or aristocratic patrons did hope for some practical results which could be of use to the army, in improving navigation, assisting farmers or encouraging new industries. The Royal Society, founded in 1662, provided a rallying point for scientific and literary men as well as curious amateurs from high society. It extended its interest to a wide field of practical questions. This was even more true of the Society for the Encouragement of Arts, Manufactures and Commerce in Great Britain, founded in 1755. It set out to stimulate invention by offering prizes. Numerous local societies and clubs followed a similar programme. In some branches of science Britain led the way, but a similar scientific movement took place in France and in European countries less developed industrially – and there were fields in which they were ahead.

Scientific progress was thus not necessarily correlated closely with industrial advance at this stage. The inventions in industry were more likely to be made by practical men working empirically on particular problems known to them than by scientists beginning with general principles and developing theoretical knowledge. But once technology moved on from the stage of improving existing tools and machines or solving relatively simple problems, such as those posed by spinning textile fibres, advance became more closely linked with science and its progress. This was so in the case of the harnessing of steam power, in the use of chemicals for industrial purposes, in metallurgy and the machining of accurate metal parts and, also, in civil engineering concerned with the vital infrastructure of an industrializing society. Mostly, however, the direct application of physics and chemistry to the problems of production came after the first stage of industrialization and were necessary to maintain the momentum of the process rather than to initiate it.

Although economic historians have been able to point out connections between science and technology in the eighteenth century and contributions made by scientists to industrial problems, it could scarcely be maintained that the crucial inventions that initiated industrialization owed much to science. Even less could it be argued that the Industrial Revolution was in any sense the result of a conscious application of scientific knowledge to the problems of production. The textile inventors, John Kay, James Hargreaves and Samuel Crompton, were practical men, not scientists. Richard Arkwright and Matthew Boulton, key figures in the industrial innovations of the time, were shrewd businessmen. Abraham Darby was a practical ironmaster, Henry Cort worked for the Admiralty and Edmund Cartwright was a country vicar. These were the stars, but in the industrial districts were hundreds of working artisans and small masters who had either anticipated their inventions or innovations or contributed their own small improvements to industrial technology.

Whatever the motive for invention, the man who turned an invention into a practical business proposition, the innovator, needed neither scientific nor technical knowledge, though it might be an asset. The real question is why opportunities existed to apply new techniques, and why there were men willing and able to do so. And the answer is to be found surely in the existing structure of industry. Production was already growing in response to expanding markets, but was doing so mainly along the old lines. This was most obvious in the textile industries, the most important group producing for the market and organized mainly on putting-out lines. At the same time, this meant that the technical problems of these industries were known to large numbers of people, especially those concerned with the making and repairing of existing tools and simple machines.

As it happened, the first major invention, John Kay's flying shuttle, came in 1733 and increased the already existing disproportion between weaving and spinning. It therefore intensified the need for ways of increasing the productivity of the spinners, then mainly women and girls working in their own homes, and of improving the regularity of the supply of yarn. Spinning involved the drawing out and twisting of textile fibres into a fine thread, a relatively simple and more or less continuous mechanical process performed with the spinning wheel. The transfer of more of the skill, as it were, to a mechanism while making it possible for more threads to be spun at the same time was a comparatively straightforward problem. A step forward had already been taken when the spinning wheel had taken the place of the distaff, and the early spinning machines were basically an improvement of the spinning wheel. Successive inventions brought spinning by rollers as well as by drawing out and twisting in the shape of machines requiring an outside source of power. Crompton's mule still required the manual intervention of the spinner to push back part of the machine after each movement, and it was several decades before the self-acting mule came into use. Once the new machines were available, the spinning mill, driven at first by water power, achieved a matchless superiority in cost per unit over the hand-spinners. Spinning thus became the first major, mass consumption industry to go into the factory.

That left weaving as a manual activity, the prerogative of adult men possessing a certain degree of skill. The effect of the greatly increased output of yarn made possible by machine-spinning and the continued growth in demand for textiles, especially cotton, placed the hand-loom weavers in a strong position. Weaving by mechanical means proved to be a much more difficult problem to solve technically, despite the high premium placed upon such an invention by the rise in weavers' wages. It was some decades after the success of machinery in spinning that it became possible to send the shuttle back and forth across the loom without a hitch and to weave a cloth of uniform quality without the intervention of human hands. Cartwright's basic invention of 1785 was not a commercial success. John Horrocks was more successful, and took out patents for his power loom in 1813 and 1822. In the following year it was being manufactured by the firm of Sharp and Roberts. Even so, the ousting of the hand-loom weaver took almost a quarter of a century. A similar piecemeal pattern of technological change is to be observed in other branches of the production of textiles – the preparation of the roving before spinning, bleaching, dying and finishing (all dependent upon advances in chemistry), wool-combing and so on. Eli Whitney's cotton gin for the separation of the fibre from the cotton seed was a strategically important invention in making possible the rapid growth of the cotton industry as the pace-setter in industrialization.

If technical change had taken place only in textiles, however, there would have been no Industrial Revolution. It was significant and perhaps inevitable that in the early stages of industrialization textiles led the way; but this does not mean that they, and particularly cotton, dragged the rest of the economy behind in locomotive fashion, as the theory of 'leading sectors', popularized by W. W. Rostow, supposes. More properly, the advances in what was the most important and

47

widely scattered industry in a still largely agrarian economy are to be seen as part of a development of technology taking place over a much broader front. The prototypes of the factory were already to be found in industries that needed large amounts of fuel or that were carrying out large-scale processing of raw materials, but they contributed only a small part to total output. The rise of coal-mining and the growing use of coal as a fuel in Britain had begun in the seventeenth century and was a harbinger of things to come. The metal industries underwent their own technological revolution, without which the supply of the basic materials for industrialization would have been impossible. Small but significant changes in production methods and organization were taking place in a great variety of industries, but without a change in the typical unit of production.

In other words, in the run-up to industrialization in Britain as well as to some extent in the more active areas of Western Europe, a growing proportion of the population depended wholly or partly upon earnings from industry without a movement into the factory. The useful concept of 'proto-industrialization' expresses this very well. It means a growth of market-orientated industry still mainly rural and still organized on traditional lines. There could, therefore, be industrial areas and a great deal of specialization in industry before a transition to the factory. It was in such areas that detailed technological change could be expected, preparing the way for the factory system, while at the same time capital was being accumulated and a wage-labour force familiar with industrial processes was available. Where, as in Britain, this was accompanied by the rise of farming for the market, a majority of the population came to depend upon the exchange economy and no longer lived within the framework of household production and local self-sufficiency.

Technological change was thus part of a wider social and economic process – the extension of the capitalist mode of production. Technology was embodied in the instruments of production, and increasingly frequently these had the social form of privately owned capital employing wage-labour. Where this was so, the owners of capital, the entrepreneurs, in the pursuit of profits had an incentive to find ways of reducing costs by adopting a new technique or increasing sales through the launching of a new product. The first in the field with any successful innovation could expect to realize more than normal profits until his competitors caught up. The shift from the putting-out system or small workshop to the factory was a major innovation carried out under these conditions because the most profitable technology could no longer be adapted to the old units of production. It was in this way, through the business decisions of the entrepreneurs, involving a calculated risk, that technology was translated into practical terms. This process can be seen to be basic to economic growth by raising the productivity of labour, and to industrialization proper by imposing the concentration of production in large-scale enterprises.

If a leap in technology is essential for industrialization, industrialization in turn requires the substitution of the power-driven machine for the workman and his tool. Machinery came before new sources of power, as has been seen in the case of the textile inventions. The point of the machine is that it took over from the workman the actual transformation of the material with the tools it activated. The worker operated the machine, seeing that it was carrying out the process properly and correcting it where necessary. Small and simple machines could be driven by the operator, say by turning a crank with his hand or moving a treadle with his feet. As machines became larger, heavier and more complex, and as it was conceivable that a single worker could operate a whole battery of machines, so it was necessary to make use of some other source of power. Animals, wind and most of all water were used to drive the early textile machines. Of these only water was really satisfactory and only then, of course, where there were suitable fast-running rivers and streams that could be harnessed. What was required was a motive power independent of nature and universally applicable, no longer tied to a particular location, but able to furnish a constant source of energy.

This vital revolution in power came with the inventions of James Watt, one of the few inventors in contact with and directly influenced by the science of his day. Working with the existing Newcomen steam-engines, which required the cooling of the cylinder after each stroke, he devised the separate condenser. At first this only provided a more efficient pumping engine, and the next stage was to adapt the engine to rotary motion. When this was done it could be linked up by belts or gears to drive machines of any sort. Watt's association with Matthew Boulton, one of the leading businessmen of his day, is well known. His enterprise and capital was vital in bridging the difficult period between conception and the production of a marketable product and finding purchasers to make possible the financial success of the firm. Continuous progress was subsequently made in the design and construction of steam-engines and their use was constantly extended.

The manufacture of machines had already raised new problems in the making and machining of metal parts. From the beginning Watt's engine depended upon the ability of the firm of Wilkinson's to bore a cylinder of the requisite degree of accuracy. The construction of steam-engines and machinery, mainly of metal, was the basis for the rise of a wholly new industry, that of engineering, and revealed a new range of technical problems in the working of metals. The production of a single example of every machine or steam-engine would have greatly limited their use. In fact, it was in the nature of such machinery that its parts should be produced in series, each interchangeable and of a standard pattern. This required more accurate ways of working metals and of checking measurements – nothing less than a completely new approach to the organization of production.

The growth of a complex of metal-working trades concerned specifically with the making of machines, machine tools and prime movers was central to continued industrialization. The textile industries might have initiated the Industrial Revolution, but only engineering could carry it forward into new fields and make possible the transformation of the economy as a whole. A number of engineers in Britain, notably Joseph Whitworth, Henry Maudslay and James Nasmyth, made possible the quantity production of machinery able to withstand the speeds, pressures and temperatures required to keep pace with growing output. To make machines for other industries it was necessary to devise a whole range of machine tools, actually to make machines with machines, which supplemented each other. It was largely as a result of developments in machine-making that specialized machines gradually became available in those branches of industry still dominated by the workman with his tool.

It was in the second stage of industrialization in Britain that the machine process began to take command. By the end of the 1830s the textile machine-makers could provide a fully equipped mill. Machines and machine tools were available to all those able to purchase them. Technology itself became a marketable commodity whether in the shape of engineering equipment or in the specialist knowledge possessed by technicians and skilled workmen. This was crucial for the diffusion of industrialization beyond the frontiers of the pioneering country. In any case, it should be remembered that, although Britain did lead the way in mechanical industry, Americans and Europeans were soon making their own contributions to the international pool of technical knowledge.

As for the technical developments themselves, the tendency was for the machinery to become more automatic and for the whole process of production to become more continuous from the raw materials to the finished product. As Marx put it, envisaging an automated factory still in the future, 'As soon as a machine executes, without man's help, all the movements requisite to elaborate the raw material, needing only attendance from him, we have an automatic system of machinery, and one that is susceptible of constant improvement in details.'*

However, mechanization was a piecemeal process and the older forms of industry did not necessarily succumb to the offensive of the machine. On the contrary, some were given a new lease of life, it seemed. When Marx was writing, for example, he was well aware that the machine had conquered only part of the field and that domestic servants, as shown by the 1861 census, were more numerous than factory workers (1,208,648 as against 1,039,605 in textile factories and metal trades). He pointed to the 'medley of transition forms' shown by the Children's Employment Commission of the 1860s but claimed that this 'does not conceal the tendency to conversion into the factory system proper'. As it turned out, this conversion was spread over a considerable period of time, perhaps longer than Marx would have thought possible, though he indicated some reasons for its protractedness.

On the one side there is the fact that, as Marx puts it, for the adoption of the new technology, 'less labour must be employed in producing machinery than is displaced by it'. In other words, an entrepreneur will not go over to the factory form of production unless it is profitable to do so. He needs sufficient capital to make the transition and will have to face new risks, including those arising from an increase in his overhead costs, requiring a larger volume of sales to ensure adequate returns. On the other side, there must be the technical means to warrant the change. For a long time, in many industries the workman with his tool was able to survive simply because machinery had not been invented to take over his job. Meanwhile, the very increase in wealth made possible by industrialization meant that middle- and upper-class consumers were disposing of larger incomes, constituting a growing market for commodities still made in the old ways as well as for personal and domestic services. Consequently, in the industrializing countries of the nineteenth century, the older forms of industry survived and could in some cases adapt themselves with success to the new conditions precisely because the economy was growing. This would apply to high-quality goods consumed mainly by the better off. But it also

* Marx, K., *Capital*, Vol. I, pp. 376–7 in the Allen and Unwin edition. References to the 1861 Census are on p. 448 of the same edition.

included outwork for firms running factories in, for example, the toy or clock industries. Moreover, there was actually an increasing scope for small workshops concerned with repair and maintenance, of which the modern garage/service station is a good example.

Thus, although the factory conquered the field more or less rapidly in the major industries as technological advance took place there were limits to its conquests. For a long period the small master, artisan or domestic industry might survive or even grow in some fields, while they were being driven to the wall in others.

Industrialization, when seen from the standpoint of technology, assumes an uneven and contradictory character. Some sectors of industry were transformed by machinery and steam power at the start; others remained for a long period in a handicraft stage. Some machines, such as the sewing machine, could give new life to the older, decentralized forms of industry; others could be operated only on a large scale in centralized units. While the early transformation of the textile industries was the result of inventions requiring little scientific training or knowledge, continued industrialization depended upon the more systematic application of scientific principles. The old, empirical approach, never as universal as has sometimes been supposed, was to be superseded by continuous experimentation and laboratory work favouring the large enterprise as against the inspired tinkerer.

The industrial late-comers, including the United States, were from the start more conscious of links between science, technology and industry. Yankee inventors and innovators soon began to make their own contributions to technological advance influenced by an environment relatively rich in resources but short of labour. By the time of the Great Exhibition, held in the famous Crystal Palace in London in 1851, a distinctive 'American System of Manufactures' had appeared, based upon standardization and interchangeable parts – a big step towards modern mass production. Scientific training developed on the Continent ahead of industrialization and helps to account for the lead which Germany took in the development of the chemical industry, particularly in the manufacture of synthetic dye-stuffs. Germans were also prominent in electricity and in petrol and oil-(diesel) fired engines. Scientists and technicians frequently held important executive positions in industry. Machines and processes worked out in Britain could be transplanted to other environments: they could also be analysed, improved upon and more successfully applied when examined from a scientific point of view. Thus, during the nineteenth century British industry tended to fall behind in the use of scientific knowledge while some rival firms abroad went ahead on an impressive scale. Technological superiority, especially in the new industries, passed to those able and anxious to apply science in a conscious way to the problems of production.

CHAPTER FIVE

Industrialization and the transport revolution

The rapid movement of large masses of goods and people regularly over short distances or more permanently over long distances is very much a product of the modern age. It has, in fact, been a necessary accompaniment of industrialization and a condition for its extension. Now something that is taken for granted, movement of this kind was exceptional in past ages. Indeed, the characteristic of pre-industrial society was its immobility. People generally lived and died in the place in which they were born. Local areas were largely self-sufficient, with little contact with the outside world. At the same time, the forces that broke up the traditional societies of the past were associated with movement: conquering armies, traders and merchants, immigrants from outside or the escape mechanism provided by transport improvements.

The growth of the market economy and the advance of capitalist dealings would have been impossible without greater mobility of the factors of production and the goods produced. The effective operation of the market requires that production should be responsive to quite small changes in demand; the extent to which this is possible, and the area over which the market can operate, depends upon available transport. This is as true of the labour supply as of the mobilization of capital. For the market to impose itself greater mobility is required. The provision of this mobility becomes a subject for technological development and investment; transport itself becomes a major business with problems of its own.

It is easy to see how the operation of market forces is linked with the development of transport and communications facilities as a whole. There has to be access to markets and knowledge about them. This accessibility is a function of cost, whether of moving raw materials, mobilizing labour or distributing finished goods. In turn, and reciprocally, possibilities for investment and for specialization in production and trade will grow as these costs decline proportionately. Improvements in transport, translated into lower costs, extend the market area, making possible the growth of national markets and of a world market for major commodities. But, of course, it is the market working through transport, and not transport improvement as such, that determines this process. Transport does not add to production but is a necessary part of it, since without the movement of goods and labour the possibilities for production are limited, as in the pre-industrial economy. Conversely, therefore, transport improvement becomes a powerful factor making for growth through the expansion of markets, greater specialization and the lowering of costs.

The nature of transport facilities in a given area conditions the type of economic activity that can be carried on. Their actual or past extent, the routes they follow and the relative costs of different types will be a major, perhaps the main, factor in determining the location of particular kinds of economic activity. For example, because water transport is relatively cheaper than overland transport, and this advantage is particularly great for commodities of heavy weight and bulk in proportion to value, access to rivers or to the sea has been a major determinant in the location of the industries extracting or producing such commodities. In the past, too, large centres of population, possible only through the constant movement of food and other goods into them, have mainly been on sea-coasts or waterways. Likewise, the introduction of new forms of transport, altering the pattern of relative costs, brings about shifts in the location of industry and movements of population. Obviously, the development of transport links makes it possible to bring natural resources that had previously had no economic significance into the market area and promotes a redistribution of population. Such shifts are constantly taking place as part of the process of economic development.

Although transport is usually thought of as a means of moving people or goods, its development has always been associated with the movement of information. Horsemen or ships' captains could carry information about battles won or lost or bring vital news for those about to make business decisions. Modern means of communication – the telegraph, the telephone and radio – makes supplying information of this kind a specialized and equally indispensable activity, intimately related to the market and to the general structure of the economy. Improvement in the transmission of information has conditioned the scale of business enterprise as well as of government. The movement from local to national trade and from local banking to branch banking, and even more the rise of big business and multinational firms, would have been impossible without the improvement of transport and new means of more or less instantaneous communication over long distances. All this has tended to expand the market area, to make markets more effective and to produce a world market. At the level of the individual enterprise, the development of communications facilities has made it possible to exercise closer control over stocks and reduce the proportion of capital tied up in stocks and goods in transit; to reduce business risks or make them more calculable; and to make possible the growth in scale. The whole nature of the distributive system and 'merchandising' has been shaped by the improvement of transport and communications.

For all these reasons, an industrializing economy is one in which transport and communications facilities are being improved and usually innovations are being made. More than that, however, it is evident that even before industrialization became the main trend in economic development, that is to say in the last two centuries, economic change has been linked with improvements in transport. Now that the process of economic growth can be seen as a whole, transport facilities can be improved in order to prepare for industrialization in less developed areas suitable for it.

In historical terms, the improvements in transport of the eighteenth and nineteenth centuries neither preceded the expansion of trade and industry nor followed it in any simple way. Without transport improvement industrialization could not have been carried out, for the reasons already given. Industrialization grew out of a long preparatory phase of growth in capitalist trade and production based on markets, so that the prior changes necessary for it also implied corresponding improvements in transport. These were less spectacular and far-reaching in their effects than the later innovations, but they were none the less real. There were, for example, improvements in ocean shipping, such as the Dutch fly-boats and their emulators; better use of rivers; the building of bridges and the making of harbours; more effective use of animals and so on. These led the way for more systematic improvement in the existing facilities, and for the development of new ones: canals, new types of road construction and surfacing, more intensive use of coastal shipping and river transport. Again, transport must be seen as part of the general process of economic change, not something separable from it. Distance, the cost of movement and the need for greater mobility raised themselves as problems to be solved as soon as economic activity was placed upon a profit-seeking basis. Providing the means to overcome these barriers itself became a profit-making activity, or so promoters hoped. Thus the surge of transport improvements and inventions was not fortuitous but was the product of the market and its needs operating through the active agents in the industrialization process.

The relationship between the improvement in transport and communications and industrialization will be clearer after a consideration of the factors that have to be present before such improvements can take place.

In the first place, there has to be a need, and a consciousness of that need, on the part of those who think they are in a position to satisfy it. Such a need arises from dissatisfaction with existing facilities on the part of merchants, farmers, mine-owners, industrialists, bankers and financiers who want cheaper and more reliable methods of moving raw materials and finished goods or communicating information. The first step is usually a local improvement which the interested parties may initiate or promote, or which one of their number may be encouraged to undertake. For an as yet non-existent facility the need cannot be expressed as a market price. To some extent it has to be provided ahead of demand, or at least in anticipation of it. Thus all transport undertakings are subject to uncontrollable risks: will there be sufficient traffic at a price that the market can bear to cover outlays and make a profit? Does the promoter merely take what business is available, or can he create new opportunities by the services he offers?

The satisfaction of a need can only come about if capital is available for the financing of projects in the hands of those ready to take such risks. There has, therefore, to be a prior accumulation of capital before substantial outlays are possible. A capital-poor country may benefit greatly from expanded transport facilities but is unlikely, from its own resources, to be able to generate the necessary capital. The surge of transport improvement in seventeenth-century England and to some extent in other parts of Europe was a sign of prior capital accumulation and the existence of a need. Moreover, transport facilities are usually capital-absorbing and can be expected to yield a return only over a fairly long period of time – certainly longer than in most other forms of business. This made transport undertakings particularly suitable for corporate forms of organization; also, because special legal powers were often required, the state might take a hand where it did not itself assume an entrepreneurial role.

Finally, the improvement of existing facilities usually requires a technical advance or a more effective way of applying existing techniques. Thus in the early stages of industrialization a considerable improvement was possible through the application of known principles, organizing constructional work more effectively and employing experts, notably civil engineers, to plan out and direct operations. Indeed, the first stages of the Industrial Revolution in Britain were carried out along these lines before new sources of power or radical changes in technology came on the scene. The river improvements, the new bridges and harbours, the canals and turnpike roads that were built would have been technically feasible in previous centuries. Organization and expertise were more important than technology, and as construction proceeded experience was gained, making possible further advances. Civil engineering thus assumed a major role, laying the basis for railway engineering in the next stage. The railway was the major transport innovation of the nineteenth century. It built on the lessons learned from the already existing constructional projects and was itself the fruit of a long process of industrial development and experimentation with steam power and its application to locomotion as well as with the old principle of running wheeled vehicles on a prepared track. The practical success of the railway depended on the ability of the industrial system to turn out cheap iron rails in large quantities, to furnish the locomotives and rolling stock and to generate the capital required. Technology was only part of the process.

From what has been said so far it can be concluded that an industrializing society will have to devote a large, and perhaps a growing, proportion of its investment to the provision of transport facilities. The ability of the early developing countries to finance both their own needs and those of other parts of the world reinforced their advantage over the less developed countries in the nineteenth century. Railway building and investment were effective instruments of imperialism in the primary producing areas, linking them to the world markets in a dependent position in the international division of labour.

Although in the early stages of industrialization the general picture is of transport improvement taking place in response to economic need, the state was often interested in transport for political and strategic reasons. This motive was less prominent in insular Britain but it could not be neglected in those countries with land frontiers and where, as in Germany, state-building was still going on. Moreover, on the Continent, where capitalist forms of enterprise were weaker, initiative was more likely to devolve on the state by default.

In any case, the provision of highways lay generally within the state's province; in Britain the private turnpike was a departure from common practice. The analogy of the roads could thus be applied to canals and railways, usually giving the government some stake in the transport network. Thus the state might intervene to determine the routes followed and exercise an overall control. It might construct and finance improvements or assist and subsidize private enterprise. Its own agents and engineers might have a major responsibility in construction if not in running transport enterprise. Politicians were thinking of transport as an adjunct to government, extending and consolidating central control over the regions, facilitating the flow of information and instructions and, perhaps above all, moving troops to the frontier in time of international tension or war. The routes determined on political grounds such as these were not necessarily the most suitable for the promotion of economic development. They tended to heighten the role of the capital city, as with Paris, and to lead to excessive centralization. However, once laid out they naturally exerted an influence on the direction and extent of economic activity. Even where the state, as in Britain, surrendered part of the road network to private undertakings and left canals and railways to the capitalist promoter, it could not remain indifferent to the social and political aspects of new forms of transport. They required powers, such as the acquisition of land or the passing of by-laws on their property, for which state backing was required. The state found that it had to adopt a regulative function from the start and that its interest grew as the monopolistic character of the railway and other forms of transport became clear.

Nevertheless, it was as a branch of business that most transport undertakings must be considered; and even state concerns could not escape the laws of the market. As already noticed, transport was subject to some additional business risks: these arose from the heavy outlay required and the danger of over-shooting.

It was characteristic of the new forms of transport associated with early industrial capitalism that they were promoted in booms when over-optimistic expectations prevailed. Of course, some projects might never be put in hand when the boom ended, but others were that might never have been started if more sober judgements had prevailed. Thus there were early canals and railways that could never expect to earn a profit – or at least not one sufficient to justify their existence on purely commercial grounds. Besides under-used facilities, the boom – bust pattern also meant over-capitalization in relation to the real value of assets and their economic benefits.

59

Transport businesses, canals and railways, were among the first modern joint stock companies at a time when few if any manufacturing businesses used this form. This gave the ever-optimistic (in some cases fradulent) promoter wide scope and placed the losses on a large number of shareholders, and may have encouraged irresponsibility. For the society as a whole there was some loss when capital was sunk in unremunerative projects. On the other hand, from the public point of view worthwhile undertakings may not have produced the average rate of return on capital for shareholders because of heavy or inflated capital costs. In this case the economy as a whole benefited at the expense of the investors whose money had been sunk in the low-profit or loss-making enterprises.

In the incessant search for cost-reducing innovations, new forms of transport emerged to challenge those already established and to establish new, unstable competitive patterns. To some extent, it is true, different forms could be complementary: some roads might feed canals or the railway trunk lines. More often there was competition for traffic, sometimes consisting of aggressive rate-cutting as in the war between the early railways and the canals in Britain. At this time the railway seriously undermined the competitive position of other forms of transport and virtually drove its competitors out of business. Until the coming of the self-propelled road vehicle, long-distance road transport could not resist rail competition, and folded up. Long-distance inland or coastal shipping could hold its own only where there were no entirely alternative rail routes or in the carriage of bulky, low-cost cargoes in which speed was not essential. Thus some American and continental canals increased their traffic after the coming of the railway as their share in general economic expansion. In Britain, where short hauls predominated, the railways ousted both the long-distance road and effective canal competition. The power of new forms of competition left the community with costly under-used facilities, no longer profitable but perhaps socially desirable. It happened in Britain when railways superseded canals. The railway system faced a similar plight with the extension of the use of the private car and the building of motorways suitable for long-distance freight traffic. It was the fate also of the luxury liner in the face of competition from jet-propelled airliners.

Each form of transport has had its specific relation to economic development in the period of industrialization and illustrates the points already discussed. After a review of the contribution of these forms to economic development it should be possible to cast further light on the role of transport as a whole.

The track, path or road for the pedestrian, pack-horse or wheeled cart is the basic facility for overland transport. The peasant beat out his own path from cottage to field; the lord imposed *corvées* on the peasantry to build roads to the market centre, while the inter-city roads came within the province of the ruler. What sort of results this gave depended less on technology than upon other factors, political as much as economic, until the capitalist era. There could have been no Roman Empire without roads, and they were an essential part of European state-building. Roads built for administrative purposes did not necessarily assist the economy. Eighteenth-century France had some good roads but they were not much used; the peasant needed local roads, connections with the town, and those he seldom got. In most countries compulsory road work was perfunctorily carried out and road surfaces were of poor quality, breaking up in dry weather and becoming waterlogged under heavy rain. Road transport in pre-industrial societies was usually slow, expensive and perhaps danger-ous, with the forces of law and order constantly being outwitted by bandits and highwaymen. A map of roads purportedly existing in the eighteenth century might disguise the fact that many were little more than pathways, suitable for horsemen and pack animals but not for wheeled carts or coaches. Even so, the extensive use of pack animals shows how badly improved transport was needed and also that goods were moving on an increasing scale despite high costs.

Cost was the basic problem. As long as roads remained unim-proved, and, in the carriage of bulky, heavy goods even when they were, commodities sold at any distance from their place of origin would cost much more. Only the lighter, more valuable goods could be traded at great distance overland. Heavy capital expenditure and new constructional techniques were necessary before the roads could be made fit for wheeled traffic, thus greatly increasing the hauling capacity of the horse. The attention given to road improvement in Britain and all developing areas in the eighteenth century is thus understandable; roads were needed to widen the market, to expand opportunities for profit-making. Civil engineering and road-surfacing and road-making techniques improved considerably. New roads were made and old ones improved. The device of the turnpike shifted financial and administrative responsibility on to *ad hoc* private enter-prise and made the user pay. The turnpike trust was widely used in Britain, and in the United States private corporations controlled many main highways in Pennsylvania and other northerly states; even so, publicly controlled turnpikes or state roads were the general rule. In Europe as a whole the state took over road-building and maintenance, often continuing to use compulsory labour until the breakup of feudalism rendered it obsolete. In any case, in the more backward areas private enterprise was unwilling as well as unsuited to shoulder such tasks, while strategic considerations were often paramount in forcing the state to develop its highways. In France and other European countries officials in the relevant departments of state developed a strong professional interest in technical and administrative efficiency. The state was thus the main employer of the civil engineer. In England the state was weaker and responsibility for the roads had been laid upon the smallest administrative unit, and not a very efficient one – the parish. So either the state had to step in, or the task was taken over by the turnpike trust. Significantly, however, the turnpike road did not necessarily mean an improvement.

During the first phase of the Industrial Revolution in Britain improved roads made possible the operation of regular coach services and an improvement in the time taken by horse-drawn vehicles to link the main towns. This was valuable in making possible greater personal mobility – though it was still confined mainly to those able to pay the relatively high fares – and the transmission of information. Commercial travellers could move around to display their products and seek orders. Catalogues and samples could be sent to prospective customers. Bankers could transmit bills of exchange and perhaps notes and money if there was not too much risk of robbery. Light merchandise and the more valuable commodities could find a national market. Road transport continued to have its hazards and its delays, and it could only move at the speed of the horse, relays being necessary over long distances. Attempts to develop a horseless carriage driven by steam power proved a failure; the heavy weight of fuel necessarily carried by such vehicles left little or nothing for the payload. Movement of bulky goods by road remained prohibitively expensive, while little impact was made on the mobility of labour and the development of a national labour market.

Once the railway had proved itself, there was little place for long-distance road transport. However, the railway did not reach everywhere. The horse remained as indispensable as ever for urban as well as rural transport until displaced by the electric tram. The roads remained significant as feeders to the railway and improvement of local roads enabled the railways to exercise their full effect on agriculture.

The rapid adoption of the motor vehicle in the United States before 1914, and even among the landed gentry and prosperous farmers in Europe, indicates the enormous gaps left by the railway in providing an adequate transport system. Not every village or every farmer or peasant could be served by rail even in the countries best endowed with railway track. The railway could handle bulk supplies of grain and milk better than it could other products. For the trip to market the farmer still had to harness his cart and spend many hours on the road; the rural transport revolution waited on the internal combustion engine. It was the motorcar and truck that broke down rural isolation and completed what the railways had only begun.

Water transport enjoys a considerable cost advantage over overland transport in the movement of goods that are bulky but relatively inexpensive in proportion to their weight. The long-distance carriage of the basic fuel of early industrialism as well as of the main constructional materials was made possible by rivers, canals and coastal shipping. Hence the importance of rivers and ports, inland as well as coastal, for commercial development everywhere. This had, of course, long predated the industrial age and partly determined the location of the new forms of economic activity. The improvement and enlargement of ports, and the deepening and widening of rivers to improve their navigable capacities, were objects of attention wherever an active business class came on the scene.

The cutting of artificial waterways grew directly out of the interest in rivers and ports and implied the existence of the preconditions already noted: a commercial need, technical ability and available capital. The canals raised constructional problems of an entirely new kind and went ahead earliest and most rapidly in the more advanced areas. They involved knowledge of hydraulics and skill in mastering the problems offered by the terrain. They required ways of mobilizing capital and of organizing a hired labour force to carry out constructional projects on a large scale and as a profit-making venture. To a much greater degree than with previous types of transport improvement, therefore, the canals required innovation and were symbols of the new capitalist age.

Canal-building came into its own in Britain by the 1760s at a time when industrialization is traditionally assumed to have begun, and followed some decades of river improvement, mostly in the areas in which canals were built. The canals were built to carry those bulky commodities upon which the developing economy depended, providing new and vital arteries of trade linking complementary areas together. In the United States canal-building reached its peak from the 1820s, while in continental Europe it continued much later and was connected with the realization of the economic significance of the river systems. Everywhere canals gave new flexibility to the movement of heavy industrial materials and stimulated the mining of coal and the opening up of other deposits of natural resources. They could also move building materials, farm products and bulk imports such as cotton and timber.

In Britain canals were a private enterprise, in most cases financed through the sale of shares on the capital market. They were the object of speculative manias, resulting in the construction of canals that could never make profits or give a return on investment. The profitability of canals was finally destroyed by competition from the railways. State finance and promotion were prominent in European countries and also in the United States, where canals were regarded as public improvements. Generally in other countries rail competition proved less damaging than in Britain. The canals went on to become, together with the natural waterways, irreplaceable links in national transport networks and in some cases in international trade.

Canal companies did not usually provide carrying facilities, but collected a toll from barge or boat operators to provide for mainten-ance and the return on capital. As long as canals had exclusive command of long-distance bulk transport they tended to exploit their monopoly position. As transport links canals had distinct and obvious disadvantages: they might freeze in cold weather or run low in time of drought; they were slow and therefore unsuitable for the carriage of perishable goods; delivery times were liable to be uncertain; and the delays to which barges were liable at locks or in backwaters encouraged pilfering. Clearly, they could not match the railway for speed of delivery and timetable punctuality.

Coastal shipping was inseparably connected with port development and the growth of the internal market in the early industrial period. Its cost advantage, which it shared with inland waterways, gave those countries and regions possessing a long coastline and suitably shel-tered ports an important potential for growth. In the case of Britain this was made full use of. Coastal ships were small and versatile enough to sail up estuaries and into rivers, so their use for carrying bulk goods helped widen the market and permit regional specializa-tion as in the case of the famous Newcastle – London coal trade. But this was only one of many examples of regular seaborne trade between different parts of the country. Coastal trade could also handle the distribution of bulk imports coming in by sea.

As a means of passenger transport coastal shipping was slow and uncomfortable, and it had certain disadvantages in the carriage of goods. Sea transport even within sight of land could be hazardous; a sea voyage might mean a long and time-consuming detour and there was the risk of the loss or deterioration of the cargo. As long as inland transport was deficient and costly, however, these disadvantages did not deter users, even passengers. In England and other regions coastal shipping, like the canals, suffered severely from rail competition.

Railways have been accorded a privileged position in the explanation of nineteenth-century economic development because of the scale of the investment effort that went into them, the propulsive effect that they are supposed to have had on the rate of growth and the way in which contemporaries reacted to this new mode of transport. More recently, however, historians have adopted a more sceptical attitude, based upon attempts to measure the contribution of railways to the growth of particular countries and calculating what additional costs would have been entailed in depending upon other forms of transport. While it cannot be assumed that any innovation was indispensable to economic growth, and while both the first stages of the Industrial Revolution in Britain and of westward movement in the United States were carried through without the railway, in practice it proved to be of enormous strategic significance.

Unlike the other forms of transport preceding it, the railway was a product of industrialization and presupposed prior technical and industrial development as well as the accumulation of capital on a large scale. Moreover, it proved to be a key factor in promoting industrialization in areas where other prerequisites were available and existing forms of transport were not apparently adequate to make possible the extension of markets on a national scale. Notwithstanding the work of some 'new' economic historians in downgrading the railway as an instrument of growth in the United States, the more traditional appreciation of its role retains much of its validity for Germany, France, Russia and other European countries. In particular, they were able to take over the railway virtually as a going concern, importing technology, capital and enterprise from outside.

The running of wheeled vehicles on rails reduces friction and thus enables a given load to be moved with a smaller effort. This principle was discovered centuries ago and was particularly useful in mining operations, where heavy loads had to be shifted from the pithead, say, to nearby waterways. By the eighteeenth century some colliery railways had become fairly elaborate, using horses or inclined planes with several miles of track, tunnels and bridges. While still an adjunct of colliery operation, the iron rail had been improved and the flange transferred from the rail to the wheel. In the early years of the nineteenth century some advance was made in England with the construction of public railways for short-distance haulage using horses. About the same time experiments were taking place with the horseless carriage. The development of Watt's rotary steam-engine had led naturally to thought of its use for traction, but for this to be practical further improvements had to be made in the steam-engine, notably the tubular boiler. By the end of the first quarter of the nineteenth century the practicability of the steam locomotive running on rails and drawing trucks had been established, although it was some time before the stationary engine and alternative methods of propulsion were finally abandoned.

By the late 1820s, therefore, short commercial lines were being built and longer ones were projected. This could only have occurred in an economy possessed of the technique, productive capacity and capital resources already provided by industrialism. With the opening of the Livepool and Manchester line in 1830, in direct competition with the canal and linking the port and the main metropolis of the thriving cotton-manufacturing area, the triumph of the railway was assured. Within a decade it had become an important factor in the British economy and was being adopted in other countries. It released the movement of goods and people from a dependence upon traditional means of transport using the forces of nature. The coming of the steam locomotive thus symbolized man's conquest of nature; it was, within a few years, to achieve hitherto unheard-of speeds and reliability. Its impact on contemporary life and thought was thus understandably immense and not surprisingly may have led to some exaggeration of its real cost-saving.

The railway was seized upon as a new type of profitable investment by financiers and promoters, many of them new men not belonging to the established business groups. It was first and foremost a business proposition, and even where governments were involved they were prodded and pushed by the business interests hoping for a high rate of return on capital. As a service, the railway did everything that the earlier internal transport improvements had done, but generally with a saving of time, expense and risk. It provided cheap, efficient and rapid transport for goods of all classes, from the most perishable up to the heavy, bulky materials of industrialism in which canals and rivers had hitherto enjoyed a monopoly. It proved to be unique in making possible personal mobility on a mass scale and with steadily improving convenience and comfort. It was the first entirely modern means of transport, and it set new standards for its eventual competitors to attempt to surpass.

In Britain the railway consolidated and extended a market already nationwide for many commodities, making possible greater regional specialization and the geographical concentration of industry. On the whole, in this already industrializing region it confirmed existing patterns rather than creating new ones and carried forward a national integration already relatively far advanced. In the great European states, however, the effects of the railway were more far-reaching. There the task of state-building, and even more the growth of genuinely national markets, had been painfully slow, largely because of the large distances to be traversed and the inadequacy of existing means of transport and communications. Industrial growth was impeded by the high cost of assembling raw materials from scattered areas and then distributing the finished products. Markets thus tended to be localized. The markets of agriculture were even more geographically circumscribed, and much of agricultural production was carried on outside, or only on the fringes of, the exchange economy. The railway, as it was built, thus acted powerfully to remove old barriers to growth by widening the market, and to integrate national units by bringing the different parts into closer and more frequent contact with each other. Manifestly, railways played a major role in the economic awakening and political unification of Europe's slumbering giant, Germany. Likewise, an analysis of French economy in the first half of the nineteenth century suggests that it was held back by poor transport facilities and that the railway played a vital part in its industrialization.

Both Germany and France were at first able to borrow or purchase from Britain what was necessary for the construction of railways. Within a comparatively short time they were able, in their turn, to export railway material and to finance construction in less developed parts of Europe, while British finance and enterprise turned from the European continent to the development of railways throughout the world. The railway was thus a major instrument in the formation of the world market and the international division of labour characteristic of the nineteenth century. Primary producing areas were opened up throughout the world as foreign, mainly British, capital built railways into the interior, improved harbours and port facilities and thrust them on to the historical stage as the purveyors of raw materials and foodstuffs, outlets for the manufactured goods of the advanced countries and debtors of the financial centres of Europe. In the sparsely populated areas suitable for European settlement, in North America, Australasia, South America and South Africa, the railway became an instrument of colonization. Their staple products could be delivered to the ports in ever-increasing quantities by the railways where ocean-going cargo ships brought them to the consuming countries. In the less developed areas, such as India, the railway was palpably an instrument of empire.

The railway was the great innovation of the mid-Victorian era, the symbol of advancing capitalism, psychologically stimulating for all and a source of enrichment for a few. Its linkage effects on supplying industries and on the stimulation of the economy as a provider of transport services can be discussed only on the basis of statistical measurement in each case. This has led to lengthy and involved controversies, especially in the case of the United States. Attempts to measure the contribution of the railways began with a dissatisfaction with old and sweeping generalizations. Unfortunately, nothing very satisfactory has been put in their place, and, subject to the warning about measurement, some are worth repeating for their essential validity.

Railway construction created an additional demand for iron, timber, bricks and other constructional materials as well as for labour. It thus created incomes, which were spent on other capital and consumption goods in a multiplier effect. As a going concern railways generated a demand for coal, lubricants, cloth (for their uniformed staff) and paper (for timetables, posters and the administration of the enterprise), and provided permanent jobs for drivers, porters, maintenance men and clerks. In general, railways exemplified the role of transport in economic change in the ways already outlined. Because of their speed and reliability they were able to do things that previous means of transport had not been able to do, with correspondingly important social and economic effects. For example, perishable foodstuffs like fresh fish and milk could be distributed over a wide area; a cheap mail service became possible; books and newspapers circulated on a national scale. Besides influencing the rate of urbanization and making possible the first suburban sprawl around large cities, the railways created new towns, such as Crewe and Swindon, and influenced the growth of resorts and ports. In fact, there was hardly any aspect of social and economic life that was not affected. Business could grow in scale without loss of centralized control, national administrations could become more effective and labour mobility was increased.

While internal transport systems were being improved, the nineteenth century also witnessed a great expansion of ocean shipping, the vital link in the creation of a world market. It made a fundamental contribution to industrialization by permitting the advanced countries to extend their markets overseas and to obtain necessary raw materials and foodstuffs at economic cost from distant sources. Large movements of population took place, principally from Europe to the other continents, as by that time the slave trade had been outlawed, but there were also sizeable movements by sea of Asiatic peoples.

Changes in the design of vessels, the substitution of steam for sail and the development of the screw-driven ship as well as the change-over from timber to iron and then to steel brought about a continuous increase in efficiency and decline in costs. This long process of technical improvement was made possible by a reorganization and expansion of shipbuilding, by new forms of organization and by the provision of capital in the shipping industry itself.

Shipping and the shipbuilding industry had long been recognized by governments as factors in national political power. The English Navigation Acts were a typical and successful example of a protective policy, contributing to Britain's success in the long series of wars for maritime and colonial supremacy which began in the mid-seventeenth century and came to an end only in 1815. Once Britain's superiority, not only in maritime trade but also in industrial technology, had been established, the whole protective system became obsolete and in 1849 the Navigation Acts were repealed. By the 1830s international trade began to grow at a more rapid rate, with Britain in a key position. The repeal came at the very time when the technical changeover was making shipbuilding a branch of engineering and was ending its dependence upon the forest. Until then, however, British shipping was being seriously challenged by the rise of the United States mercantile marine.

American shipyards were able to exploit cheap and abundant supplies of softwood. They turned out improved sailing ships with a greater expanse of sail and a greater speed and carrying capacity. American ships were worked by smaller crews, by skippers of great skill who exacted the utmost effort. Their owners were sharp and enterprising and were assisted by discrimination against foreign flags modelled after the English Navigation Laws. In the 1840s the famous clipper ships were introduced, and American competition won control of the China tea trade and made a bid for the North Atlantic, Australian and Mediterranean trades. But the cost of construction was rising in American yards. The clipper ships were effective only in trades where speed was the significant factor. They were more expensive to run and carried less of a payload than more orthodox vessels. Speculative construction in the 1850s led to over-competition. With the repeal of the Navigation Acts British shipowners bought American-built ships. But in any case the sweep of technical change favoured British yards and placed the Americans in an increasingly unfavourable position. American enterprise and capital, including capital accumulated in the maritime industries, was drawn towards the development of the vast hinterland. The Civil War completed the undermining of the competitiveness of American shipping and ship-building and left the way open for British domination of the carrying trade until the First World War.

Freight rates declined markedly during this period. Average freight rates on a pound of cotton shipped from New York to Liverpool fell from 0.5 pence in 1823–25 to 0.16 pence in 1851–55. Exceptional falls in rates were reported in the 1850s, by almost 50 per cent in some trades. There was intense competition for return immigrant cargoes for vessels sailing across the Atlantic with their holds full of cotton, grain or timber. Further falls in freight and passenger rates were to come in the depressed years of the last quarter of the century.

The outstanding charge in organization of shipping services was the rise of specialized shipping firms, often concentrating on particular routes and a general carrying business. This form of business organ-ization superseded the earlier system, under which ships were owned and managed largely by private merchants or privileged companies whose own merchandise formed a large part of the cargo. In the main ports shares in vessels, divided into sixty-four parts, were used to raise capital, and this method continued well into the nineteenth century but could not properly cope with the new demands. The shipping firms provided tramps, or transient ships, or might offer scheduled sailings on a particular route. Packet lines, developed for the passenger trade, required at least two ships; competition stimu-lated improvements in the vessels and in the accommodation offered. Rivalry became intense, with speed becoming a major consideration. Big capitals entered the field to run ocean liners, as happened in the case of Inmans of Liverpool. The sixty-fourths system was recognized by the Merchant Shipping Act in Britain in 1854, but the Company Act of 1862 speeded up the use of the joint stock company without which the big shipping lines, with their increasingly expensive vessels, would have been impossible.

Although technical change was continuous, it was hardly revol-utionary. Ships were highly durable pieces of capital equipment and, barring accidents, could pay their way for years, or even decades, after they had become technically obsolete. The newer types involved heavy and risky investment, and many owners and ships' officers were reluctant to depart from traditional designs, materials and methods of propulsion. The early steamboats were inefficient because of their heavy fuel consumption which restricted cargo space. Composite sail and steamships, with sail only gradually becoming the auxiliary, were useful throughout the century. The screw took the place of the paddle-wheel only slowly. Steamships came into use on rivers, lakes and short sea routes before they took command of transoceanic traffic. The steamship began to take over from the mid-century. Its voyage time was more predictable than that of the sailing ship, whose arrival could never be counted upon with any accuracy. Thus the steamship won the favour of all those concerned with punctuality of arrival: cabin passengers, postal authorities and shippers of high-class or perishable merchandise. As steamships grew in size and reliability they were able to offer better passenger quarters and hotel-type service. Even so, the early steam packet lines were, actually or in effect, subsidized by governments (for example through payment for carrying mail) and required extremely careful management to prove a financial success. In fact, it was not until the 1870s that steamers were able to compete really effectively with sail in the long-distance carrying trade.

The newer industrial countries, such as Germany and Italy, seeing the importance of ocean shipping for trade and colonial expansion, gave it subsidies and special favours. Governments were obliged to step in to lay down standards of safety, stipulate the qualifications of masters and officers and regulate the living conditions of the crew and passengers. National legislation thus tended to become increasingly detailed and could be used to discriminate against foreign flags.

The growth of the shipping industry necessarily encouraged shipbuilding, a field in which Britain retained a competitive advantage until the twentieth century. It also had as a necessary corollary investment in harbours, port and dock installations, navigational aids on land, around the coast and in estuaries, and the creation of feeder services in inland transport. The success of particular ports depended on their geographical position relative to the great trade routes, but also upon the availability of capital and the vision and enterprise of local business leaders. Success tended to breed success, with a few large ports capturing a major part of the traffic at the expense of their rivals. Big ports had to provide a range of facilities for handling trade and financing it. Processing plants and servicing activities of various kinds tended to be drawn to port areas and internal transport links radiated from them. Thus the market of each country involved in trade was linked through ocean shipping to the world market and the international division of labour.

Industrialization made necessary transport facilities of growing scale, complexity and expense. Therefore special financial problems arose with which the small entrepreneur or partnership was unable to cope. Transport businesses tended to be above the average size and in some cases were giants, the first big businesses. Capital had to be raised from a wide investing public through the sale of shares, or in some cases was provided wholly or in part by the state from the general revenue. The early canals and even more the railways put on to the capital market a large volume of paper titles to ownership and familiarized a wider public with their activities. The services they provided, together with the telegraph and the cable, made possible rapid communication within and between countries. Capital became more mobile, more easily mobilizable for the projects of advancing capitalism. At the same time, the reduction of transport costs, the expansion of the market and the enormous growth in internal and international trade made it possible to generate the ever-larger volumes of capital required. The huge capital costs of transport facilities gave the advanced countries an enormous advantage over the dependent countries in the global economy that was coming into being.

While transport improvements ostensibly drew countries closer together and, with the coming of jet transport, literally shrank the globe, they were also instruments of national economic integration and political unification. As such they tended to sharpen international competition and rivalry. Already at the time of the Franco-Prussian war use was made of the railway timetable to speed up mobilization. In preparation for war, or war itself, transport facilities are the first to be requisitioned. This is one part of the industrialization of war, an important matter which, is, however, not pursued in this book.

CHAPTER SIX
Banking and industrialization

Of all the institutions of a modern capitalist society, banks are perhaps those generally found to be most perplexing. Their apparent wealth, symbolized by the possession of impressive office premises, the operations by which they achieve it and the occult power they are supposed to exercise, make them objects of wonder, fear and admiration. Banks have become an indispensable and integral part of the economic system and their role, like that of other institutions, is best understood through their history. At the same time, it can also be said that the development of industrialization cannot be understood without examining the role of banks, and that an effort must therefore be made to bring this relationship into focus and to do so historically. It is necessary to emphasize the latter point because, as will be shown, banks arose under various historical conditions, to satisfy diverse needs; and they performed different functions, under the general heading of banking, according to the level of economic development in the different societies in which they arose. The history of banking lends itself particularly to comparative study because national banking systems today reflect very much these varied national patterns of development. Into them enter many factors, including the policy of governments, the influence of foreign models and the attempt to deal with specific needs arising from the nature of the economy at a particular time. Moreover, within a particular country there may be found a diversity of banks whose functions relate to particular sectors of the economy, such as agriculture or foreign commerce. Other institutions like loan or mortgage companies may carry on banking functions; the government and the labour and cooperative movement may run banks; while banks themselves fit into a wider framework of institutions concerned with short- and long-term credit needs.

The history of banking obviously antedates the beginning of industrialization though the great institutional development of banking has accompanied it. Banking emerges out of the needs of trade, that is of commodity exchange. Once commodities are produced for sale and bought and sold on the market for money, some people will come into possession of more money than they need for immediate purchases, while others will not have enough cash to make the purchases they would like to make. This will be particularly true of those who act as intermediaries in trade, as distinct from the final consumer or even the producer. Such men, traders or merchants, are all the time finding themselves in one or another of these positions – of having too much ready money or not enough. Moreover, there may be other people on the scene, such as landowners, farmers and inactive businessmen, who have spare funds for which they are seeking an outlet. In even quite backward societies that have been penetrated by money relations, lending and borrowing goes on; we have, thus, the ubiquity of the usurer as in early modern Europe or nineteenth-century India. Various groups seek to borrow money while others are willing to lend it – at a price, the going rate of interest. Borrowers and lenders, debtors and creditors are thus found in most societies in which commodity production and the use of money are prevalent. These relations, based on credit, provide the need for financial intermediaries able to bridge the gap between those needing to borrow money and those willing to lend it, as well as for lenders who use their own surplus cash. The intermediary clearly makes his profits, or the payment for his services, out of the difference between the interest paid by those to whom he lends and that which he pays to those from whom he borrows. The appearance of such intermediaries also requires the existence of some instrument, usually a piece of paper, testifying to the debtor's willingness to pay off the loan, with the specified interest, at a given date.

In this way we have described the embryonic form of banking, the basic need it satisfies, the type of service it provides and the means through which it does so. But the existence of these transactions does not mean the appearance of banks in a formal sense. They may be carried out by merchants as a side line to their trade in commodities, especially where they handle large sums of money, have payments to make or receive payments in various ports and towns. Banking history shows innumerable examples of merchants who became bankers – the Rothschilds for example – and nothing could have been more natural. It merely represented a shift from a trade in commodities to a trade in the universal equivalent of all commodities, i.e.

money. The trade in money could be, and often was, the most lucrative trade of all; it was also the most sophisticated trade of all, requiring dealing in the precious metals, exchanging one form of money for another and taking advantage of variations in the rate of interest prevailing in different trading centres. Moreover, while it was easy to understand how a trade in commodities could enable men to get rich, the wealth of money-dealers appeared to depend on a special alchemy. Its existence defied the Aristotelian precept that money cannot beget money, and the teachings of the Church directed against usury. Money-dealers, embryonic bankers, were, therefore, in medieval and early modern times under somewhat of a cloud, recruited from minorities or foreign groups, such as the Jews or the Lombards in England. Not only did their wealth give them consideration, however; governments and many members of the ruling class, with the growth of money dealings, found themselves chronic borrowers, forced to resort to the financiers and money-dealers to make both ends meet. The rise of state expenditure, and particularly the growing cost of wars, meant that in the seventeenth and eighteenth century the states of Europe had to borrow on an increasing scale. Not only private credit, but also public credit, became a profitable field for the emerging bankers.

A bank properly appears when a firm offers to accept money on deposit, pay interest to depositors and effect the transfer of such funds by loans and drafts. This involves the existence of notes and bills of various kinds. But it may take some time before banking detaches itself from other forms of business, and even after banks appeared banking functions for a long time continued to be provided by merchants or, indeed, by anyone able to act as a financial intermediary. For example, notaries and solicitors having charge of clients' funds often found profitable employment for them because, through their activities, they knew of other people able to make use of them and ready to pay for the privilege. Though the varied origins of banking firms may be interesting, it is with the operations of banks recognized as such that we shall be principally concerned. Under the fractional reserve system banks need only hold a part of their deposits as cash reserves, sufficient for day-to-day needs. In this way banks can multiply their lending powers, or create credit. Confidence is essential; depositors must believe that their money is available if they need it. If their confidence in the bank comes to an end for some reason there will be a rush to withdraw deposits, thus hastening its collapse.

Strictly speaking, England was by no means a pioneer in the

development of the practices so far described, but in the course of the eighteenth century she not only went ahead in industrialization but also established a banking structure that was in some ways to be a model for the world. It certainly permitted England to dominate the world market financially until the First World War. English banking followed the two lines of development mentioned above: it was concerned with public credit and also with private financing. The first began with the foundation of the Bank of England in 1694; the second is usually traced to the London goldsmith bankers of the seventeenth century and the provincial banks growing out of a business in trade and industry, for the most part after the Glorious Revolution of 1689. By this time internal commercial expansion was in full swing with a continuous growth in the volume of money transactions, and foreign trade was of increasing importance. There was a growing demand for capital and credit, exactly the kind of atmosphere for the embryonic bankers to spread their wings in. The network of commercial transactions, including those arising from the main form of industry at this time, the putting-out system, gave rise to complex transactions between middlemen of various sorts, many of whom used credit, not cash, in much of their business. Daniel Defoe estimated that about two-thirds of internal commerce was conducted on a credit basis.

There is no means of telling whether Defoe exaggerated or not, but his instinct was sound; credit played an indispensable role in the expansion of trade. At the various stages between the time when raw material left the producer's hands until finished goods passed to the consumers, traders used bills of exchange or promissory notes instead of cash whenever they could. In other words, the purchaser would hand over his promise to pay, at a future date, with interest on the sum involved. Thus a credit instrument arose acknowledged by the signature of the borrower on the note. Bills of exchange could pass from hand to hand in settlement of debts, and in eighteenth-century Lancashire were so widely used in this way that business was able, for a long time, to dispense with banks. In a commercial community where most of the participants were known to each other default was unlikely. The widespread use of the bill of exchange, originating in a transaction in commodity trade at home or overseas, provided in England a network of credit on a scale not paralleled elsewhere at this time. It was the basis upon which some merchants and even manufacturers having to transmit funds or handling bills in the course of their own business could offer facilities to their neighbours or associates and perhaps metamorphose themselves into fully-fledged bankers. Instead of trading in commodities, they could trade in credit, holding bills until maturity or passing them on to others willing to do so. London houses came to occupy a central place in supplying credit to areas unable to generate enough by 'accepting' bills, placing their signatures on them and passing them on to areas with spare funds. Such activities became the occasion for the growth of specialized banks in the provinces, the country banks. Like other bankers, they discovered that they could issue notes in exchange for deposits or in the course of discounting bills and thus create additional credit for their customers in excess of their cash reserves.

The eighteenth-century English economy was characterized by a growth of the internal market as well as of foreign trade, facilitated by and at the same time calling for credit facilities and thus favourable to the development of banking. In practice the banking structure was shaped by the state of the law, or rather by the interpretation of the Bank of England's charter, held to restrict banking to partnerships of not more than six people. The Bank, by cautious management, developed its activities as a lender to the state and a recipient of government funds, using the 'fund of credit' thus made available to discount bills, lend on mortgages and other security, accept deposits and perform other banking services. In the course of these activities its notes were put into circulation, but they were of high denomination and circulated mainly in London and among a select clientele of big merchant houses to whose bills its discount business was mainly confined. In these circumstances the Bank of England had little effect on the growth of industry. It did not come into contact with the active centres of industrial growth, make capital available for long-term investment or discount bills arising from the trading and manufacturing activities of such areas. However, it helped to place state finance on a stable basis and to create an atmosphere of confidence beneficial to the development of credit relations. Its monopoly powers restricted the growth of banking and meant that English banks were limited in their supply of capital and were confined to one or a few branches in one area. This made it more difficult to spread risks and tied the bank closely to the fortunes of the type of agriculture or industry prevailing in the area in which it was established. In the 1750s there were still only a handful of banks, properly speaking, outside London, but the number grew rapidly and by 1800 there were about 400 and many more were started in the following decades.

These banks issued notes as well as dealing in bills of exchange. Opinions vary about their contribution to industrial development. They were formerly thought not to have played much part in the financing of long-term capital investment and to have confined their lending to the provision of short-term credit. The existence of a network of credit using the bill of exchange certainly provided the country banks with business and, through London acceptance houses, brought them into touch with something like a national structure of banking. The early factory entrepreneurs, who required large amounts of working capital, could insert themselves into this credit network by means of the bill of exchange. They could also use the banknotes which, especially because of the poor state of the coinage, made an important contribution to the monetary means of payment. The relative ease of obtaining short-term credit enabled the entrepreneur to employ a higher proportion of his own capital in investment in plant and machinery than he could otherwise have done. Short-term credit might be continually extended, so that it virtually became a medium or long-term loan. Personal or family connections with local bankers enabled some entrepreneurs to borrow from banks for long-term investment. It was dangerous for a bank to become too involved with the less liquid forms of investment, and 'sound' banking practice in England eschewed long-term loans to industry on that account. It was an instinct influenced by practice. Early banks were accident-prone; many had a short life and in some cases it may have been because of imprudent investment, a failure to distinguish between the short and the long term. Of course, the credit created by failed banks might enable real assets to be increased – at the expense of depositors or the bankers themselves. Banknote issues, for example, probably had a stimulating influence on the economy adding to the circulating medium, driving prices up and opening up a market for commodities. On the other hand, bank failures could create havoc, ruin many investors and put a blight on new enterprise until the effects were overcome.

In the early decades of country banking it is clear from the rapid growth in numbers that there must have been many who entered the profession with more enthusiasm than experience. The theory of banking had to be worked out pragmatically and was the source of endless discussion and controversy. Moreover, after 1797 and until 1821 England was on a managed paper currency. During this Bank Restriction period there was steady inflationary pressure resulting from government finance of the wars with France, in the course of which the National Debt increased almost fourfold. Excessive note issues by the Bank of England and the country banks were held responsible for the inflation; but they were, in effect, only accommodating the government and business themselves directly or indirectly affected by government contracts and paid in government paper. Throughout this period, in England, the prohibition on joint stock banking was maintained. In Scotland, however, banks were permitted to have more than six partners, although not limited liability, and branch banking developed, drawing deposits from a wide circle of even small savers. To meet the need for earnings to pay interest to depositors, the Scottish banks engaged in various forms of long-term lending. On the other hand, they resisted the temptation to over-issue notes and, although there were failures and runs on the banks, the Scottish system was relatively stable. In the 1820s the Scottish example was held up by the advocates of joint stock banking south of the border.

By the 1820s most provincial towns were well supplied with banks and their services were widely used by all the active economic agents of Britain's industrializing economy. Even though the banks may not have provided much direct long-term capital for industry, and despite their defects, largely attributable to the state of the law, as well as to the uncertainty of banking practice, it cannot be doubted that the banking structure was very much in advance of anything to be found elsewhere. Even the more developed areas of the Continent lacked the network of credit facilities available in Britain, mostly because the internal market was still narrow and fragmented rather than national in scope with a powerful financial centre such as London. Banking services for industry were notable by their absence. Those that did exist were provided rather by merchant bankers dealing in state loans and large-scale international transactions.

During the second quarter of the nineteenth century the banking structure in Britain, centred on the City of London, reinforced its early lead and contributed in major ways to the country's international economy predominance. The Bank of England had strengthened its position during the period of the managed paper currency. With the resumption of cash payments in 1821 the gold standard was adopted. The Bank was the custodian of the national bullion reserve and its note circulation was linked to the holdings of gold in its vaults. The operation of the gold standard required that note circulation should be reduced if gold was withdrawn to meet foreign payments or increased if gold flowed in as a result of a favourable balance of payments. It took some time for the bank directors to accept the responsibilities that followed from this, notably that the Bank had to adjust its own credit policy accordingly, subordinating its own short-run interests to the stabilization of the situation in the money market. The growing complexity of this market has briefly to be described.

Instability still characterized the banking structure, as was shown by the many failures in the crisis of 1826, in which sixty country banks collapsed. In that year an alteration in the law permitted the setting up of joint stock banks (though not with limited liability) outside a sixty-five-mile radius from London. The Bank also opened a number of branches in the larger provincial cities. At the time of the renewal of the Bank's charter in 1833 joint stock banks were permitted also within the London area, provided that they did not issue notes. By this time the London money market had become more specialized, with firms of bill brokers assembling bills of exchange and passing them on to the banks for discounting and to money-dealers, who actually held bills for which they gave cash. These bills, assumed to originate in a genuine commercial transaction, gave the banks, whether private or joint stock, a convenient, profitable and self-liquidating outlet for their funds. The money-dealers, of whom Overend and Gurneys was the best known, used their own funds or money borrowed from the banks for their discounting. This organized market gave great mobility for short-term capital and provided unrivalled facilities for the financing of trade whether at home or overseas. The firms concerned acquired experience and reputations, but the system was also fragile. For one thing it was difficult to guard against fraud and abuse; for another, all the firms involved were tempted to involve their funds to the utmost. Thus the banks lent money 'at call' to the money-dealers. In the event of these funds being recalled to meet a demand for increased cash on the part of the banks' customers – and all banks would be withdrawing funds at the same time – the dealers would find it difficult to meet bills as they fell due. From 1830 they were permitted to hold accounts at the Bank of England. As a result of the increased volume of bill-dealing owing partly to this the Bank moved reluctantly to the position where it had to re-discount bills for the money-dealers in an emergency; that is, it became a 'lender of last resort'. This became one of the classic functions of central banking in the latter part of the century.

The joint stock banks, though not at first as stable as their advocates had hoped, built up their business during the mid-Victorian expansion, setting up numerous branches, attracting customers by their favourable rates of interest and the services offered and helping to spread the banking habit widely among the propertied and middle classes. Nevertheless, periodical crises continued to decimate the money market about every ten years – in 1826, 1837, 1847, 1857 and 1866. Veritable panics swept the financial world on such occasions, revealing much unsound business and fraudulent practices and causing much heart-searching on the part of anxious Victorian editors and public men. Meanwhile, those of a theoretical bent were trying to systematize what banks were doing and lay down principles to observe if future panics were to be prevented. Some held that banknote circulation should be tied strictly to the gold reserves of the Bank of England, with the assumption that other forms of credit could not get far out of step. This was the view of the Currency School. Their opponents, known as the Banking School, argued that note circulation should reflect public demand and mistrusted government control of banking. Members of this school of thought claimed that if more notes were put into circulation than the public required they would be returned automatically. They stressed the smallness of the note circulation compared with other forms of 'money' or money substitutes. Their theories had a modern ring, but the government and, rather naturally, the Bank of England's directors, preferred the theories of the Currency School.

The Bank Charter Act of 1844, confirming the privileges of the Bank of England, was based on these latter theories. Despite serious flaws, it was to be the fundamental law of British banking until 1914. It divided the Bank's business into two departments, one concerned entirely with issue, the other with banking. Note issues were to be tied to gold, with the exception of an agreed fiduciary issue of £14 million in the first instance, backed by government securities. Provision was made for the eventual extinguishing of other note issues to centralize them in the Bank. In terms of central banking development, the Act represented a step backward, since it was claimed that, once the note-issuing functions had been separated from the banking department, the latter could behave in the market just like any other profit-seeking bank. In any case, the Act was far from living up to expectations and soon had to be breached when, in October 1847, the government authorized the Bank to increase its discounts and advances to end the panic then raging in the London money market and promised a Bill of Indemnity if this should result in an infringement of the Act. On that occasion the Bank did not have to exceed its note-issuing powers: the psychological effect of knowing that it could helped to calm the market. However, critics point out that it was a queer kind of law that only worked when, every ten years or so, the government had to give permission for it to be ignored.

Despite these controversies and defects in the working of the law and in the money market itself, the British banking and financial system became something of a model in the course of the nineteenth century and ensured Britain international financial predominance. Long-term projects of expanding capitalism could be financed in London through the great merchant banking houses with their cosmopolitan connections and wide experience. They were able to tap an unrivalled pool of idle funds from the wealthy, especially the landowners, and from a broader layer of middle-class *rentiers* produced by the expansion of the British economy. These people had spare funds but no direct contact with industry or other investment outlets. They were retired businessmen or their widows and heirs, professional people, small property-owners, farmers, entrepreneurs wishing to spread their risks. They were attracted not only by the prospect of an income from the holding of paper titles but also by capital gains during the speculative waves through which the economy passed. Railways provided a vast amount of paper to attract these funds, as did foreign and colonial investment; but company law, until the reforms of the 1850s and 1860s, denied limited liability to most enterprises and little of this *rentier* capital found its way into industry. The long-term capital market acquired a foreign bias which it was to retain until the twentieth century.

British practice influenced those countries which were part of the empire, though not always with the best results. Thus Indian banks resembled those in Britain and were geared mainly to providing short-term credit for the needs of trade when investment banks on the German model would probably have been more appropriate. On the other hand, in Canada the many small banks which existed earlier were combined into a small number of networks thus avoiding the weaknesses of the American banking system based upon many local banks not permitted to operate outside the state in which they were established.

The same sort of people who held shares in railways, government stock and foreign paper also, together with the business community at large, made up the clientele of the expanding banking system, especially the joint stock banks. The latter tended to consolidate into regional groups and to open offices in London, dropping note issue and concentrating more on loans and advances through the overdraft to customers. This proved more flexible than the bill of exchange, though it too was intended mainly for short periods. The bill of exchange therefore declined as an instrument for the financing of internal trade, retaining its importance in foreign trade. The railway and the telegraph, improved ocean shipping and then cable connections between the main international centres brought London into ever-closer contact with the world financial system which it continued to dominate. However, London also became more sensitive to conditions elsewhere, and the Bank of England was forced to become the continuous watchdog of the external situation. The pound sterling became the key currency of the world financial system and the Bank had to develop rules for running the gold standard and apply them. Central banking became more formalized, in a pragmatic way at first, in response to these unique conditions. In principle this meant that some measure of financial autonomy was lost as the internal credit situation and the level of economic activity became bound up with the external balance. Britain's financial pre-eminence meant that the practice was somewhat different: the burden of adjustment could, before 1914, be thrown on to other parts of the world economy.

To consider the role of banking in the industrialization of Britain in isolation from the whole context of the money market would be unrealistic. Nor is it very meaningful to ask whether the banking facilities were adequate. Banking did not develop to provide long-term funds for industry; that it found most of its own funds for expansion was only normal as it became the main source of surplus capital for investment. In the main, in Britain, the banks had other functions arising from the mutiplicity of financial transactions generated by internal business and from the central role of the country in the international market. No doubt institutional factors, notably the state of the law and the position of the Bank of England, dominated as it was by conservative interests in London in close relation with the government, brought weaknesses as well as advantages. The Bank Charter Act of 1844 was not the wisest measure taken by Parliament at this time and could have been improved upon. However, it became, as it were, part of the established order of things; it worked pragmatically, it proved to be flexible enough not to impede expansion, and it may have added to that confidence in the system which was all-important.

In most other countries the banking structure remained weak and lopsided until industrialization began. Then the banks, or some of them, were called upon to play a more active role in propelling economic growth. However, banks are founded in response to a demand for their services, and the kind of business they offer is related to needs. Once a certain pattern of business has proved safe and profitable there will be some inertia built into the institutions concerned. Equally, banking business, just like any other, may be a field for innovation: new methods, new techniques of financing may be tried and tested by pioneer institutions. Conservative inertia as well as innovating entrepreneurs are to be found throughout banking history. Not surprisingly, opinions differ about the role of banking in the industrialization of particular countries, if only because it is difficult to separate its specific contribution from all the other factors in the process.

France was the country that most nearly approached Britain in industrial development in the eighteenth and early nineteenth century, but she remained behind as far as the concentration of capital and the application of new techniques were concerned. There were many reasons for this and the absence of a banking system reflected the absence of a need arising from an active network of internal transactions already typical of Britain. Such banking as existed was concerned with raising loans for the state and financing large-scale trade and currency exchanges with foreign countries. It was in the hands of a small number of firms, mainly Protestant in religion, forming *la haute banque parisienne*. They were joined by a branch of the Rothschilds and other Jewish bankers concerned with the same type of business. These bankers achieved considerable influence and Napoleon I called upon them when he founded the Bank of France in 1800. This was intended to be a central bank with note-issuing powers, similar to the Bank of England. By the time of Louis Philippe's reign (1830–48) *la haute banque* had acquired still more influence and took a leading role in the financing of the railways, but large-scale foreign trade remained a major source of profits. Both the Protestant and the Jewish bankers had extensive foreign connections, but they were looking for other outlets for investment – in insurance, mining and large-scale industry – by the 1840s. Some provincial towns had their own version of *la haute banque* carrying on a similar kind of business, but most of the country had no banks at all before the Revolution of 1848. The only innovation came with the establishment of a number of what were called *caisses* (as distinct from banks issuing notes). These institutions accepted deposits, discounted bills and made loans to industry; they raised additional funds by issuing interest-bearing certificates repayable at short term. The most famous of these *caisses*, established by Jean Lafitte in 1837, collapsed in 1847 during the financial crisis: it had borrowed at short term and lent at long term, always a dangerous thing for a bank to do. The other *caisses* either died in a similar way or were swept away during the Revolution of 1848.

In fact, as late as this most transactions in France were still carried on with metallic money. Bank of France notes were used mainly in large-scale business. Credit facilities for ordinary business dealings were virtually non-existent. According to one calculation, in 1850 notes were used in only 7 per cent of commercial transactions; silver changed hands in 90 per cent and gold in 3 per cent of the remainder. The shortcomings of the banking and credit structure could hardly fail to limit the scale of internal transactions and the volume of industrial investment. As in England, most of the initial capital for mining and manufacturing was provided by small partnerships and family firms. French law did offer the device of the *société en commandite* under which, while the liability of the active directors was unlimited, that of the sleeping partners was limited to the extent of their investment. By the 1840s a number of industrial firms were using this form, some with their capital divided into shares. Ordinary limited liability companies required special government authorization under the legislation of the Second Empire (1863 and 1867) and it was given sparingly, as a privilege, to certain types of large-scale enterprise.

It cannot be concluded that, because France lacked banks in the first half of the nineteenth century, this was the reason for her industrial lag. For one thing, steady growth was recorded, and the failure to transform faster can be accounted for by other causes: lack of adequate transport facilities, for example, or the heavy weight of peasant agriculture resulting from the revolutionary land settlement. However, some businessmen and ideologists, like the followers of Claude-Henri Saint Simon, believed that banks should play a leading role in industrial development and the building up of the infrastructure. They studied foreign models and urged their adoption in France. They aimed to mobilize the savings that existed in abundance in the hands of big property-owners and many smaller ones in the shape of hoards of gold and silver. For this it was also necessary that the political regime should inspire confidence by upholding the rights of property. These conditions were provided after the defeat of the working class in 1848 and the overthrow of the Second Republic by Louis Napoleon Bonaparte. The Second Empire he established was to see the foundation of the modern French banking system.

Napoleon III favoured the projects of the brothers Pereire, Emile and Isaac for an investment bank to be called the Crédit Mobilier. Its model was the Belgian Société Générale and it owed something to Lavitte's *caisse*; in turn it influenced banking practice in other countries, notably Germany. The Crédit Mobilier was both a deposit bank and an investment bank. That is to say, it accepted deposits from customers and carried on a discounting business; it also sold bonds and investment in industry proper, but it became deeply involved in the financing of railways in France and abroad and in the public works programme of the Empire. Its weakness, like that of the *caisses*, was a tendency to borrow at short term and to tie up its resources in illiquid, long-term investment. By the 1860s the financial methods by which the great public works schemes of the Empire had been made possible were falling into disrepute. The Pereires had incurred the enmity of the Rothschilds and other bankers prominent under the Orleanist monarchy. A first shock came with the financial crisis of 1857. The Pereires survived this and the Crédit Mobilier was again active in the early 1860s; their rivals even did it the honour of copying its methods. But its continued prosperity depended upon property speculation and foreign railways, in which it was heavily involved. Taking advantage of the Pereires' embarrassments, their enemies moved in for the kill, and, abandoned by the regime, they were squeezed out of the firm in 1867. The Crédit Mobilier had had its day. And yet, despite its failure, it embodied important principles which could be taken over whenever banks were called upon to play a promotional role.

The Pereires were not the only banking innovators in the period of the Second Empire. For the long-term development of French banking the initiative of Henri Germain, founder of the Crédit Lyonnais in 1863, was perhaps of greater importance. Germain's model was the English system of deposit banking; his aim was a network of banks with a large number of depositors. While long-term investment in industry was not ruled out, the main source of profits would be short-term lending, mainly by discounting. Some banks, like the Société Générale, tended to follow its example; others, the *banques d'affaires*, resembled the Crédit Mobilier in that they invested their capital in industry. But the distinction was not always clear-cut. The specialized *banques d'affaires* in any case did not appear until the end of the nineteenth century or early in the twentieth, corresponding probably with the need for ever larger masses of capital in the leading branches of industry.

What stands out in French economic history, however, is the slow and inadequate development of the banking structure, the lack of financial facilities and the belated (even post-Second World War) spread of the banking habit among the middle classes. Transactions continued to be carried out on a cash basis, perhaps because many of them were performed by peasants or small entrepreneurs suspicious of bankers. Even larger firms dreaded dependence on the banks and sought to protect themselves by holding large reserves and liquid funds. This provided a powerful motive for self-financing, adequate enough while business was on a small scale. By the latter part of the nineteenth century, however, in for example the steel industry, a closer tie-up of the banks with industry was discernible, and the tendency in this century has been for the formation of close links between banks and industrial groupings.

The French banking structure, as it developed, owed something to British models but it also adopted its own methods. Other Continental countries, late-comers compared with Britain and even France, developed yet a different model which can be described, not altogether accurately, as the German system. Again, it was not altogether original; nor, in practice, does it appear in a pure state. Its prototype is to be found in the Société Générale de Belgique and to some extent in the Crédit Mobilier which followed it. The German system of banking, according to the model, sets out to mobilize funds from the public and uses them to finance the industrial firms it promotes and whose affairs it supervises or controls. This does not preclude it from offering other services, but its particular role, particularly appropriate in the late-comer, is to promote industrial development, to act as entrepreneur and capital-provider by breaking down the reluctance on the part of savers to invest at long term.

In fact, German banks did not conform exactly with this model and it would be misleading to attribute to them major credit for the rapid German industrialization in the middle decades of the nineteenth century. Until the creation of the *Zollverein* in 1834 and the construction of a railway network there was no national market in Germany, and banking, like other activities, was very much influenced by the situation of each separate state. In the more active commercial areas, such as the Rhineland and the northern ports, private banking houses existed, similar to those found in other parts of Western Europe. Industry was financed mainly from its own resources, and in the rural areas and small towns such financing as there was came from the ubiquitous usurer or the local grain-dealer or notary. The governments of the German states limited the growth of banking and the formation of joint stock companies. Until the 1830s or 1840s government stock provided the main outlet for investors and it is likely that there was a shortage of investment outlets. The private bankers concentrated on the financing of trade, the provision of working capital for merchants and government loan operations. They had already accumulated a great deal of experience and skill which could be transferred, as it were, to the financing of industrial projects. To some extent, through such devices as the bill of exchange, the private bankers in the Rhineland did provide a permanent pool of credit that was short-term in form but that made possible the building of larger fixed capital investment by the borrowing firms.

What is referred to as the revolution in German banking came in the 1850s and its starting point was the foundation of the Darmstadter Bank, modelled on and associated with the French Crédit Mobilier. Launched by Rhineland bankers, it was intended that it should promote and finance long-term investment. Credit banks on similar principles were founded in Prussia and other parts of Germany during the following decade or so. They established themselves and proved successful in the areas of rapid industrial growth, but industrial financing comported enormous risks and the banks ran into trouble during the 1857 and subsequent financial crises. These banks also undertook the usual banking services for customers and they were less interested in holding large blocks of industrial shares than in encouraging the sale of such shares over their own counters. This was increasingly possible as railways were floated and industrial firms adopted the joint stock form of organization. Banks could provide working capital for the firms they had promoted or in whose fortunes they were interested, and bankers might then sit on the boards of these firms to protect their interests. In general there was a closer tie-up between the banks and industry than was the case in Britain, or even in France, despite the Crédit Mobilier – a readiness on the part of bankers to play an entrepreneurial role and an acceptance by industry of its dependence on the banks. However, the differences should not be exaggerated. Until the last quarter of the nineteenth century the role of the credit banks remained comparatively modest, and most German banking business was mixed in character and on fairly orthodox lines. Despite their role in promoting some firms, most of industry and particularly the medium- and smaller-sized firms were financed by their owners and by reinvesting profits with banks only appearing to supply working capital. Moreover some of the larger firms steadfastly opposed outside finance and, like Krupps, remained family firms.

German investment banking, which started in the 1850s and assumed a prominent role in the later decades of the nineteenth century, provided an alternative model to that of Britain for the later developing countries. It obviated the need for the slow build-up of capital by small firms and, by making it possible to raise large amounts of capital, enabled big plants embodying the latest techniques to be established from the start. It would, for example, have been more appropriate for India than the English-style banking that was actually adopted during the period of the Raj. Investment banks could also finance the building of the infrastructure, such as railways, requiring huge amounts of capital and could if necessary act as a conduit for foreign investment. They could also provide the necessary entrepreneurship in fields in which it might be lacking. It is tempting to generalize the model and see it as the answer to many of the problems of the late-comer. This indeed, is what Gerschenkron has done, drawing his argument mainly from Germany and more particularly from Russia where in the modernization programme of the last phase of tsardom the banks did play a leading part. But the fact that the investment banks may play such a role does not guarantee that they will do so. Historical studies of banking in Europe, Japan and the United States show how varied the pattern has in fact been.

Sharp contrasts between the different banking models are easier to draw in theory than in practice. Banks provided a multiplicity of services, varying from place to place and in the course of economic development according to local needs. Foreign models could be important in determining development, but bankers had too much common sense, or business acumen, to follow them slavishly. It would have been as foolish for a country developing in the late nineteenth century to adopt the English banking system of the early stages of industrialization as it would have been to power its factories with the Watt steam-engine. Generally, such countries had to work out a banking system by selecting bits and pieces from foreign practice; but unless they could be adapted and developed according to local conditions and the existing legal and institutional set-up, they would be doomed to failure. That is why in practice national banking structures varied so widely, while at the same time having much in common. Moreover, in trying to understand the industrialization process it would be as hazardous to attribute successful cases mainly to the role of the banks as to blame shortcomings and failures on the weaknesses of the banking system alone. Banks play a necessary and indispensable role in capitalist development; they are the product of particular conditions, the response to a need. At the same time, as business enterprises seeking profits, subject more or less to legal control, they enjoy a measure of autonomy. At a particular juncture in a country's economic history what bankers do may be of crucial importance; at other times they may be powerless or themselves become victims of other forces, as is very plain during financial crises and panics. They may speed up economic growth or act as a brake upon it; only historical enquiry into particular cases can determine what their role was.

CHAPTER SEVEN

The state and industrialization

The increasing scale of government services since the 1930s, as well as the large armed forces in many countries, has obliged the state to appropriate through taxation and borrowing (adding to the national debt) a substantial part of the national product; disbursement of funds by the state has had widespread and perhaps decisive effects on the level of economic activity and the rate of growth in many countries. Such intervention was called for, in the first place, to deal with the effects of the Second World War as well as to prevent a return to the depressed conditions of the 1930s. Here the thinking of John Maynard Keynes was an important influence until growing state spending seemed to lead to inflation without stimulating growth or bringing down unemployment. The post-Keynesian period (since the 1970s) has thus seen a reaction against state intervention and a return to belief in market forces. This tendency has been reinforced by the collapse of the so-called 'planned economies' of the Soviet Union and Eastern Europe. The influence which Soviet-style planned industrialization had on the developing countries, such as India, embarking on industrialization for the first time was considerable. Even in the advanced countries after 1945 a certain amount of borrowing took place. France and other countries drew up national economic plans, though of an indicative rather than an imperative variety, attempting to co-ordinate the policies of private industry and the state sector.

The question of the role of the state in industrialization and more generally in the economy as a whole became increasingly contentious in the 1980s. Until then, since the Second World War, there had been considerable agreement that the state should play a propulsive role in industrializing countries, drawing up plans for the different sectors of the economy, establishing the necessary infrastructure, and itself perhaps acting as entrepreneur, building and running some of the new plants. Even where private ownership of the means of production was not in question, it was often assumed that the state would set targets for industry and undertake functions which private capital was unable or unwilling to undertake, such as investment in the infrastructure – the transport system, communications, power generation, traditionally parts of the public sector in many countries. The latter would include most West European countries as well as such industrializing countries as India, Brazil and South Africa. Japan, South Korea and Taiwan were among countries with highly successful industries in which there had been pervasive state support for the main growth sectors.

Looking back to earlier examples of industrialization it was clear that there had been a variety of patterns from the predominance of market forces in Britain to the rigid state planning of the Soviet Union, Eastern Europe and China. By the 1980s not only had these models been discredited but there was disappointment with the results of interventionist policies in the 'developing countries'. More particularly, Keynesian economic policy, which was based upon the state playing a positive role in the management of the economy, had lost its appeal. Economic opinion, under political pressure from the right wing, especially in Britain and the United States, reaffirmed its belief in the virtue of market forces and the reduction of state intervention to the minimum possible. This was a return to the views held by economists (and many economic historians) a generation or so ago. Revived and refurbished it now became the official ideology of governments and of bodies, such as the World Bank, laying down policy guidelines for the 'developing countries.'

It may be useful, therefore, to look at the evolution of the doctrine of economic liberalism (the best description of the anti-statist ideology) in its heyday before 1914 and why it went out of fashion. It was then accepted that the forces of supply and demand operating on the free market would tend to produce the optimum allocation of resources and distribution of goods. The state performed certain indispensable tasks, such as national defence, the protection of private property, the upholding of contracts and the maintenance of order, and for that purpose it had to tax the citizenry. Its spending powers should, however, be kept to a minimum; it could only take away from the private citizen income that he would otherwise have used to secure personal satisfaction; the state could not add to wealth. This was, in short, the outlook of so-called *laissez-faire*, the dominant mode of thought of West European and American capitalism from the late eighteenth century. In practice, *laissez-faire* in a doctrinaire form was never applied; it remained 'an untried utopia'. Nor was it advocated without major qualifications by the classical political economists like Adam Smith and David Ricardo, who codified the theory of the market economy. They and their successors were marked by a strong strain of empiricism, shared by law-makers, ready to concede that facts came before theory. Indeed, even in Britain, where *laissez-faire* as a policy was most nearly carried out, the functions of the state in the social and the economic spheres exceeded those approved by the dogmatic popularizers.

It is important to point out that, when the theory of the free market was put forward in the eighteenth century, it was a novel and in a sense a revolutionary doctrine. It appeared at a time when two major historical processes were in full swing: the development of capitalist trade and industry in the advanced centres, and the formation of national states as the basic political units of the modern world. Nor were these processes separate; they had been closely related from their inception. The process of state-building had gone on under the aegis of the old dynasties as the monarchs and their advisers sought to impose on the territories under their jurisdiction a more uniform and centralized system of laws and administration. This required the reduction of the powers of the privileged orders, the nobility and the Church, and the establishment of a corps of officials appointed by and responsible to the central government and carrying out its orders. In other words, a more complex state apparatus, a hierarchy of officials, had to be established. It had to draw resources from the underlying population in a more efficient manner, and possibly at the expense of the ruling class of landowners who had received most of the surplus before. These resources went to a large extent, it was true, into unproductive uses, since this was a period of frequent and ever more costly wars. The bureaucracy itself was built up largely in connection with the need to tax the population and maintain the armed forces, and it was through military power, in an incessant conflict with other dynastic states, that each state identified itself on the international arena. In doing so it tended to assist the forces of nascent capitalism. The interests of the merchant class in foreign trade and colonies could be harnessed to the needs of the state. Trade was assisted by the power of the state against that of rivals through privileged companies, like the East India Company. National merchants were given exclusive rights in territories acquired by the state so that they could keep up the price of the products they sold and buy colonial staples for sale in the world market at a lower price than if they had been sold in a free market. Likewise, home industry was protected by prohibitions and tariffs and encouraged by export bounties and subsidies. The prohibition of the export of certain raw materials was designed to keep down the costs of home producers, while materials they required might be admitted duty-free. There was, in short, a close intermingling of the state in formation with the growth of commercial capitalism, ripening in a kind of hothouse provided by these policies, usually designated as 'mercantilist'. It would, however, be wrong to see them as systematic attempts to plan the growth of the economy or to raise national income on behalf of the subjects. It was more a temporary correlation of interests. The state promoted trade and industry for its own power-political reasons and could play off the merchant capitalists against opposition to its centralizing pretension from the nobility. The different commercial and industrial interests were far from homeogeneous; they pushed and pressed this way and that, each on its own behalf to win favours from the state. Some succeeded; others did not. Policy therefore lacked coherence, but it was based on the assumption that the state could, indeed should, intervene in the economic concerns of its subjects.

The emergence of the modern state from about the end of the fifteenth century took place against the background of a regulated economy. The urban crafts were regulated by guilds and corporations while in the agrarian sector most of the peasant population was in some kind of unfree status. The growth of the market economy took place within a framework of controls, of accepted traditional restraints and limits. The penetration of money dealings became increasingly rapid during the sixteenth century and proved to have alarming corrosive powers: thus the state intervened, for example, to try to check enclosure, to regulate certain industries itself and to provide for the casualties of the market economy through poor laws. This kind of regulation can hardly be separated from that which took place for other motives, such as to raise revenue for the crown by selling privileges to particular promoters or to strengthen the state by promoting industrial development. In any case, in the developing states of Europe such intervention was routine and widespread. In France it was practised by Louis XIV's famous minister Colbert, whose policy aim was ordered economic progress under state direction. Besides the usual mercantilist policies in foreign trade, Colbertism included a minute system of industrial regulation imposed by government officials with wide powers. It tended to put industry into a rigid strait-jacket. During this period, and throughout the period of the old regime, the French state subsidized some enterprises and ran others through its own officials. Foreign inventors and technicians were encouraged to come to France to set up new industries.

A similar policy was pursued in Prussia, where the state owned coal and other mines, set up manufacturing enterprises run by officials and gave assistance to some private entrepreneurs. In fact, most states in continental Europe actively intervened in this way, especially in the promotion of large-scale industry either to meet war needs, to manufacture luxuries otherwise needing to be imported or with the hope of raising revenue. It was, in general, part of an attitude on the part of the governors to see the realm as a vast estate to be managed much as the big landed proprietor might open a mine on his land, distil his grain into alcohol or even set up a workshop. While it would be an exaggeration to say that these enterprises had no influence on industrialization, so long as the state was involved with the preservation of social structures of the old, traditional or feudal kind it was as likely to inhibit as to encourage enterprise. Moreover, where state regulation extended to small-scale artisan and craft production it definitely held back innovation and technological change. The large-scale enterprises subsidized or promoted by the state, while they may in some cases be seen as prototypes of the later factories, usually produced goods with a limited market – either the state itself or the nobility. There was little interest in those industries capable of tapping mass demand by large-scale production at low unit cost.

In France, at least, in the closing passage of the old regime the officials supposed to be enforcing the regulations themselves became advocates, in some cases, of a greater degree of economic freedom. They were thus responding to pressures from the entrepreneurs and tended to see themselves more as counsellors and intermediaries with the government than as controllers of industry. Indeed, before 1789 statist action was in full retreat before the growing demand from merchants and manufacturers for greater freedom, as least as far as the internal market was concerned. To that extent the French were only following a path mapped out more than a century before in England. There too the Stuart monarchy had applied a policy of mercantilist controls and industrial monopolies and regulations, only to run up against the opposition of the business groups resentful at being held back from accumulating and investing capital according to the impulses of the market. Hostility to state economic intervention played an important part in the overthrow of the monarchy, and although some restrictive legislation remained on the statute book it largely fell into desuetude during the eighteenth century.

Industrialization in Britain, then, as is well known, owed little to the state or to public action, apart from the very important exception of the continuation of mercantilist policies in the field of foreign trade, shipping and colonies. It was only in the 1770s, notably after the publication of Adam Smith's *Wealth of Nations*, that what he described as 'the mercantile system' came under attack, and even Smith accepted that defence was more important than opulence, in other words that strategic and national interests could justify a policy of trade restrictions such as the Navigation Acts. As for restrictions on the operation of the free market at home or regulations applying to industrial production, they were small in extent by this time and there was vigorous hostility on the part of the trading and industrial classes to any official interference with their business activities. No doubt this derived from their own experience. The exigencies of state-building in an island kingdom virtually immune from foreign invasion and with a small standing army had not imposed the need for the creation of an hierarchical bureaucracy of the continental kind. Many administrative functions, under statutes passed by Parliament devolved upon amateurs, the justices of the peace appointed from among the landed gentry in the shires. These men had neither the desire nor the competence to become entangled in detailed regulation of trade or industry and were no doubt responsive to the clamour for freedom of local farmers and businessmen. The paid officials of the state were few in number and in many cases they were placemen, owing their sinecures to wealthy patrons or were too incompetent and corrupt to administer anything. Hence, for example, customs and excise men could be persuaded, for a consideration, to turn a blind eye to evasions of the law.

State officials in Britain were thus of low repute, and in the eyes of the businessman the idea that one of them could tell him what to do was simply laughable. Both through the advanced character of commerce and the results of the revolutions of the seventeenth century, the demand for economic liberty was irresistible and the doctrines of the political economists found the soil already fertilized by a long process of development. On the Continent the situation was different. Merchants and entrepreneurs were less powerful, as a group, and less self-reliant in their individual business efforts. The bureaucrats were more numerous, enjoyed greater respect and possessed greater power. They were even capable of mastering the new doctrines themselves and selecting those parts that fitted in with the interests of the state as they conceived them. Thus officials went to school with Adam Smith as the inspectors of the old regime in France

95

had gone to school with the Physiocrats, the first advocates of economic liberalism and *laissez-faire*. They did not thereby renounce interference in the economy, but they tried to make it more selective, perhaps also having learned that *laissez-faire* carried out too completely could be destructive, for example by driving worthy artisans out of business.

The significant difference between the character of the state in Britain as compared with the Continent did not arise out of doctrine but out of material conditions. Britain was the ideal territory for the application of the doctrines of economic liberalism its development had produced. Most continental countries, with the partial exception of France, received them as an alien import, not fully applicable in any case. Traits already well marked by the end of the seventeenth century were confirmed by subsequent development. Industrialization in Britain surged ahead under conditions of economic liberalism. To some extent it acquired prestige as a result, but observers from afar could not fail to note that while permitting market forces to operate with maximum freedom making possible impressive technological achievements and an enormous increase in output, it also had unpleasant side-effects. *Laissez-faire* thus tended to become synonymous with a disorderly, anarchic development of production, with speculative excesses and slumps, with a miserable factory proletariat crowded into stinking slums: hardly a model to be emulated. For that reason, on the Continent there was some demand for the state to prevent such happenings.

The rising commercial and industrial bourgeoisie in Britain desired a state responsive to its will and cheap to administer. There were few offices in the state offering it better prospects than business and, at least in the eighteenth century, dissenters might be barred from them. On the whole, therefore, politics could be left to the old landed oligarchy, or rather that party called the Whigs, 'the aristocratic representatives of the bourgeoisie', as Marx called them. In return, the middle class obtained most of what it wanted to permit the free operation of the laws of the market – but not everything. Policy was not determined by one party alone but as the outcome of a party struggle in which the landed interest represented by the Tories played a part. The Tories in power were less ready to see market forces prevail because they would harm farmers and landlords. And out of the contest between manufacturers and the landed interests measures were passed from which other classes, including workers, could benefit.

In Britain, while Whigs and Tories struggled for public office, the middle class in the main pursued business and professional careers, and not until the second half of the nineteenth century did the now-reformed civil service come within its purview. But the civil service was itself permeated with the ideology of economic liberalism and only reluctantly embarked on policies conflicting with it, and then under the pressure of necessity, as in the case of factory legislation and public health but not in economic matters. In France, on the other hand, and wherever the old regime was reformed along modern lines, reducing the power and privileges of the nobility, the middle class opened a way for itself in state service, a major outlet for the educated bourgeois élite. Prussia and other parts of Germany and central Europe also possessed a corps of bureaucrats to which middle-class aspirants could gain admission. Growing nationalism in Germany, Italy and Eastern Europe focused on the state and required an enhancement of its power, not least to protect and extend the commercial interests of the bourgeoisie. The British state acquired colonies and extended its hand to assist its subjects in trouble all over the world. The citizen of Prussia or Bavaria had no such helping hand until the formation of Bismarck's empire. Moreover, in the period after 1815 the gap between British industrial efficiency and that of continental producers had grown wider. Everywhere the state was looked to as a protector against low-priced British imports. It seemed that in order to get off the ground with the use of the new techniques the aid of the state was necessary, at least in the form of tariff protection. Friedrich List put this into coherent form as the continental answer to free trade. British manufacturers ceased to need protection of the home market because foreign competitors produced at higher cost and that, together with the cost of bringing in imports, gave them near complete command. On the other hand, they wanted free import of food and raw materials to keep down wages and costs of production and thus to assist still further in the conquest of foreign markets. Continental businessmen and economists were not slow to perceive that free trade served the interests of the dominant economy, that it favoured the strong against the weak, the rich against the poor, and that it was an instrument of British nationalism as much as the tariff. They could not bar the door to British goods if only because the agrarians and some sections of industry were against it, but they could advocate tariffs to blunt the edge of British competition. Politicians were generally ready to oblige.

How far the tariff was an instrument of development in continental Europe is difficult to say. It is always virtually impossible to disentangle the effects of a tariff, or the lack of it, from all the other interacting factors in the situation. It could be argued however that, given the onslaught from Britain after 1815, the tariff saved parts of Europe from de-industrialization and enabled industries to get a foothold which might not otherwise have come into existence. In so far as that raised incomes and purchasing power by assisting the movement of resources from less productive to more productive uses, it served not only the interests of the European population but was in the long-run interests of Britain as well. There was no future for a single industrial country in an exclusively agrarian world.

When it is asked in what ways the state in continental Europe contributed positively to industrialization, the reply, despite some contrary impressions, must be that it was not generally of great importance. There was in most countries an inherited body of state regulation and intervention belonging to an earlier era, the economic old regime. It was usual for the state to provide highways, bridges and similar facilities nowadays conveniently described as the infrastructure. It did so in large part for administrative and strategic purposes: to permit information and commands to be transmitted back and forth from the seat of government to the provinces and to enable troops to be moved for attack or defence in time of war. In states like France and Prussia this meant the training of specialists to supervise and plan the building and maintenance of such facilities. They were clearly of basic importance for the growth of wider market areas necessary for the encouragement of large-scale investment in industry. The coming of the railway involved the state inevitably because of its national and strategic importance. Most governments therefore exercised some control over railways as far as routing and finance were concerned from an early stage. The most usual practice, as in France, was for the state to contribute towards the cost of railway building and to guarantee interest on the investment of private capital. Railways thus became a privileged form of capitalist enterprise. In some cases, as in Germany, the state's commitment was deliberately extended because of the military as well as economic significance of the railway network. Since lack of transport facilities was a major barrier to the growth of the market, and thus of the economy as a whole, throughout continental Europe, if state action made possible railway building or speeded it up then it played a positive role. However, it is not always clear that this was so. Governments and government engineers tended to be conservative and cautious about new projects. Constructional standards tended to be high. The involvement of government opened the way for a struggle of interests and for delays in launching new lines. This was especially true in France during the 1840s. On the other hand, in the next decade the regime of Napoleon III pushed forward new construction by agreements on favourable terms with the railway companies to restore prosperity and add to its own stability and prestige.

Railways and similar public works were the main sphere of direct government intervention in the internal economy during the early stages of European industrialization. On other matters, however, the industrial and commercial middle class were as committed to economic liberalism as their British counterparts. They desired and eventually secured the abolition of remaining state regulation of manufacturing and mining, with usually the bigger firms taking the lead. In Germany, for instance, legislation during the 1860s threw open most trades and occupations to whoever was able and qualified to carry them on. In most countries the state removed itself from the arena or at least did not attempt to extend its stake in manufacturing and mining as the economy grew. Its intervention was generally haphazard and piece-meal. Even in the late developing countries such as Germany, Italy or even Russia, it is difficult to argue that industrialization followed a deliberate course mapped out by the state in advance. Experience generally showed that rapid growth could best be achieved by opening the way for the investment of private capital. State action was thus confined mainly to assisting railway development, and offering generous contracts to private business firms, concessions to foreign capitalists and favourable rates to investors. Russian experience in the period of the 'great spurt' of the 1890s confirms this; although the state provided the stimulus it was an enormous wager on the capitalists. In the end it can be said that even so it was not carried through with sufficient singlemindedness to achieve fully sustained growth. Once state spending slackened so did the level of private investment.

Another example is provided by Canada after Confederation in 1867. Although the business community fully accepted the ethos of free enterprise, nevertheless it was evident that in a country of new settlement there were tasks that could only be undertaken by the state. This was recognized in the so-called National Policy of 1879 by which the federal government charged itself with the promotion of railways across the barren Canadian Shield which could not hope to pay their way, raising the revenue necessary to meet the cost and at the same time encouraging manufacturing industry for the national market by imposing tariffs. Moreover, only the government had the credit-worthiness necessary to raise the required loans in London. Private capital was thus left free to seek other outlets, notably those opened up by government spending; some of the biggest fortunes made in the subsequent period came, in fact, from railway contracting. In Canada, therefore, it was accepted that the state had perforce to play a promotional role, as a path-breaker for private accumulation and national development.

In India the situation was very different. Nationalists claim that under the British Raj the state did not play its proper role by promoting development. Because India was governed from London through an alien civil service, policy was responsive to pressures from interests in Britain. These demanded that the Indian market be kept open for Lancashire textiles and other manufactured goods, and that railways, ports and harbours be built so that primary products could be drawn out of India for sale by British merchants in the markets of the world. Even railways did not speed up industrial development as much as in other countries since most of the material was imported from Britain. For economy reasons, from the 1880s, government purchasing policy, it is true, moved towards a larger proportion of locally made goods. The state did not do much to encourage the privately owned manufacturing industry, either by British or Indian entrepreneurs, but it did not discourage such activity, assisted as it was by railways, harbours, telegraphs, roads, waterworks and other enterprises in the public sector. However, government spending did little to change the economic basis of the country, and there was no intention to promote industrialization. Policy aimed to keep the Indian market open for British imports and capital investment and to ensure the production and export of primary products saleable on the world market. It conformed broadly with the norms of economic liberalism, this time applied to a dependent country for which *laissez-faire* would have been inappropriate.

Indian nationalists sometimes refer to Japan as an example of what might have been achieved in India. Whether Japan provides a satisfactory model for a developing country is doubtful. Industrialization began there after a revolution from above which brought to power a new governing élite, firmly rooted in traditional society but aware that, unless Japan adopted Western technology, it could not remain independent. Authoritarian nationalism provided the ideological grounding for the policy of the new regime after the Meiji Restoration of 1868. The only issues were how far and in what ways the state should intervene to promote modernization. In fact, it acted positively to remove trade and industry from feudal restraints, began to establish a modern infrastructure and financed and organized new, modern industries. Some of the foundations for economic growth had been laid under the previous regime and could not have been provided through the market alone. However, there was no intention of establishing a controlled or planned economy. Economic liberalism had been imported along with foreign techniques and business methods, but in the early stages the business classes depended upon the bureaucracy and the military to reorganize society and establish a strong centralized state, a necessary basis for independent economic development. The state therefore established strategic industries and assisted the initial stage of industrialization by financing and running factories. After 1880, however, most of these factories were sold off to private capitalists on favourable terms. Once some basic industries had been established and the economy had acquired a momentum of its own the government withdrew, having prepared the way for giant private concerns, the *zaibatsu*, to dominate the modern sector of the economy. Businessmen generally accepted the necessity for some state supervision and indulged in professions of selfless devotion and patriotic motivation. Their behaviour did not differ fundamentally from that of foreign counterparts; capitalism was adapted to the social environment but operated according to the same laws. There was a close relationship between business groups, especially the *zaibatsu*, and the state; at the same time, the bureaucracy and the military succeeded in conserving an independent role.

As these examples show, the role of the state in industrialization has varied considerably according to the timing of the process and the national conditions in which it has taken place. At least for the period before 1914 there is a danger of exaggerating the role of the state even in countries like Russia or Japan. Although economic liberalism was weaker in late-developing countries, they all counted mainly upon the incentives to private entrepreneurs operating through the market to achieve industrialization. There was at this time no ideology of state intervention coherent enough to stand against belief in private enterprise, the profit motive and the benefits of the free market economy outside the socialist movement. But although economic liberalism was widely accepted by businessmen, bourgeois public opinion and bureaucrats, practice never went as far in non-intervention as in Britain and the United States. Moreover, national goals took precedence over liberalism. The freer trade era opened up by the Anglo-French treaty of commerce of 1860, imposed by Napoleon III on a hostile business world, proved to be an aberration and was felt to be so by most French and many other European industrialists. The national state became more sharply defined in economic terms through tariffs, currency systems, commercial laws and practices, even while

101

the different components of the world economy were being drawn more closely together. Economic policy was national and often nationalist in character.

Also, few businessmen or members of the propertied classes were prepared consistently to advocate the principles of economic liberty and non-intervention when their application would harm their own private interests. Even in Britain, when foreign competition began to hit industries such as the silk industry in the 1880s, those affected clamoured for protection and supported the Fair Trade League's demand for tariff reform. In case of labour disputes employers expected the state to intervene on their behalf while often opposing the right of their workers to organize. In periods of depression producers turned to the state for help and sometimes obtained it in the form of loans, tax relief or support for measures to control prices. This tendency became more pronounced in the latter part of the nineteenth century; in the following century it was to become systematized into the 'mixed economy' composed of counterbalancing corporate groups demanding the attention of the state.

Certainly an examination of countries undergoing industrialization shows different degrees of state involvement, and if Britain be taken as the yardstick there was clearly more of it in most of the others. But Britain was a special case, because of her priority in industrialization and the great advantages derived from it. Almost everywhere else some degree of state support, at least in the shape of tariffs, was necessary. Overall, however, it was the relatively small contribution made by the state that stands out in most other cases. Outside the provision of part of the infrastructure it was rare to find the state owning and managing industrial enterprises or attempting to pilot the economy as a whole. Even in the field of banking, for example, private enterprise was supreme. Central bankers, though having a special relationship to the state, none the less in most cases jealously preserved their independence and even tended to recognize a common cause with their counterparts beyond national frontiers. Belief in the virtues of the free market economy remained deeply rooted practically everywhere until the war of 1914 forced governments to establish a command economy substituting administrative fiat for free market forces. But even that experience was felt to be exceptional and offering no lessons for peacetime; the cry at the end of that war was 'back to normalcy and the end of all controls', so deeply rooted were the doctrines of economic liberalism.

It would be anachronistic to expect to find in the nineteenth century, even in the case of the 'late-comers' to industrialization, that the state's role would be analogous to that regarded as normal at the present day in advanced as well as in developing countries. The state lacked the trained personnel, the experience and the financial resources to exercise more than a generally watchful eye over the running of the economy as a whole. To do more would not have had the support of the commercial and industrial bourgeoisie or the sanction of expert opinion at a time when even civil servants were often convinced of the virtues of the free market. Before 1914 the idea of a planned and purposive development of the economy under the aegis of the state had little appeal outside socialist circles, and the fact that it smacked of socialism weakened that appeal. Not until 1914 was there an example of the state playing a controlling role in an advanced economy. Where the state intervened it did so either on the old lines, or in response to special interests, often to preserve them from the effects of the workings of the market. Thus the East German landlords obtained special benefits in the shape of tariffs and railway facilities. Hit by falling revenues in a period of depression, French railways in the 1880s obtained state assistance through the Freycinet 'plan', enabling unremunerative lines to be built with state support. True, some states conserved state enterprises in mining and manufacturing inherited from the past (as in the case of formerly Prussian state enterprises in Germany) or run for revenue purposes, as with the French tobacco monopoly (dating from 1810). State intervention in the provision of public works, or as they would be called today the 'infrastructure', was widely accepted even by non-interventionist economists. Arms-spending tended to rise in the quarter of a century before 1914 and brought the state on to the scene with its own ordnance factories and shipyards or as a principal purchaser of the output of private arms firms, mostly the latter. There may have been some 'spin-off' in a stimulus to advanced technology, but this was unintended. Such examples show that there was no necessary connection between state intervention and socialism, and that the 'mixed economy' was not a twentieth-century invention; but they do not do much more than this.

Generally the respective roles of the state and private enterprise were well defined and understood both by entrepreneurs and by public servants. The borderline could vary from one country to another and might shift over time in one direction or another. Despite some impressions to the contrary, the period immediately before 1914 was very much the heyday of economic liberalism rather than one of growing state intervention. There was no doubt that the market held sway and resort to the state was made only in cases of emergency, to supplement or support private enterprise. Even in Russia and Japan it cannot be said that the state pursued a policy of planned development or had any intention of supplanting the private capitalists: rather the contrary. The state in such countries, when it played an entrepreneurial role, did so by default and with the intention of promoting private investment in industry. And this remained the main difference, at this time, between the late-developing countries and those more advanced in their industrialization, particularly Britain and the United States, where the ideological roots of economic individualism were deepest. If this led to the conclusion that this was a necessary concomitant of all Anglo-Saxon countries it would not be confirmed by the experience of the new countries of European settlement such as Canada and Australia, where the state was expected to play a more positive and promotional role. Everywhere, in fact, the state was expected to facilitate the working of the market and open the way for capitalist development; the way it did so naturally varied according to the national conditions and peculiarities.

In the sphere of social policy it is possible to discern a more definite pattern of state involvement as industrialization spread. This was required for two main reasons: to assist the functioning of the market mechanism, and to moderate or prevent its negative side-effects. Under the first heading would come the assistance given by the state in the various fields of education, whether to produce a directing élite for business, the professions and the service of the state itself or to raise the literacy level of the masses of the population. Under the latter would be placed factory legislation, social insurance schemes, the laying down of minimum standards in public health and hygiene, the purity of food or the quality of other goods and services including housing, and intervention in these fields.

It was usual in continental states for the state to undertake the provision of higher education or to subsidize it in one form or another, although a good deal of the cost actually fell upon the families of students. This arose not exclusively out of a concern for culture or the promotion of knowledge, but because education was a necessary mark of upper-class privilege valued as much or more by the bourgeoisie as by the older ruling classes it displaced. Thus in France Napoleon I carried forward a policy begun under the old regime of training a technical and scientific élite for the service of the state and to supply the needs of the liberal professions. The products of the institutions of higher learning did not necessarily fit in with the needs of developing industry and might have a too narrow or conservative point of view, placing technical excellence or conformity with the rules above market considerations. However, it was certainly better to have a supply of trained people than none at all, and industry was able to draw upon a pool of experts for specific functions whose training had been financed in part by the state.

Primary education tended to lag on the Continent as it did in Britain. It posed quite different questions, such as the desirability of educating the masses and the relationship between secular knowledge imparted in the schools and religious instruction, over which the Church insisted on maintaining control. Extended education at the primary level had to be made free and compulsory before it could become really effective. This required the exclusion of children below school age from the labour market, notably by enforceable factory legislation. It meant the provision of an adequate supply of trained teachers, possibly only with extensive financial provision by the state. Buildings also had to be provided and finance made available for their maintenance. In sparsely populated rural areas there were special problems in establishing continuous full-time education for the majority of children, usually meaning, for a long time, a one-teacher school for children of all ages. With problems such as these it is not surprising that development was slow and that intentions expressed in law were not always translated into practice even in the most advanced countries. Literacy might therefore remain minimal into the late nineteenth or early twentieth century. What is certain is that it had by that time become indispensable for the masses of the population to fit them for industrial and other employments and enable them to shoulder the responsibilities of citizenship. Opposition to the spread of education tended, therefore, to fall away, and wider provision was made by the state to ensure the spread of literacy to the entire population. The gap remained wide between the primary and later stages of education, still mainly the preserve of the middle and upper classes.

Of the second type of social intervention, the regulation of working conditions was the first and the most significant. In fact, hardly had the old forms of interventionism in industry come to an end than this new form entered the scene, first of all in Britain and then in other countries in which factories were established. Regulation of working conditions began with children and females who were not regarded as fully free bargaining agents in the wage contract and was intended to prevent abuses by unscrupulous employers and, in a sense, to ensure the long-term welfare of the working population and thus the quality of the future supply. There were, of course, other humanitarian considerations, and once factory regulation began it developed with a logic of its own. It required trained and independent inspectors if it was to be applied uniformly and successfully. In Britain, the pioneer in this respect, the inspectorate became the agency for extending and tightening up the regulations. They were extended to wider categories, took in mines and workshops, included regulation not only of hours but also of standards of safety, ventilation, health precautions and the control of occupational hazards. They set a precedent for other forms of state intervention in the wage contract, including the way wages were paid (as with the Truck Acts in Britain) and even the establishment of minimum wages in some cases.

The rapid growth of an industrial labour force and its concentration in larger towns created new social problems, or rather brought existing problems into the public arena. Poverty in the sense of low incomes was endemic in pre-industrial societies, but overall want did not create a special problem as far as the state was concerned. Moreover, as long as the vast majority of the population was composed of peasants or those working under the old conditions in small communities, the sick, the old and infirm, the incapacitated and other categories deprived of means of their own could generally be cared for within the family or by some kind of charity. It was only as the old structure began to be penetrated by market forces that the appearance of large numbers of landless and masterless people without means of support created a major problem for the public authorities. Generally it was from the sixteenth century that these problems began to become acute, both as a result of economic change and because religious upheaval was undermining the religious institutions whose role it had been to dispense charity in the past. Post-medieval society thus begins to experience large-scale mendicity and destitution, a more or less permanent problem carried into the industrial era and tackled in various ways by national governments. Some, like that of England, gave the destitute a minimum right of assistance at the discretion of the local administrators, the justices of the peace, amateurs appointed from the gentry and paid for by a rate levied on householders in each parish. In other countries, like France, there was no general right to assistance; the poor depended upon what help was available from private charity, the Church foundations and municipal handouts. Even declarations made during the revolutionary period in favour of a national system of relief for the poor, sick and aged came to nothing in practice. The need in France and other countries, still predominantly rural and peasant, was less pressing than in Britain until the old economic order began to break up under the impact of industrialization.

As this took place, larger numbers of people became entirely dependent upon the labour market for their means of existence. Where it was overcrowded wages were low; in many cases, particularly where there were children to be maintained, wages were insufficient to pay for adequate housing or to enable money to be put by for periods of unemployment, sickness and incapacity or to provide for old age or the emergencies and hazards of life. In the face of these mounting problems it was hardly possible for the state to do nothing. The more widely the market spread its influence, however, the greater was the scale of these problems and the more acute. Middle-class writers spoke of the industrial workers moving into the factory centres as an encamped horde and of the dangerous classes inhabiting the big cities where, indeed, a large floating population existed, as it were, on the fringes of society. Fear of revolt or revolution, as well as humanitarianism, motivated the beginnings of social reform. Adherents of economic liberalism were reluctant to interfere and did so circumspectly, afraid of destroying the incentive to work or creating a sub-proletariat existing on relief, the accusation generally levelled against indiscriminate charity as well as public assistance. British policy-makers tried to deal with this in the Poor Law Amendment Act of 1834 by imposing a workhouse test on the able-bodied applicants for relief and making their condition 'less eligible' than that of the worst-off worker dependent upon wages. In practice it was impossible to impose entry into the workhouse and the splitting up of families, especially upon industrial workers temporarily without means of a support as a result of trade depression, or to organize workhouses in such a way as to make food, care and the general environment as bad as required by the principle of 'less eligibility'. The law was successful in reducing expenditure on poor relief and attaching such a stigma to the system as to undermine the old 'right' to assistance and deter self-respecting workers from applying to the Guardians of the Poor except in the direst circumstances. Even so, a large proportion of the urban working class could expect to end their days in the workhouse.

When an alternative was devised it took over the insurance principle already adopted by the workers themselves in friendly societies, mutual aid clubs and some trade unions, of which examples were to be found in most countries, as well as by some paternalistic employers. The pioneer in this regard was Germany and the architect of the scheme, the Chancellor Otto von Bismarck, expressed its essence as follows in a speech made in 1884: 'there are purposes which only the State as a whole can fulfil . . . To these belong the help of the

107

necessitous and the removal of those just complaints which provide Social Democracy with really effective material for agitation. This is the duty of the State, a duty which the State cannot permanently disregard.' The German Social Insurance Laws of 1883–84 provided compulsory insurance against sickness, including sick pay, medical and hospital treatment for certain categories of workers and insurance against industrial injuries. Later, old age insurance was added and the scheme was extended until, after the Workman's Insurance Code of 1911, it included most categories of wage-earners in a text of no less than 1,805 clauses. The German scheme was the most comprehensive in Europe and exercised considerable influence on the social insurance systems adopted in other countries. For example, Lloyd George studied the scheme in Germany in 1908 and acknowledged its influence on the National Insurance Act of 1911 in Britain. Other countries followed more or less belatedly. A comparable French law was not effective until 1931 and the system did not compare with that in Germany until after 1945. By that time the 'welfare state' had become general in most industrial countries with the exception of the United States, where the Social Security Act of 1935 was intended to encourage the states to set up their own unemployment insurance and old age pensions schemes.

The development of social policy in the capitalist countries has tended to safeguard society against the ill effects of an unregulated market economy by providing for its casualties. It can be seen, therefore, not as something antithetical to the market system but rather as complementary to it. True, pressure from the labour movement has hastened the pace of reforms either directly through Parliament or indirectly, as with Bismarck's attempt to steal the thunder of the Social Democratic Party. Social security schemes have been financed in large part by contributions from workers and employers with some subsidy from the state met out of general tax revenue. Since the employer contribution can be said to be a part of the wage bill, paid into the insurance fund instead of to the individual worker, and the workers pay part of the taxes, they can be said as a class to have paid what its various members receive in the shape of benefit. Social insurance schemes recognize that the wage system alone cannot provide adequately for social needs, but it does not abolish that system. Wages are still determined by bargaining and contract; but in addition, by compulsory deductions from the wages of all workers, a social wage is provided for those not able to work owing to sickness, injury, disability, old age, unemployment and the other risks covered by the insurance scheme. Other benefits, such as a minimum level of education, health services, subsidies to housing and so on, may be paid for directly from taxation: collective use is made of these facilities without payment or at a fee below the full cost of the service. From one aspect state intervention in these ways confirms and reinforces the wage system and the market economy; from another it conflicts with them by a recognition of need and the satisfaction of needs independently of the furnishing of an equivalent on the part of the recipient. Taken as a whole, the social policy of advanced societies, of which the bases were laid at the end of the nineteenth or early part of the twentieth century, had the effect of maintaining the health, quality and working capacity of the labour force. It thus contributed to increased production and productivity enabling the societies concerned to pay for such schemes. The working class may have gained, but so have the employers and society as a whole, and a more or less conscious recognition of this has contributed to their general acceptance, though obviously not without criticism of their details and their practical working out. Their contradictory aspects provide a continuing basis for such criticism.

In conclusion, it may be said that the course of industrialization itself imposed on the state new and wider functions in the field of social policy earlier and to a greater extent than in the sphere of production itself. In the first place the state was called upon to remove the barriers to the free operation of market forces, especially by creating the conditions for a free market in the factors of production and to dismantle much of the old apparatus of control. But hardly had this process been completed than new forms of interventionism were required to deal with the social consequences of the operation of the market on labour and to some extent on the consumer (e.g. through Pure Food and Drugs legislation). A distinction can be made between the economic sphere, or at least production, where before 1914 the intervention of the state remained minimal almost everywhere, and the sphere of social policy, where positive action by the state has proved to be inescapable to prevent market forces from acting in intolerably destructive ways. Also, the state has had to provide a range of necessary services and facilities which private enterprise has been unable or unwilling to supply through the market. This has included education at all levels, much of the infrastructure and certain public utilities. The extent and nature of state intervention in these different fields has varied considerably from country to country though it has not differed very much in principle. States of the most varied political complexion have operated very similar types

109

of interventionist policy. It is the needs of industrial, urbanized society that have prevailed, rather than the choices of policy-makers or the teachings of ideologists. A society governed purely by the laws of the market has never existed. The choice for capitalist countries has never been between the market and statism, but more practically of deciding how far the free operation of market forces could be tolerated or, alternatively, how much state intervention was necessary to achieve the desired ends, including the preservation of private ownership of the means of production and the market system.

CHAPTER EIGHT

Late nineteenth-century industrialization

Until the middle of the nineteenth century Britain can be considered as the *only* industrial country, with her leadership in no doubt. Only in a few areas, such as Belgium and some parts of western Germany and France, were there signs that industrialization properly speaking was taking place. On the other hand, areas of 'proto-industrialization' were becoming more clearly defined as part of moderate but cumulative growth in income levels. There has been a tendency in economic history to see Britain as the typical or model case for the study of industrialization. In fact, stress should be laid rather on the unique characteristics of the British experience, which could not be duplicated in different environments where technological and industrial development took place as a process of diffusion and assimilation. This is accounted for in the analysis of the specific characteristics of the 'latecomers', mainly in terms of national economies. The upshot of such an approach is to suggest that later developing countries enjoyed advantages enabling them to speed forward in the early stages of industrialization and overcome their backwardness. On the other hand, 'the early start' thesis asserts that by the last quarter of the nineteenth century Britain was handicapped and falling behind mainly because her industrialization had begun much earlier.

If the historical process of industrialization is seen in a world perspective it had, by the latter part of the nineteenth century, become a generalized process. It was rapidly transforming the societies of Western Europe and North America. It was penetrating into Eastern Europe and Russia. Japan was demonstrating the capacity of an Asiatic country to adopt techniques worked out in the West and to modernize her traditional economy on capitalist lines. There were a few other outposts of industrialism and enclaves in some countries still underdeveloped, such as India. In the main, however, what was stiking was the fact that the more highly industrialized countries were not only far in advance of other parts of the world but dominated them economically. By the end of the nineteenth century most of the globe had been parcelled out among the advanced countries, with Britain enjoying the lion's share.

This meant that, despite the challenge to her industrial leadership, Britain remained the premier imperialist country with a vast colonial empire and an 'informal empire' of client states. Britain's ability to assume such a position was, of course, one aspect of the all-round economic leadership she had acquired as a result of her priority in industrialization. It was built upon financial as well as industrial foundations and upon the domination of the world market established earlier in the century. The City of London was the pivot of the international trading system; it provided the system's key currency in the shape of the pound sterling and was the main source of short-and long-term credit for world development. The erosion of this dominant position can also be said to have begun in the decades after 1870, but decline here proved to be a much more long drawn-out process.

The main deleterious change in the economic environment for Britain as it seemed, was the rise of new and vigorous industrial and exporting rivals. This new phase of multiple industrialization, however, not only imposed strains on the pioneer industrial country, but was also accompanied by a number of characteristic features indicating that a new stage in capitalist development was in the offing.

The last quarter of the nineteenth century, or at least part of it, has been described by many economic historians as 'the Great Depression'. The appropriateness of this term has been questioned mainly because these years were not all depressed, because the economy continued to grow overall and because the symptoms of 'depression' were not so much unemployment and falling production as falling prices and profit margins. Without entering into the details of the controversy, there seems to be a case for claiming that the conjuncture of enterprise was different in significant ways from that of the mid-Victorian decades. There seem to be reasons for agreeing with Hans Rosenberg that there was something in the nature of a 'downswing' lasting from 1873 to 1896, and that 'it was a trend of world-wide scope which, despite sharp national, regional and local differences, displayed in its fundamental tendencies, and also in many of its particular features, a far-reaching degree of unity'.*

* Rosenberg, H., 'Political and social consequences of the great depression in Central Europe', in *Economic History Review*, Vol. xiii (1943), p. 59.

The overall tendency of the period was for production (and productive capacity) to grow faster than markets, thus exerting the pressure on prices and profits of which businessmen in many countries complained. Production continued to grow, but at least in the older industrial countries, Britain and France, it grew more slowly than before; 'deceleration' had set in. The problem of 'overproduction', a feature previously only of short periods of depression, now afflicted industry as a permanent nightmare. The spread of industrialization had made the international struggle for markets more intense. British exporters, accustomed to enjoying a virtual monopoly in many markets, now found themselves up against German, American and other foreign competition. Moreover, the industrializing countries were competing on an unprecedented scale in each others' home markets.

As the new period began in the 1870s the structure of the market inside each country was still broadly competitive. Few firms were large enough to influence prices, and tariff walls were low, or in Britain's case non-existent, so that in a time of depression foreign manufacturers tried to push sales inside their competitors' home markets. This was most pronounced after the continental crisis and slump beginning in 1873 following a boom period which had seen a massive build-up of industrial capacity. French and German manufacturers, for instance, complained bitterly about British competition. Entrepreneurs could try to meet this competition by technical change or improvements in organization. They could step up their aggressive search for markets and thus aggravate the situation from which they were trying to escape. But they also began to turn in a new direction: (1) towards the control of competition by means of cartels and trusts. and (2) towards the exclusion of foreign competition by a return to protective tariffs. From this practically universal trend, only Britain was exempt, and that for special reasons. The older established British basic industries were controlled by many competing firms with their own individuality, business and trade secrets. There was little basis for them to influence the market through monopoly control of raw materials. The ideology of the free market had a stronger hold than on the Continent and was backed up by the presumptions of the law regarding restraint of trade. Free trade enjoyed the prestige associated with the prosperity of the Victorian era and indeed seemed to be indispensable for the maintenance of Britain's world position in trade and finance. For a nation of consumers and townspeople it seemed more important to ensure a supply of cheap food and raw materials than to protect the home producers. The landlords and farmers were too small a proportion of the population to swing the balance back to protection, and there was little support for it in industry.

In the other industrializing countries, however, different considerations prevailed. Industry had developed later; its centre of gravity tended to be more in heavy industry than in the light industries. In heavy industry and in the industries based upon advanced technology the economies of large-scale production were being recognized; plants tended to be large in relation to their market, thus making competition inherently unstable. It was easier for a small number of firms to get together and recognize an interest in controlling prices and dividing up the market among themselves. The belief in the dogmas of the free market was less deeply rooted; public opinion and governments were less influenced by them; and the law looked more favourably upon combinations among producers. However, a price-fixing agreement or any combination to control the market would be ineffective if foreign competition remained unregulated. Whether or not to make such arrangements effective, industrialists on the Continent were clamouring for protection. The influx of cheap food from other continents and the slide in prices that followed converted the big agrarian interests to protection and prepared the way for the German tariff law of 1879 and the Méline tariff in France in 1892. A definite movement away from free markets and free trade may therefore be dated from the 1870s.

The downward price trend and the tendency to overproduction bore down with special weight on the older industries and industrial areas. This tended to set up a self-reinforcing process of deceleration. The rate of investment declined and the proportion of aging and obsolescent equipment tended to grow; the firms affected became less competitive while technological leadership passed to the newer industrial areas or countries. The weight of past investment, made at an earlier technologicial stage, limited the possibility for changing over to new methods. Especially in an uncertain economic climate it appeared safer to continue with obsolescent equipment, and this could, indeed, be rational in cases where it had been wholly or largely paid for. But a heavy price could be paid for such attempts to maintain short-run profitability in the face of sagging markets.

It is difficult to disentangle the effects of short-run responses to conjunctural situations from the long-run consequences of having been first in the field. Certainly the late-comers were not subject to the incubus of an inheritance of a deadweight of obsolescent equipment. Generally speaking, they had a larger proportion of more modern equipment embodying later techniques and giving them certain advantages. However, this capital equipment had to be paid for, and the conjunctural factors already noted could not be evaded; indeed, it was in the newer industrial countries that the retreat from the free market and into protection was most marked. Artificial means were necessary to maintain the profitability of this equipment in the face of intensive competition. The protected home market could be used as a base from which to go forward to conquer foreign markets by ensuring that the heavy fixed costs were spread over a larger volume of output.

Multiple industrialization had, however, other characteristics. The industrial structures of the new industrial countries and areas did not precisely reproduce those of the old. As already mentioned, they did not necessarily follow the British model as far as the leading position of textiles was concerned. More emphasis tended to be laid from the start on the mining, metallurgical and engineering industries – those concernd with producers' goods. Consumer goods industries were transformed too, but they had less determining weight in the economy. Moreover, paradoxically, as in Germany and France, the preservation of a relatively large agrarian sector kept alive many small-scale producers and artisan-type industries. In short, before 1914 they were not as completely modernized, or as industrialized, as Britain.

Also, during the latter part of the nineteenth century new advances in technology had opened up wider possibilities for industrialization. It no longer had to follow the old pattern of dependence upon coal, steam, iron and textiles. An industrial vocation was opening up for areas that could never have industrialized on the basis of the techniques of the first Industrial Revolution. More highly mechanized methods of production enabled populations with little or no prior industrial experience to become as proficient as workers in the older industrial countries.

The new technologies had as their main distinguishing feature that they depended closely upon applied science for their development and application. The changeover from iron to steel was itself of profound importance. Cheap mass-produced steel opened up entirely new potentialities for engineering and thus for the advance of mechanization in a wide range of industries. Electricity made its appearance as a new source of power in competition with steam. It enabled industry to be carried into new areas where electricity could be generated cheaply, especially from water power. It was also the basis for an important new development: electro–metallurgy, notably the production of aluminium (a patent was taken out in 1888 and production began two years later). The electric furnace for steel-making dates from 1900. No less important were the often-linked advances being made in the chemical industries, making available inorganic chemicals for a wide range of uses, from pharmaceuticals to fertilizers, not forgetting their potentiality for warfare. The first steps were being made in the development of the gas, diesel and petroleum engines, the full revolutionary consequences of which were to unfold themselves in the twentieth century. The introduction of the rotary kiln in the cement industry made possible the large-scale production of concrete for building, and thus the steel-framed blocks and sky-scrapers of the modern city.

It is true, of course, that these inventions and innovations did not effect a radical change all at once any more than did the much better known inventions of the eighteenth-century Industrial Revolution. Their impact was not felt until well into the new century whose industrial and technological aspects they were to typify. They did not so much constitute a new industrial revolution as represent the working out and continuation of preceding trends, demonstrating the continuous and cumulative character of the technology released when industrialization began. They did not bring about a fundamental change in the structure of production or in social relations; there was no sharp break with the past. Nor was there even, at that time, qualitative change in methods of production or the productivity of labour. The new innovations only affected a relatively small part of total industrial output and do not show up powerfully in the overall indices. Even in the newer industrial countries it would be difficult to claim that they played the role of 'leading sectors', or if they did it was only much later. It was in what they promised, rather than in what they did, in the late nineteenth century that the new technologies were of major historical significance, making possible the further extension and spread of industrialization.

As a symbol of the new possibilities, however, the period from the 1870s saw the rise of a number of new industrial areas based essentially on the new technology. A striking example in Europe can be found in the Alpine regions of France, Italy and Switzerland, hitherto rather poor pastoral areas. By making use of abundant sources of hydraulic energy to generate electricity, new industries were established and what was in some ways a new pattern of industrialization emerged. It was becoming apparent that industry was no longer tied to coal and steam power but that entirely new locational patterns were possible.

On the side of organization, late nineteenth-century industrialism witnessed a growth in the scale of the business unit and the rise of new financial methods in which the banks played a more prominent role. Here again, these new features of advanced capitalism – of which there had been signs before – grew up side-by-side with the older forms of organization and did not necessarily supersede them. Rather was there the possibility of collision and conflict between the new and the old. Industrial capitalism had grown up largely in the form of family businesses and partnerships, passed on from one generation to another in many cases. These firms often survived, especially in textiles and light industry. But some were equally long-lived in other sectors where there were veritable industrial dynasties like the Krupps in Germany and Peugeot in France. However, many firms changed hands as a line expired or heirs evinced no interest in the business, and some, of course, collapsed. At least it can be said that the entrepreneurs were dominant personalities, and that in them was generally vested ownership as well as decision-making. What was new in the later nineteenth century was the foundation and growth of big firms, requiring large amounts of capital and thus adopting from an early stage the joint stock form of organization. The joint stock company proved to be a powerful engine for mobilizing capital from wide sources while concentrating control in the hands of a small number of business leaders. What was remarkable about British industralization was that it took place without its use in manufacturing industry and mining, mainly for legal reasons.

Industry in the later industrializing countries made use of the joint stock company at an earlier stage in their development, especially where large amounts of capital were required. Even in Britain it grew rapidly in importance from the 1880s and further industrialization would have been impossible without it.

Once the capital of the great business enterprises was divided into transferable shares, the way was open for a greater weight of financial control. Combinations and mergers could be effected more conveniently to deal with 'excessive' competition. The huge outlays needed to exploit the new technologies, especially in heavy industry, made the stock market itself inadequate without the support of the banks. Again, Britain remained to some extent an exception to these general trends. Finance, as pointed out, was interested in foreign trade and investment rather than in providing capital for industry. Bank assistance to long-term industrial financing was informal and personal, largely on the basis of renewable credits and loans, not of direct participation through the holding of shares and representation on the board. It was particularly in Germany and central Europe that industrial and bank capital drew closer together and promoted the growth of cartels and mergers.

These associated changes in business organization and the growing intervention of the banks were sufficiently striking, at least on the Continent and in the United States, for economists and historians to look around for a general descriptive term that would comprehend them. As yet the state seldom intervened in the business arena, except through tariffs and in generally providing a favourable environment for national capital. Nevertheless, it was widely felt that capitalism was passing through a new phase of 'high capitalism', 'organized capitalism' or 'finance capitalism'. These and other terms, invented in the early part of this century or later, suggest that the undisputed rule of the market was coming to an end and that some form of self-regulation by business or of intervention by the state would take its place.

Early industrial capitalism had been everywhere associated with competition. Markets were never in practice completely perfect. Firms might enjoy locational advantages, privileged access to raw materials or patent rights, for example, giving them a monopolistic position. It is significant that the market situations intermediate between perfect competition and pure monopoly were not analysed theoretically until the 1930s – but they had become typical of many industries much earlier. The old-style capitalism as found in textiles and the early manufacturing industry as a whole was based on the small partnership or family firm, growing by the reinvestment of profits. The scale of fixed capital was still modest, and working capital could be obtained through existing commercial channels using the bill of exchange, or by personal and informal connections with the banks. Successful businesses grew, driving out or absorbing their competitors, and as access to permanent sources of finance and the conversion to the joint stock form of organization became more important the survivors tended to account for a larger share of the market. Competition became less stable as strong and seemingly indestructible firms emerged from the early struggles.

Moreover, technical changes worked generally to favour bigness. Capital equipment became more expensive and this deterred new entrants into the existing industries. In the new industries growing up as a result of the application of science and technology to production the initial capital could be very large indeed – beyond the capacity of individuals or a small group of partners. The economies of large-scale production encouraged producers to reach backward to control their supplies of raw materials and forward towards further fabrication and marketing. Vertical as well as horizontal combinations appeared. To finance these developments firms had to resort to the stock market to raise capital or to establish closer relations with the banks, as many firms of the continental 'late-comers' had done from an early stage in their careers.

These new tendencies in advancing capitalism that were discernible in the later part of the nineteenth century grew up side-by-side with the old structures and did not necessarily supersede them. The process was always very uneven. Small-scale production held out and even expanded in some sectors as an accompaniment of growth; even so, it was sometimes dependent on the bigger firms for whom it worked as sub-contractors or suppliers. The new phenomenon was the growth in the scale of the business unit and the rise of new methods of accumulation related to the capital market and the banking system and bringing greater integration into the system as a whole.

In the United States, for example, this was the period in which the great modern business corporations – forerunners of the present-day 'multinationals' – had their beginnings. By the early 1900s, in fact, these large firms, operating nationwide and already beginning to look abroad, had become the central business units of American industry. The new-type twentieth-century industries were built upon the nation-wide economies of large-scale production and distribution as well as integration between the different stages from raw material to consumer. The giant firms that now set the pace built up national organizations, taking over competing firms or forcing them out of business. This meant, in a number of major industries, that the market was effectively divided up between a small number of large firms, the typical market situation later to be described as 'oligopoly'. There was less emphasis on price-cutting and more on advertising the product, differentiating it and establishing a brand name with a distinctive package, and on increasing the market share.

The United States was also the theatre for the application of new methods of controlling the labour process to increase the productivity of labour. The object was to be achieved by tighter management control over all the operations down to the last detail of the worker's movements on the factory floor. The best-known and most elaborately worked out system was that of 'scientific management' devised by an American engineer. Frederick Winslow Taylor, and better known as 'Taylorism', first applied by him in 1881 but not becoming influential until twenty or thirty years later. Taylor subjected the traditional way of performing a particular job to minute examination and measurement. Then a more 'scientific' method was prescribed for

Historical Patterns of Industrialization

the worker designed to increase his output. The application of time-and-motion study thus removed all discretionary power from the workers, preventing them from setting their own pace or deliberately slowing it down to a more comfortable one. Doubtless few factories, even in the United States, applied 'Taylorism', at least for many years, but it reflected a trend which accompanied industrialization: to extract the maximum output from the workforce, indeed, to eliminate the worker as far as possible from the process of production, replacing him with automatic machinery. New methods of wage payment were devised, giving the worker incentives to work harder and produce more. A somewhat later innovation, again American in origin, was the moving assembly line introduced by Henry Ford in his car factory in 1913, though the principle was well-known and had long been used in the Chicago stockyards. In the nineteenth century, however, there was still a place in industry for the skilled craftsman, especially in engineering plants, where he set up machines, made dies, carried out repairs and maintenance. The general trend was towards the predominance of the semi-skilled.

In Germany the crisis of 1873 and the subsequent depression convinced many businessmen that unchecked competition was ruinous. Within the next thirty years most major products were regulated by price cartels, quota controls or marketing syndicates. Under the latter device, the most sophisticated way of controlling the market devised up to then, the entire output of the member firms was in the hands of a single marketing agency, disposing of competition altogether. The formation of the Rhine – Westphalian Coal Syndicate in 1893 was a significant landmark in the advent in Germany of the new 'organized capitalism' that was to dominate the coming century. At the same time, the major firms in heavy industry – the 'leading sector' in German industrialization – were being reorganized into complex, interlocking concerns, based on vertical integration and large-scale production, making maximum use of by-products and internal economies. Market strategy could thus be devised on behalf of the grouping as a whole, which at the same time, through the concentration of economic power that it represented, was able to exert considerable social and political influence. The connections between industry and the banks became closer still with 'an almost inextricable network of personal and financial links'. The object of these arrangements was clearly to keep up the rate of profit, threatened as it had been by the competitive response to the post-1873 downturn.

Heavy industry was particularly affected by these trends because its capital outlays, already relatively large, were made even larger by technological demands imposed by the mass production of steel, now the key material of industrial development. The same motive, the need to guarantee profits on heavy capital investment, was behind the industrialists' demand for protection and their alliance with the big agrarians to get it in Germany in 1879. In other continental countries, including France, the growth of huge new industrial complexes using the Bessemer and Gilchrist-Thomas steel-making process led to the same coagulation of massive units of capital. In these countries, too, influenced by the German model, relations between industry, or heavy industry at any rate, and the big financial institutions became more intimate. These pressures were not absent in Britain, but they were less powerful in an older industrial country with dominant family firms still prominent and able to avoid resort to the capital market or dependence on the banks. However, it may be that this was now a factor of weakness and dragged down Britain's competitiveness in the new era of multiple industrialization. Old plants tended to be kept in operation, and there was a noticeable loss of technological leadership to the 'late-comers'.

One of the reasons for the slowness with which these trends appeared in British industry was the advantages it still enjoyed in the privileged markets of the formal and 'informal' empire. The continued growth of the old-style export industries and the comparative lack of urgency about modernization resulted from the ability to find new markets in the colonial and semi-colonial territories, the traditional preserves of British exporters. In areas such as India, British capital enjoyed a dominant position in extracting raw materials, drawing a profit from the operation of the transport system and exploiting a captive market. The huge flows of British capital assisted this process. The surplus flowing from India bridged Britain's growing trade deficits with the newer industrial countries and cushioned the effect of the deterioration in her world economic position that was visible from the 1870s onwards. As two Indian scholars remark with perceptible bitterness: 'It is no exaggeration to say that towards the end of the nineteenth century the export products secured from India's villages supported the entire structure of Britain's worldwide commerce and empire.'*

Britain's rivals had no India, and very little empire at all of

---

* Ray. Rajat and Ratna, 'The dynamics of continuity in rural Bengal under the British imperium', in *Indian Economic and Social History Review* (Delhi), Vol. x, No. 2 (June 1973), p. 121.

economic benefit; therefore a substitute had to be found. The emphasis on technical efficiency, on the economies of large-scale production, aggressive marketing and credit-financed expansion, was a response to the privileges the pioneer industrial country still enjoyed. Of course, it did not stop there. Germany's determined strides towards world power, the construction of a high-seas fleet and the build-up of alliances – notwithstanding the struttings of Kaiser Wilhelm II – represented imperative needs for German heavy industry and big business. Real or assumed, it seemed that German expansion depended upon access to markets and territory obtainable only at the expense of others or on terms that Britain and France would not be willing to accept. In that sense, the new-style capitalism was sowing the seeds of conflict.

To return to Britain, however, here the pace of change was more measured and sedate. Britain was a satiated power, with no need for territorial conquests. Despite the trade challenge of the last quarter of the nineteenth century, it was Britain's continued world financial, and commercial predominance that made the transformation to 'organized capitalism' less urgent. The older and more traditional methods appeared to yield adequate returns on capital, despite the profits squeeze of which businessmen complained. They had less to complain about as the new century began. In the long run, the effect of this cushioning – and the shaping of policy according to the interest more of the City of London than of industry – was that the old, increasingly outdated structures derived from the early Industrial Revolution were preserved. Perhaps it could not have been otherwise: economic historians are not agreed about whether there was anything to criticize, whether businessmen were blameworthy or not. Undoubtedly Britain conserved great gains from the past, at least down until 1914. By destroying, in large measure, the special conditions favouring Britain as a result of her financial and imperial pre-eminence, the First World War revealed the disadvantages to her of having been first in the field.

While Britain's problems are familiar, they were not unique. All the older industrial areas suffered from them – in continental Europe and even in New England. They also underwent a pronounced deceleration in the last quarter of the nineteenth century. Some industries declined or moved away as a result of changes in market demand or relative costs. There was nothing extraordinary in that in a competitive market economy. But, as the twentieth century was to show, Britain's history had endowed her with a particularly high proportion of industries and firms vulnerable to these changes.

As industrialization continued, production became more 'round-about'. As shown by the figures of the German statistician, Hoffman, the ratio of the output of producer goods industries to consumer goods industries tended to increase★. Workers in industry became more productive because they operated more machinery, concentrating in itself a higher level of technological specialization but also entailing higher installation costs. And because workers were more productive, creating larger incomes and a bigger surplus, so services and non-factory trades could also grow faster than before. The proportion of industrial workers to the occupied labour force, increasing in the earlier stages of industrialization, tended to slow down.

The continuation of growth and technological change on a widening front meant a growing market for plant and machinery of every kind, for transport equipment and constructional materials – hence the rising ratios discovered by Hoffman. But a major factor behind this development was another characteristic of the industrial age: the continued movement of population into towns and the growth of the urban market thus created as the major dynamic factor in the period; in the United States urban population rose from 28 to 40 per cent of the total between 1880 and 1900. It was a pattern not confined to the United States but characteristic of all the industrializing countries. Urban living was now becoming characteristic of a large part if not the majority of the population. City people, involved in a complex system of job specialization, produced practically nothing for their own consumption. They had to earn a money income and satisfy their needs by purchasing them in the market.

Towns, and especially big cities, created big standardized markets, huge worker populations, a large, more affluent middle class and even a concentration of the very rich. It was to serve this market, or rather this series of markets, that new forms of distribution developed (the department store, chain stores, delivery services). Fortunes were made in the mass production of prepared foods and ready-made clothing, footware and furnishings for the relatively high-income urban market. Much entrepreneurial talent went into these fields, especially in Britain (as names such as Lever, Boots, Lipton and Cadbury testify), which was supposed to be short of it according to some economic historians. Some of the big firms prospering in this period were to be found in the processing and packaging of food –

★ See Hoffman, W. G., *The Growth of Industrial Economies* (translated from the German by Henderson, W. O. and Chaloner, W. H.), Manchester U. P., 1958, especially Ch. II.

doing things in the factory that the housewife had previously done in the home.

But the home market did not grow fast enough to satisfy the imperative need for markets of the large-scale production industries. A major consequence of multiple industrialization was that the major firms, located in the different countries, sought to extend their markets abroad in a severe competitive struggle. Heavy fixed costs, coupled with high-productivity technology, meant that firms produced under conditions of increasing returns over a longer range of output than in the past. They sought to spread the heavy fixed costs over the largest possible volume of output. They called on the state to protect their home market from foreign competition at the same time as they sought its support in conquering the market abroad. This clamour became louder during periods when home market demand slackened. The United States was blessed with a large and growing home market, the sheer size of which reduced the pressure for exports. Even so, American firms were pressing into the world market, especially with the products of the new engineering and mechanical industries. Some, like Singer, had already set up their branch plants, and in new industries like motorcars this was early to become a feature. By the 1900s in Britain the fear of an 'American invasion' of the home market, both from imports and from the activities of US firms, added to the nervousness provoked by the 'Made in Germany' scare*. In fact, the 'American challenge' was already making headlines in Europe. The huge home market gave American exporters an advantage from which they were not slow to profit, and in some fields, such as office machinery, farm machinery and some kinds of machine tools, they had a clear lead over their rivals.

The economic imperatives pushing industrial nations into a struggle for markets were particularly marked in the case of Germany, the classic late-comer. The powerful and growing German industries had to have markets abroad to continue to remain profitable and grow. 'Export industrialism' was a characteristic of German economic development from the 1880s. It meant in particular an aggressive search for markets, mainly at the expense of Britain.

The struggle for markets, the new conditions of international competition in the age of multiple industrialization, brought a drive

---

* A book called *The American Invaders* by McKenzie, F., was published in 1901; the much better-known *Made in Germany* by Williams, E. E., which caused something of a scare, appeared in 1896. The term 'the American challenge' was popularized in the 1960s by J-J. Servan-Schreiber's book of that name.

for colonies and economic satellites. Industry was becoming increasingly dependent upon raw materials, and to a less extent foodstuffs, that were to be found only in underdeveloped areas, mostly in tropical or semi-tropical climes. Besides the old staples like cotton and jute, there were new ones – tin, rubber, oil seeds and nuts, cocoa, petroleum and some non-ferrous metals. Businesses and governments felt more secure if they had supplies of these commodities under their control. Likewise, they sought soft markets which their industry could virtually monopolize in the way that Britain did with India. The new economic imperialism was not always successful, however, and in some cases, as with the German colonization programme, proved to be a delusion; but that did not stop it. Britain's colonial power was regarded jealously by German businessmen, among others. It was backed up by a massive outflow of capital, or really a continuous reinvestment abroad of the proceeds of past investment. This 'export of capital' was a main source of Britain's continuing economic power before 1914.

The world market, like the gold standard, was very much a creation of Britain's during the period of her unchallenged economic supremacy. The international division of labour had been stimulated by Britain's voracious demand for raw materials and, from the 1850s, for food as well; and by the ability of the City of London to supply capital for development. The multilateral system of trade pivoted on Britain, and continued to do so. It enabled highly specialized economies to be brought together in the same system, but it was primarily a division between the industrializing countries and the primary producers, limiting the latters' development. International trade was predominantly an exchange of commodities between the more advanced countries, located in Europe and North America, or an exchange of their manufactured goods for primary products. The less developed countries carried on little trade between themselves because control of their foreign trade was mainly in the hands of foreign merchants or their local intermediaries.

Britain dominated the world market with little challenge until the 1880s. From then on, however, her relationship to the world market began to undergo a significant change. As the competing industrial countries took the lead in fields like light engineering and chemicals, Britain's trade deficit with them tended to grow. British industry became dependent upon imports of semi-finished goods from other industrializing countries, and some foreign specialities simply could not be duplicated, under conditions of free trade, by British firms. This was normal in a peaceful, free-trade world of the kind that economic liberals had assumed; it was a sign that the international division of labour was giving results. At the same time, continued urbanization and the relative decline of agriculture in Britain increased dependence on imports from the newly developing countries. With some of them, too, a trade deficit developed. By the early twentieth century Britain could count on a trade surplus with few countries – the role of India in bridging this gap has already been noted – those, indeed, still ready to buy the traditional exports. The existence of these markets was intimately connected with Britain's imperial position. Britain's ability to retain her world position was bound up with the continuing flow of income from past investment.

By the late nineteenth century the era of British economic predominance was drawing to a close. The type of capitalism represented in Britain preserved many archaic features as compared with the newcomers, challenging her position in one field after another. The seeds of Britain's relative decline were undoubtedly sown in this period. In a fuller sense than previously, capitalism had become a world system. Its leading centres had become delineated. A few favoured areas able to apply technology to production were growing economically and yielding a relatively high, though unequally distributed, income per head. They had imposed upon most of the rest of the world a position of economic dependence that held back or stunted the latter's development, preventing them from following the path of industrialization and thus raising incomes. At the same time, they had entered into a competitive struggle among themselves for markets, sources of raw materials and investment fields and had carved out most of the world into empires and spheres of interest or influence. This process was propelled forward by the imperatives of capitalist development and was not simply, although it was also, a power struggle between states for political hegemony. It was accompanied by a closely related process: the breakup of the older forms of capitalism and the emergence of new structures in which free competition gave way to 'monopoly' and banks and credit institutions took on a new role in financing production and distribution. Whatever the differences in the terminology used to describe this new stage of the disputes in detail over causes or its significance, it can scarcely be denied that the late nineteenth century was the watershed for a new stage in industrialization. For the Marxists the phenomena were part of the era of imperialism. Others have preferred to speak of 'organized capitalism', 'neo-mercantilism' or 'late capitalism'. It should at least be agreed that the newly emerging economic forms required a fresh analysis and a new theoretical approach.

CHAPTER NINE

India: the economic performance of a colony

Considering the length of time that India was under British rule, its history, and particularly its economic history, suffers chronic neglect. It is possible to read many accounts of British industrialization with scarcely a mention of India and certainly without any serious examination of the economic relations between the two countries. Although the contribution made by the earnings from India to the British balance of payments in the period 1880–1914 is well documented, the claim that the plunder and exploitation of India was a major source of capital accumulation necessary for the British 'take-off' has been neither proved nor disproved. Equally controversial is the degree of responsibility of the British Raj for the poor economic performance of India in the period of its existence. At the time of independence in 1947 per capita income in India was one of the lowest in the world. Nationalists claim that India's potential for growth was no less, say, than that of Japan but was frustrated by imperialism. Apologists for the Raj, on the other hand, stress the backward nature of Indian society and Hindu culture in particular, suggesting that whatever change and growth took place was the result of British effort.

These crucial but unresolved problems, together with the fact that India today contains something like half of the population of the so-called 'developing countries' in the capitalist world, gives the study of its economic past a particular relevance. It may provide information on the sources of growth in the advanced countries, particularly Britain, and do something to shed light on the question of whether the legacy of colonialism or inherent factors in local culture and institutions is the main barrier to development today. Of course, in a short treatment it is possible to do no more than introduce such questions.

When Europeans began to open up trade with India, the sub-continent, or at least a large part of it, was under the control of the Moguls, Muslim conquerors who had come in from the north-west. The predominant features of the mainly Hindu society remained intact through the duration of their rule, which was that of military conquerors and administrators interested in drawing tribute from the underlying population. The overwhelming majority of the people lived in more or less self-contained villages concentrated on the more fertile land. Families holding land mostly cultivated it with their own labour and had a definite place in the village community, giving rights and imposing obligations on the members. Land could be passed on by inheritance, but it was not individual private property in the Roman or modern European sense. Hindu society had devel-oped a particular form of division of labour, sanctified by religion – the caste system. This made for an extremely rigid and stable rural social system.

Formally Hindu society was divided into four main castes. At the top stood the priestly caste of Brahmins, defiled by contact with lower castes and exempt from manual labour. The other three castes consisted of warriors, traders and peasants. Outside the caste system were the untouchables, who did the most menial and degrading tasks unacceptable for a caste Hindu. There was a substantial minority (perhaps 20 per cent) of Muslims and converts as well as members of other religions and sects such as Jains, Sikhs and Parsees not bound by the same caste system and rules as the Hindus.

In the course of some thousands of years of its existence, the caste division of Indian society had become incredibly complicated. In each region the many sub-castes (*jatis*) carried on particular trades and occupations. Economically, therefore, the caste system corresponded to an intricate division of labour within a backward agrarian society, reinforced by ritual and supersition. Within the framework of the village community, members of particular sub-castes carried out certain tasks, making it a largely self-sufficient entity.

Mogul rule was essentially a type of feudalism superimposed upon the villages and extracting a surplus for the maintenance of its military and civil apparatus. However, the villages were not parcelled out into manors in the hands of local lords to whom sovereignty was delegated in return for a vow of allegiance. Instead, local representatives of the Mogul were endowed with revenue-collecting power over the villages in a given area. These *zamindars* received only a subordinate share of the taxes they were responsible for collecting; the bulk went to the central government. The land revenue was thus a share of the peasants' crop, but often it had to be paid in cash and could amount to between a quarter and a half of the gross product. The *zamindars* might in practice be hereditary, and the state could carve out territory for the support or reward of leading members of the ruling class. On the whole, however, these lords merely skimmed off the surplus and did not concern themselves with the organization of agriculture.

The Mogul agrarian system thus had little tendency to change or to increase production. The revenue system might impose the need to sell part of the crop, and there was some growth of urban markets for special crops, but the peasant had little or nothing left over for investment and the lords were interested in the amount of the surplus, not in increasing it through directing agriculture, which was left in the hands of the direct producers.

The political struggles in India were not over acquiring land but over the right to acquire the surplus produced by the peasantry in the shape of land revenue, and in this the British were no exception, as we shall see. This surplus went to maintain the Mogul court and local potentates living in towns. For their time, Indian towns could be very large and European visitors in the seventeenth and eighteenth centuries were duly impressed. But these towns were something like a military encampment of warriors and retainers living on the surplus and therefore creating a demand for services and manufactured goods, mostly of a luxury or semi-luxury type for the needs of the ruling class. Thus, while the surplus was drained off from the villages, little found its way back in the shape of mutual exchange between town and country. Most of the manufactured goods required by the peasants were provided by the artisan castes in the village, and, in any case, once they had paid their taxes they had little left over for anything else. Probably already in Mogul India peasant indebtedness to the local usurer was widespread. Not the land itself but the labour of the peasant was what rulers sought; the peasant was thus tied to the land, his place in the social hierarchy determined by the caste system. Moreover, there were many landless labourers belonging to low castes or untouchables who formed a village labour reserve. Passivity in the face of this situation was encouraged by Hinduism, which called on men to accept their fate in this world.

The need to turn crops into money to meet revenue demands and the urban market based on the circulation of the surplus left a place for merchants, financial operations and money-lending in Mogul India. Some of the artisans and small producers worked to the orders of merchant-manufacturers as in Europe. However, the nature of Indian society gave little scope for the emergence of an independent middle class in the towns. Merchant capital remained in a subordinate position; it could only snatch part of the surplus on its way from the peasantry to the ruling class or as profits on the supply of consumer goods to the latter. The merchants could accumulate capital and extend their activities as buyers of commodities produced by the artisans and handicraft workers, but little if any merchant capital found its way into industrial investment. Moreover, the conditions of arbitrary government by a military depotism, and then the insecurity that prevailed when the Mogul regime began to break up in the eighteenth century, offered little incentive for such investment.

By this time, however, European influence began to make itself felt as a factor in Indian development. The European traders who went to India were well organized in companies, and they possessed a superior technology – ships and firearms – and a coherent goal: to acquire riches by whatever means. The Mogul regime, already torn apart by conflict and facing challengers from among rival states, was ill-prepared to resist. Europeans largely took over India's foreign trade and harnessed artisans and small producers in the hinterland of the ports to the production of goods, mainly textiles, for export. They were able to take advantage of low costs of production resulting from the use of local raw materials, low wages and the existing division of labour, and Indian products could therefore compete successfully in Europe. Even so, there was no systematic improvement of technology, far less the introduction of machinery. What happened in some parts of India, under the stimulus of foreign trade, was what has been called 'proto-industrialization', which could perhaps have led to industrialization proper but showed no signs of doing so.

The eighteenth century saw the breakup of the Mogul empire, the steady encroachment of the Europeans and a struggle between the latter for the monopoly of plunder and trade in India from which the English East India Company emerged victorious. A steady process of territorial conquest began in which the British established their administrative system, restored law and order and organized the collection of land revenue and other taxes to place the exploitation of the conquered territory on a more systematic basis. The changes going on in Britain subsequently determined the changing relations between the metropolis and the colonial country. In particular, with industrialization India was to be developed as a market for industrial goods, to the detriment of the old handicrafts which had previously furnished goods for domestic consumption and export. However, real as this process was, it can be exaggerated. It cannot be asserted that India was on the road to industrialization before the British took over, nor were all parts of India affected by the competition of machine-made imports.

Wherever the British went, however, they introduced fundamental changes into the groundwork of the traditional, feudal society. This was most strikingly the case in agrarian relations. Here, the main concern was to ensure the collection of land revenue. In the first occupied region, that of Bengal, the *zamindars*, who were basically tax-farmers, were identified as the owners of the land. It was hoped that they would continue in this role, behaving in much the same way as the improving landlords of contemporary England and providing much needed allies in the countryside. This was the purpose of the famous Permanent Settlement of 1793. The *zamindars* acquired an hereditary right to that part of the revenue not handed over to the British, a right that could be bought and sold as well as passed on to their heirs. They did not become landed proprietors in the fullest sense, and they certainly did not fulfil the hope that they would behave as improving landlords.

The Permanent Settlement in Bengal reflected the British administrators' background and experience with the landed aristocracy in their own country where in the eighteenth century it was actively concerned with improving their estates to increase their incomes. The British saw the assurance that the *zamindar* would have a share in the surplus produced by the peasantry as the basis for investment in agriculture, but they were mistaken. The larger landlords tended to be absentees, living in towns and with no interest at all in agricultural improvement. As the Company took over other parts of India, and as officials tended to be influenced by the Ricardian theory of rent, an attempt was made to avoid the mistakes made in Bengal. Later land settlements thus left the land in the hands of the peasants (*ryots*) with the hope that they would improve the land and that both they and the state would benefit. But *ryotwari* tenure, and other attempts to compound with the village community, met no better fate. A new class of owners was created; the original owners were often forced to sell or mortgage the land granted them. Subletting flourished, the land tended to pass into the hands of larger, absentee owners and money-lenders who battened on the insecurity of the cultivators. The combination of private property and money economy with the old communal relations and feudalism proved a disaster for Indian agriculture and introduced a built-in depressor from which the agrarian sector has never recovered.

Agrarian relations did not change overnight, and in many ways they displayed a powerful continuity right through from the Mogul period to the present day. In all, the principal sufferers from this hybrid of European and Asiatic forms were the mass of the peasants, condemned to indebtedness and poverty. The old village society was steadily undermined, but it was not replaced by a vigorous capitalist agriculture. The Indian peasant thus suffered from the worst of both systems. A large part of his product was paid to the state, the landlord or intermediary, and the money-lender. Little if any of the surplus found its way back into the agrarian sector, despite the anxiety of British administrators that this should be so. The income of the peasants remained on, or scarcely above, subsistence level – meaning both that they were unable to make much improvement themselves in the land and that they were unable to buy very much in the market. The process of differentiation went on at different rates in different areas with strong peasants, mostly from the superior sub-castes, emerging and producing for the market. At the same time the rural proletariat and semi-landless peasants also grew in numbers in the course of the nineteenth century. Pre-capitalist forms of exploitation continued to exist, particularly in those parts of India that were still ruled by the princes in the British period.

The torpor and stagnation of the rural sector scarcely provided an auspicious basis for a dynamic economy. The peasant remained desperately attached to the land as a means of livelihood. To the vagaries of the monsoon were added the fluctuations of the market and the implacable demands of the money-lender. The peasant was forced to sell his crop under the most unfavourable conditions because of his chronic need for cash. The creation of a land market – the accompaniment of private property in land – favoured the landlords and 'strong' peasants and weakened the defences of the poor. Land-lords and money-lenders flourished and continued to show a conspicuous disregard for agricultural improvement. The heritage of the British in the sphere – and they were the main beneficiaries, as recipients of the land revenue in the place of the old rulers – was a negative one and with some grounds it could be claimed that it was, and is, the source of India's underdevelopment. The vested interests built in over 150 years have proved resistant to change and still condition the character of Indian agriculture today. It is not surprising that, in what is still overwhelmingly a rural country, agrarian questions should be the key to economic advance or that the nature of the social relations in Indian agriculture should be a source of controversy.

The survival of much of the old agrarian system helps to explain the continuing force of tradition, including the caste system, as a restraint on growth. For example, the undermining of the village community and the uncertainties and insecurity resulting from the growth of a market economy probably gave the caste added import-ance and led to emphasis on caste differences. At the same time, the slowness of change in the agrarian sector reflected the weakness of the forces acting upon it from outside. But when such influences began to make themselves felt it was in a particular way, arising from India's status as a colony: its growing involvement in the world market as a producer of primary products for export. Once again, therefore, a distorting factor was introduced into growth in which one side of agricultural production was developed in line with the needs of the advanced countries.

The results of the British intervention in Indian agrarian relations were not, of course, intended, but they did arise out of the pursuit of specific goals which did not include the rounded development of the economy of the sub-continent. There was no question, for example, of providing rural credit to break the stranglehold of the money-lender, or of fostering industrial development. From the time that the East India Company began to extend its territorial dominion the country was seen as a source of revenue and an economic appendage of Britain. But, as the economic transition proceeded rapidly in Britain from an agrarian to an industrial basis, so India was seen in a changing light. With the expansion of the cotton industry in Lanca-shire India became a vast market for cheap British factory-made textiles. Mercantile capital expressed in the Company, which had won concessions at the point of the sword for its trade, had to face the challenge of industrial capital, which saw India as a market and as a source of raw materials and was hostile to the Company's monop-olistic position. The Company operated with the assistance of a comprador class of Indian merchants. The continued development of trade further opened up opportunities inside India for the enrichment of a merchant class.

Colonial rule by its nature requires a strong state, and with reason the civil service built up by the British in India is described as a 'steel frame'. The Raj rested on the army, the police and a bureaucracy quite different from anything existing in Britain in the nineteenth century. Such a state could not fail to intervene in the economy to guarantee the interests of the dominant power: to ensure that India remained a market for British goods and a producer of raw materials. To this end the state had to promote the creation of an infrastructure of roads, railways, telegraphs, administrative centres and army camps, a whole 'public sector' tending to extend into sections of industry. In fact, the state became the largest single purchaser of industrial goods and eventually came to operate iron-works, coal-mines and ordnance factories, as well as railways., This infrastructure would not have been laid out by private enterprise alone. Although provided for the convenience of the colonial rulers, however, it was financed from Indian revenue. It riveted India more closely to the world market in a position of dependence upon Britain, using state power backed up by the sword. Growth there was, but it was confined to some areas and sectors; inherently lopsided, it slowed down some forms of development or inhibited them entirely. Particularly, British control over tariff policy prevented the use of protection to encourage industrialization. Government purchasing policy favoured British suppliers (although there was some relaxation on grounds of economy towards the end of the nineteenth century).

The case of Indian railways provides an example of the limitations resulting from colonial rule. Financed by British capital with a guaranteed rate of return, their running losses were paid for out of Indian revenues. They had few backward linkages with the domestic economy and absorbed capital which might have been more profitably employed elsewhere. One linkage was to coal-mining. But although output grew rapidly, especially in the period leading up to the First World War, conditions of production remained primitive with the mining carried out by subcontractors employing cheap labour including women and children. The mines, like the industries of colonial India, retained an enclave character.

Climatic and social conditions prevented India from being a country of white immigration. The British in India always formed a tiny minority, the highest caste in a caste-ridden society, convinced of their cultural superiority. The British who went to India did so mainly as expatriates bent on making a career in the army or civil service or in business, and they lived separate lives from those of the Indians. On the other hand, the deliberate introduction of English education following Macaulay's Minute of 1835 opened the way for the growth of a Westernized middle class of a type that India had not known under the Moguls. Later this class was to use the ideology of the conquerors to demand the right to rule themselves in their own nation-state (again, a concept hitherto foreign to India). For the period down to independence Indians had little influence on overall policy, which was determined basically in far-away Westminster and interpreted on the spot by the ruling viceroy and the Indian civil service.

India attracted British capital, but only into limited sectors. Even for railway-building investors required the incentive of a government guarantee of interest. Capital went into plantations, trade and finance, but only to a limited extent into industry: hence most pioneer efforts here came from Indian businessmen. For the nationalists the most serious indictment of British rule was expressed in the 'drain' theory. This was first put forward in a coherent form by Dadabhai Naoroji in the 1860s and argued that India was being impoverished by the export surplus in the current account; controversy has been raging ever since. No one denies that there was a net outflow from India beginning with the remittance of huge private fortunes accumulated by plunder or fraud in the eighteenth century. This overflow continued as British rule was extended and consolidated in the first half of the nineteenth century and subsequently became more methodical in its nature.

Nationalist writers may exaggerate the drain and get the sums wrong. Apologists for British rule claim that the drain was smaller and less harmful than the nationalists assert; they say that only Government of India payments overseas for the so-called 'home charges' represented a drain. The rest, they say, was payment for services or charges on borrowed capital which contributed in one way or another to India's economic development. On the other hand, Indians, and particularly the direct cultivators of the land on whom land revenue and other regressive taxes fell, had to meet not only 'home charges' and other external expenditures of the Indian government, including those for military operations in defence of other parts of the Empire, but also the costs of the British Raj in India. To British officials both outlays appeared to be quite normal; Indians were only, after all, paying for the benefits of British law and order. Such arguments were unconvincing to the nationalists and the 'drain' theory was one of the most powerful political weapons used in the drive for independence.

Statistically considered, the 'drain' may not have been large in relation to India's national income. One calculation suggests that 'the proportion of invisible and debt servicing charges in the current account of the balance of payments could not have been much more than five per cent of India's national income in this period' (1898–1914)*. That may be so but 5 per cent is a lot for a poor country, and the claim that the export surplus stimulated activity in

---

* See Chaudhari, K. N., 'India's international economy in the nineteenth century; an historical survey', in *Modern Asian Studies*, Vol. ii No 1 (1968), p. 43.

India does not carry conviction because of the limited extent of the linkage effects of the export-based sectors.

Moreover, the export surplus has to be put into a wider perspective. India was a great captive market for British goods. In the five years before 1914 63 per cent of total imports of merchandise came from Britain; this proportion did, however, fall rapidly after the First World War, and by 1938–39 was down to 31 per cent. As for India's exports, over half went to the United Kingdom in the 1870s; again, this fell to 25 per cent by the late 1930s. The significant point about the pre- 1914 situation is made by S. B. Saul, who says 'The key to Britain's whole payments pattern lay in India, financing as she probably did more than two-fifths of Britain's total deficit.'* Saul also contends that 'it was mainly through India that the British balance of payments found the flexibility essential to a great capital-exporting country'. He goes on to say 'The Indian safety-valve brought immense advantages [i.e. to Britain] from other points of view as well. It was partly through her Indian connection that Britain was able to survive the blows of tariff barriers. The Indian market was kept open to British goods and Indian exports overcame the tariffs for her.'

The ability of the British economy to weather the difficulties of the period 1880–1914 stemmed to no small extent from the hold over India, a country, be it remembered, whose masses lived in dire poverty. At the same time, the ability of British investors to lend on a large scale to Canada in this same period can, without exaggeration, be traced to the same Indian connection. As two Indian economic historians mordantly observe:

> India's export surplus was appropriated by Britain through a complicated mechanism of home charges and invisible services (shipping, insurance, etc) to cover two-fifths of her enormous trade deficit with the rest of the world. It is no exaggeration to say that towards the end of the nineteenth century the export products secured from India's villages supported the entire structure of Britain's world-wide commerce and Empire.†

Obviously this is not the last word. The whole question of the 'drain', the economic connection between Britain and India and colonial exploitation call out for further research. As has been pointed out, this is true from the very beginning of the Industrial Revolution in Britain as well as through to the end of the Raj. It should be remembered, too, that throughout this period there was little British

---

* Saul, S. B., *Studies in Britain's Overseas Trade 1870–1914*, Liverpool U. P., 1960, p. 62.

† Ray, Rajat and Ratna, article cited, p. 121.

enterprise in factory industry in India (the only important exception being the jute industry, one of those exports able to leap over foreign tariff barriers).

On the other hand, India was unique among the colonial countries in that, during the nineteenth century, a local class of businessmen emerged who began to invest in industry as well as trade. It must be said at the outset, however, that only a relatively small proportion of the economic surplus accruing to Indians found its way into productive investment. Given the conditions of Indian agriculture, much capital was invested in landlordism and money-lending in an entirely parasitic way. Conspicuous consumption on the part of the traditional ruling class was rife. Speculative activities no doubt also drew off capital. It was significant, too, that entrepreneurs were drawn mainly from particular communities, such as the Bombay Parsees, or members of trading sub-castes from particular areas, such as the Gujeratee and Marwari traders. Members of these sub-castes tended to fan out from their region of origin and to constitute, as it were, an immigrant entrepreneurial group in other areas where they were distinguished and separate from the main population groups. The reservoir for the recruitment of entrepreneurs was limited and they tended to be unpopular.

The juridical conditions for the development of capitalism in India were laid when the British introduced private property in land; the economic conditions, which had already begun to appear under the Moguls, were progressively established with the growth of foreign and internal trade, the stimulus given to the commercialization of agricultural produce and the opening up of the internal market through the improvement of communications. Although from the time of the East India Company European merchants seized control of external trade, they could carry it on and expand it only with the assistance of Indian middlemen. Members of the trading castes and other communities were not slow to take advantage of the opportunities presented despite having to accept a subordinate – and even humiliating – position. In the period after the Mutiny (1857–58), when the East India Company finally lost its territorial jurisdiction, a more determined policy for the opening up of the hinterland was pursued. This activity was still, of course, British-directed – railway building, plantations, banking – but it could not fail to open new opportunities for the accumulation of capital by Indians.

The most significant achievement of Indian capital in this period was the development of a cotton factory industry mainly in the Bombay area. Machinery was purchased from Britain, local raw material was available, and it proved possible to recruit a disciplined industrial labour force to work in the mills without particular difficulty. The industry grew rapidly on the basis of cheap lines for export to the Far East, but later in the century came more directly into competition with Lancashire for a share of the home market under the pressure of the rising cotton industry in Japan. With labour cheap and the market growing, the cotton industry proved to be highly profitable. Perhaps pressure from Lancashire limited the British investment in the industry, for the majority of the capital came from Indian sources, though in some cases it was administered by British-controlled managing agencies. British cotton manufacturers also lobbied strongly against a protective tariff for the Indian industry.

In the case of jute, on the other hand, which did not compete so directly with an established industry in Britain, much of the capital was British-owned; it could, indeed, be fairly regarded as an outpost of the British economy operating in Bengal. Consequently the secondary multiplier or linkage effects were small. But although the cotton mills on the other side of India had deeper effects, they did not lead the way for a more thoroughgoing change reaching to the roots of the rural economy: if this be identified as the source of India's backwardness, then it is significant that even the cotton industry had something of an enclave character.

Towards the end of the nineteenth century something like an ideology of industrialization began to appear, formulated by the articulate spokesmen of the rising bourgeoisie. The Indian National Congress took shape as the expression of this class; led mainly by high-caste members of the intelligentsia, it expressed the interests of the developing industrial bourgeoisie, which saw, increasingly, that its interest lay in the creation of a national state. The first demand, however, was for tariff protection and the end of the government's *laissez-faire* policy regarding industrial development. Indeed, this policy did begin to change as the economy of India became more complex and Britain's world position came under pressure.

There was a fear that India would become a dumping ground for cheap foreign manufactured goods, as happened before 1914 in the case of Belgian steel. The revision of government policy was accelerated by the First World War. Supplies of imported manufactures were cut down, acting as a form of protectionism, while the war created a demand for the kind of goods that could be produced in India such as textiles and hides. A boom period began for Indian industry, but it was not sufficient by a long way to set the country on the road to industrialization. The Industrial Commission set up in 1916 reported two years later and recommended a more forward policy, but industrial matters were placed in the hands of the provincial governments. In practice there was no fundamental change, and the world depression of 1929–33 proved to be a severe blow to the hopes of more rapid industrial development. The obstacles to growth had not been removed. Government policy remained in its traditional grooves while the nationalist movement, supported by the industrialists, clamoured increasingly for a positive and interventionist policy of development. It was apparent that such a policy would only be carried out by a sovereign and independent state.

India thus remained an example of combined development. Bullock carts and sacred cows existed side-by-side with advanced capitalist industry and a modern industrial proletariat. Religious fanaticism and superstition abounded; there was an archaic and distorted land system, stagnation, mass poverty, sloth and filth. On the other hand there were railways, factories, banks, modern city centres and a sophisticated intelligentsia in touch with the most advanced ideas. These contradictions and paradoxes were essential parts of India's historical legacy of colonial dependence.

In deciding between colonial status and the traditional heritage as explanations of India's backwardness and poverty, the balance would seem to lie with the former. That is not to say that modernization and industrialization are compatible with the caste system and the religious and cultural features of Hinduism antipathetic to change and material values. But the persistence of these traits cannot themselves be divorced from the long period of British rule. Clearly, no one can say what India's fate would have been had the British never conquered the sub-continent. The disorder and anarchy of the period of the breakup of Mogul rule was itself partly a product of the impact of Europeans. The alternative to British rule may have been another foreign yoke, say that of France. Or Indians may have worked out a solution to their differences either within some kind of union or by the creation of a number of separate states, some of which no doubt would have been capable of economic growth to a greater extent than others. By the later nineteenth century not only Europe but also Japan provided a model for development. There is no reason to suppose that Indians would have been impervious to these models, given the fact that criticism of traditional values and reform movements were under way and the alacrity with which outside influences were absorbed by the intelligentsia under British rule. There is a case for saying that the Raj gave a new lease of life to traditional elements, including the caste system. However, although what would have happened in the absence of British rule must remain a purely speculative question, it is not without sense to raise it.

Under British rule India remained an underdeveloped, primarily agrarian country with a very low per capita income, put at $50 in the 1930s. Manufacturing industry employed some 2 per cent of the active population and contributed only 6 per cent of the national income. Almost three-quarters of the population was employed in agriculture and this was the basic reason for India's underdevelopment. Much of the cultivated land was in dwarf holdings of under five acres and the cultivators led a precarious existence, a prey to debt, famine and disease. The British were much more successful in improving hygiene and thus lowering the death rate than they were in increasing production. At the beginning of British rule there had been much spare land in India, and the steady growth of population in the nineteenth century does not suggest overpopulation. In the twentieth century, however, the population began to grow very rapidly, from 236 million in 1891 to 248 million in 1921 and 357 million in 1951 (if present growth rates continue, the population will reach 1,000 million by the end of the century), making it possible to argue that controlling population growth has become the number one problem – which it certainly had not been previously.

As has been seen, unlike many underdeveloped countries India did possess, under British rule, a developed industrial and mining sector run on modern capitalist lines as well as a capitalist sector in agriculture consisting of plantations and peasant holdings or farms producing for the market. The modern sectors were the dynamic ones, attracting both foreign and native capital investment and accounting for perhaps 30 per cent of the national income. However, these sectors had specific features arising from India's relationship to the world market as a dependent, colonial country. For example, the most progressive sectors of agriculture produced for the export market principally. Industry depended upon foreign machinery and produced mainly consumer goods. Modern enterprises tended, therefore, to have an enclave character with limited linkage effects on surrounding activities.

The slow growth of industry could thus be explained by the low income and inadequate purchasing power of the rural masses; this tends to be confirmed by the current situation, where industry produces mainly for the top 10 to 15 per cent of income-receivers. It has already been suggested that this agrarian problem was a legacy of British rule, which ensured that most of the surplus found its way into the hands of the state and landlords, intermediaries and usurers not interested in productive investment. In any case, Indian industry received no encouragement from the government before 1914 and had to struggle even for the home market in competition with low-priced British imports. It was notable, for instance, that there was little engineering, apart from railway repair shops, or heavy industry producing capital goods. Some Indian capital, as with the Tata firm, began to go into these sectors in the twentieth century, partly out of a nationalist motivation. However, comparatively little Indian capital went into industry and even where it did so the use of the managing agency system meant that it was often under British control. The bias of education towards literary subjects was also unfortunate. The British were uninterested in mass education and the illiteracy rate remained staggeringly high. This was itself a factor making for economic retardation and it meant, among other things, a lack of technicians, managers and, perhaps, potential entrepreneurs. At the same time, the type of education that flourished reinforced the disdain of the high-status castes for industry and business.

These features, arising from the colonial situation, meant that India was not able to seize on the potentialities for growth possessed by the 'late-comers', including those colonies opened up for European settlement. There was no question of leaping over stages or of big spurts of growth. The built-in depressor operating in the agrarian sector limited the linkage effect of urban industry and the growth of exports. Instead of spearheading growth, as in Canada, staple exports tended to lead the Indian economy into a trap, reinforcing the existing growth-inhibiting patterns. There was little expansion of the internal market or development of the social division of labour along modern lines, and much of the increasing demand for cheap manufactured goods was met by imports (in the absence of tariff protection). The spread of monoculture enabled some peasants to prosper, it is true, but there was little local processing of raw materials, and generally speaking the peasant producer had to sell under disadvantageous conditions because of his poverty and continued indebtedness. These peculiarities arose from India's colonial dependence and the character of the economic policy of the Raj and of British investment.

The conditions of India's development under foreign rule thus precluded industrialization either on the British or on the later European or Japanese model. This conclusion seems to follow independently of any social and cultural impediments as well as of those of a physical and climatic nature. Caste divisions and the vast social inequalities of the traditional society, the real or supposed antipathy of Hindus (or Muslims) to business, or more doubtfully to material acquisition, played a role only in the context of India's subordinate and peripheral position in the capitalist world market.

CHAPTER TEN

Canada: country of recent settlement

The contrast between Canada and India could scarcely be more extreme. Canada has one of the highest income levels in the world and is one of the Group of Seven richest countries. Relatively sparsely populated, she could evidently absorb many millions more people without a drastic reduction in the standard of living. Dependent, like India, on the export of primary products, these have been a source of growth and wealth, not of exploitation through trade. Despite the role that these products play in exports, Canada is a highly urbanized and industrial country. The typical Canadian no longer conforms to the old stereotype of farmer, lumberjack or trapper, but is a city-dweller working in an office or a factory.

Canada and India were, for a whole historical period, constituent parts of the British Empire – but their relationships with Britain could hardly have been more different. After the independence of the Thirteen Colonies there was no doubt that the remaining colonies in British North America would become self-governing and would not be ruled, as India was, by an expatriate civil service. The evident reason was that Canadians were Europeans, and a large proportion of them were British, while Indians, with their own inpenetrable culture and coloured skins, were regarded as incapable of governing themselves, at least until they had been wards of their alien rulers for a considerable period.

While Canada was absorbing large quantities of British capital to become, by 1914, the leading debtor country, the amount of capital invested in India, compared with the size of her population, was more modest. No one doubts that the import of capital was the determining factor in Canada's development and that the lack of capital adversely affected India's development. Canada consequently, had, a permanent deficit on her balance of payments, while her people grew steadily wealthier; India had a current surplus while her economy stagnated and mass poverty went unrelieved.

Climatically, most of India lay in the tropical and sub-tropical zones. How this affected the character of her economic development is a controversial question; all that can be said with certainty is that modern economic growth has not taken place in such conditions as an autonomous process. However, it was the products cultivated in these climates that attracted Europeans to India, at least to a very large extent. Much of Indian agriculture was dependent on the vagaries of the monsoon or could not be carried on successfully without irrigation. Some sort of living was perhaps easy to come by in a climate not subject to extremes of cold and where sun and water could produce fairly abundant crops. In the case of Canada, climate presented a problem of a different nature. Apart from the moist seaboard regions on both coasts, the great problem over most of what became the Canadian Confederation were the extremes of cold and heat. Intensely cold winters meant a short growing season and the risks arising from drought, early frosts and crop-flattening storms. But, given European techniques developed to deal with similar, if less severe, conditions, climate was a challenge rather than merely a drag on development so long as there was a material incentive to overcome its rigours. Certainly, it was not a climate to encourage indolence or passivity; to be able to survive at all was a struggle for the early settlers and the pioneers everywhere. European ideology, derived from a capitalist background, encouraged Canadians to work hard and get on. The older settlers generally thought of the newcomers as working less hard than themselves, however, and often they were right – the work ethic flourished in a pioneer environment.

In short, Canada displayed all the characteristics of a country of recent settlement in which Europeans opened up a wilderness with advanced techniques under conditions of competitive individualism untrammelled (or almost) by traditional institutions and inhibitions. The new environment sharpened the purely capitalist elements in the culture which the colonists brought with them. In that respect, if French Canada is excluded for the moment, then like the United States, Canada represented a purer form of capitalism than the parent society. It was because at the time when French settlement occurred France had not become a capitalist society that French Canada developed from the beginning in a different way.

Colonists moving into Canada did not find, as they did in India, a strong, coherent indigenous society able to stand up to their advance if only by sheer numbers. Instead, North America represented a huge virgin zone inhabited by only a few hundred thousand Eskimos and Amerindians, adapted to the environment at a low level of technique and requiring large tracts of land for survival. On the whole, the settlers treated with the inhabitants from a basis of superior strength which resulted in a deterioration in their condition and a decline in their numbers as effectively as genocide. Under the polite cloak of treaty settlements with the British monarch, Indian tribes were deprived of their land, given a little money and a few baubles and parked in reservations, where they lived on the fringes of the new Canadian society as it came into existence. On the whole the white man did not need the Indians' labour, even had they been willing to furnish it. He learned something from the Indian way of life to help master the wilderness, but otherwise the Indian was not a very serious encumbrance.

Canada today is the second largest country in the world by area, but a small country (some twenty-six million in 1988) in respect to population size. Its history, and especially its economic history, is scarcely better known outside its frontiers than is that of India. The first settlers in the area now known as Canada, more specifically in the St Lawrence basin, were French: feudal *seigneurs*, royal officials and peasants shipped bodily from France and establishing virtual replicas of French villages on the edge of the wilderness beside the river. By the time that the British completed their conquest of North America in the 1760s, French settlements amounted to some 75,000 souls. They were the nucleus of present-day French-speaking Canadians in Quebec and neighbouring provinces; an exception to almost every rule applying to the rest of the country. Anglo-Saxon settlers were attracted first by the fisheries and the maritime industries of the eastern seaboard. Rivers and lakes gave access to the interior of the continent, and intrepid men pressed westward in search of riches, i.e. salcable commodities. The only riches to present themselves in commercial quantities were fur-bearing animals. For a long time it was the beaver in the cold, but not too cold, wastes that gave the area its economic basis for existence. But the wilderness was also a forest, dense, huge, interminable – an obstacle to the modest agriculturalist but a source of riches for the entrepreneur.

The northern part of America attracted men in search of wealth through the exploitation of the region's natural resources and their sale in the world market. Staple products were at the heart of all Canadian development in the early period. But Canada was not yet Canada. That began only when the rebel colonies to the south had fought for, and won, their independence. Canada as we know it was the creation of those determined to stay under British rule or, from self-interest or indifference, not attracted by rebellion. The scattered colonists in British North America were joined by many loyalists who chose British rule as well as by some demobilized soldiers from the wars of the 1770s and 1811–13. Politically, Canada was to be defined by its separateness from the United States and its ties with Britain – and by that anomaly, the willingness of the ruling élite of French Canada to accept British government.

The small, sparsely settled colonies at first clung to the fringes of the wilderness, then moved along the river valleys and the lake shores and began to penetrate into the interior. Furs and the forest offered a living – a hard one for those who worked, made more precarious by the rigours of long, cold winters and the vagaries of nature. But if the staples were a great magnet for expansion and development, many settlers were concerned mainly with wresting a living from the land. Land was abundant, labour was scarce, but capital was scarcer still: only by the investment of borrowed capital was there an economic future for the colonies. The seaboard colonies and those on the St Lawrence, Upper and Lower Canada, at first derived their substance from their inclusion within the British mercantile system. It was this that opened up a privileged market for staple products like grain and timber.

At this stage the colonies were an offshoot of the mother country, their trade dominated by British merchants. Merchant capital bought up raw products and arranged for their transport to the external market. The commitment in fixed capital was still relatively small. The Industrial Revolution in Britain changed many things for Canada, but only over the long term. Demand for staple products began to grow, but once British industrial supremacy had been established free trade created a new environment for international trade.

Apart from the French Canadian *habitant* (the peasant cultivator) and a few scattered farmers in Nova Scotia and elsewhere, settlers did not go to Canada to cultivate the land on a subsistence basis, but to produce a cash crop which could bring in a money income. (This was the great difference between the North American farmer and the European peasant. The farmer was tied into market economy from which even the *habitant* could not escape – for the surplus manpower of backward French Canadian agriculture had to seek by-employments in such jobs as trapping and lumberjacking.) The main requirement of the agricultural colonist was a market.

The world market was undoubtedly growing in the period after

1815, but the colonies of British North America were not favourably placed compared with the United States. The southern neighbour enjoyed a more temperate climate, ice-free ports, easier access to the interior, closer proximity to markets and more incentive for private investment. In addition, Canada lacked capital. Without capital, transport facilities to link producers to markets could not be constructed or improved. The basic infrastructure had to be laid, but the money for it had to be borrowed. Canada began its long history of debt. Something like a strategy of development emerged, in which the state had to take the initiative. Private capitalists were not rich enough to provide the infrastructure, nor was their reputation sufficient to enable them to borrow to do so. The state had to accept the responsibility, its first great task being to extend the St Lawrence system by the building of canals beginning in 1827 and comprising two boom periods: 1827–37 and 1841–49. Most of the money for these projects came from the City of London and represented a public debt. Already, from this period, certain constants in Canadian economic development for some period ahead become visible.

The additions and improvements to the St Lawrence system represented a heavy capital outlay; the capital had to be amortized and interest paid. Therefore there was a need for paying traffic and for the opening up of the regions traversed for settlement by people able to produce and sell goods and to pay taxes. However, the St Lawrence system was in direct competition with the trade routes to the south, passing through United States territory and debouching in the larger and better, because ice-free, ports of the United States seaboard. These routes were constantly being improved as capital flowed in to profit from and further stimulate the boisterously growing US economy. The investment in the Canadian transport system had from the start, therefore, a speculative element. There was always a need to expand and attract traffic to overcome the burden of overhead costs. If that could not be done, then the project would not fulfil its expectations and debts could not be paid off from increased earnings or rising tax revenues.

In this first stage the results were only modest, but the flow of immigration into Canada did increase. In the 1850s the international environment changed with the adoption of free-trade policies by Britain and the loss of Canada's preferential treatment, the lower rate of duty levied on her staple exports, in the British market. At about the same time, however, Canada entered the railway age; and, sponsored by government, heavy outlays were made on construction of lines to link up the various parts of the colony and provide access to the world market. In 1841 the union of Upper and Lower Canada took place, bringing together the French- and English-speaking colonies and providing the starting point for wider union. A broader-based government was, in any case, necessary in order to embark upon the tasks of development. It soon had to face the challenge of working out a new strategy for development in the face of Britain's change of policy. Not surprisingly, the viability of a state separate from the United States on the North American continent was again posed, and not for the last time. There were those in the Canadian business community who conceived of union. The continued rapid growth of the United States was a powerful factor. Moreover, the United States was able to begin its westward expansion into grain-growing lands attractive for settlement, while Canada faced the great barrier of the Canadian Shield, some 1,000 miles of barren scrub and waste, before it could reach its own west. Bearing this in mind, however, there was still considerable scope for settlement in the lands east of this barrier as they were opened up by canals and railways. In the favourable climate offered by an expanding world market in the 1850s, and despite competition from the south, Canada entered a boom period.

Basic to this new phase was the building of railways. Coming in the wake of canals, they opened up new opportunities for enrichment for Canadians. It was axiomatic in colonial conditions that the state should take the initiative in building the infrastructure necessary for development. There were no individuals rich enough to finance costly expenditure on transport improvements, no large investing class and no local capital market adequate for the task of floating companies. The capital had to come principally from abroad (i.e. from the City of London), and only government could borrow on the necessary scale. But outlay on canals and railways created incomes and stimulated investment in other sectors. Part went to pay for imports – and both import and export trade benefited. Canadian businessmen soon learned that 'the real money in railroads was to be made, not from owning and operating them, but from building them, provided the matter was handled properly'*.

In short, railway investment, financed from abroad and sponsored by government, made possible the accumulation of capital in the hands of the business class. Fortunes were made by contractors,

---

* The quotation is from the very interesting article by Pentland, H. C., 'The role of capital in Canada's economic development before 1875' in *The Canadian Journal of Economics and Political Science*, Vol. xvi, No. 4 (Nov. 1950), p. 467.

money was invested in supplies for the railways, and more scope was offered for investment in manufacturing industry. By the late 1840s Canada's first mining boom had begun. The local business class began to find its feet and make its weight felt more strongly in politics: it stood, however, not for *laissez-faire* but for the use of the state as an instrument for development, that is to say to widen their own business opportunities. At the same time, the problem of relations with the United States was solved, temporarily as it turned out, by reciprocity measures introduced in 1854 thus lowering or abolishing duties on a wide range of commodities. Canadian farmers and raw material producers now looked towards the US market as a compensation for their loss of British preferences.

The middle decades of the nineteenth century saw in Canada the growth of an internal market and the rise of some manufacturing industry. Staple products did not lose their importance. The staple remained the life blood for much agriculture and the source of profit and accumulation for the Canadian business class. But it always has to be remembered, when stressing the importance of the staples for Canadian development, that the very nature of the economy made possible, simultaneously, the expansion of the internal market. This was the difference between Canada – a country of European settle ment – and primary producers like India, who were led by staple production into an export-trap. We shall see later that in Canada, too, the staple meant lopsidedness and instability – but it did not mean poverty or exploitation.

The Canadian developmental project in this period was only a mitigated success, and it was in any case overshadowed by events in the United States. By the early 1860s Canada's population was still only about the same size as that of the United States in the 1790s. At the later date the giant to the south already had a market of thirty-two million people with a high per capita income able to support a powerful industrial base. Canadian manufacturers feared competition from both the United States and Britain, hence their demand for a protected market. The Civil War in the United States raised the demand for foodstuffs and also cut off the import of American-made goods, thus encouraging import substitution in parts of Ontario and Quebec. The victory of the North was a victory for the protectionists and a blow to an immediate prospect of integration. The provinces of Canada thus had to look to their own resources; Canadian nationalism took clearer shape and had protection on its banners.

Economic strategy had to take account of the changing conditions; this meant closer political union, and the formation of a more coherent

149

national unit, able to stake its claim to the land beyond the Canadian Shield known as Rupert's Land, held by the Hudson's Bay Company. The British North America Act of 1867 provided the necessary political prelude, creating the union of the maritime provinces of Nova Scotia and New Brunswick with Central Canada in a new Confederation. But the economic model was the United States. The aim was to link the different parts of Canada closer together through railway building, to bridge the Canadian Shield with a transcontinental railway to link up with British Columbia and to develop the West in competition with the United States. Rupert's Land was purchased in 1868, thus giving Canada a new frontier. The aim was further government sponsorship of all-Canadian transport routes, even though they would be more costly to build and expensive to use than alternative routes passing through US territory.

The opening up of the interior was favoured by the business interests for a variety of interconnected reasons. The heavy investment already made in the transport system had not paid off because of the effectiveness of US competition. The need for the opening of Canada's own West stemmed from the need to find paying traffic both for the routes already built and for the new lines planned by the Confederation. A bid for a growing volume of west–east traffic was necessary on economic grounds, an attempt to meet an already existing problem of debt and overhead costs by taking the risk that debts would grow and the problem of unused capacity increase. However, the main risks would be taken by government; the main gain seemed likely to accrue to the business sector. It was necessary, therefore, to attract more capital into Canada with the prospect of the development of the staple products supplying the world market, though with the knowledge that this would open up new horizons for profitable investment at home. At the same time, the Confederation suggested the abandonment of any prospect of North American integration. The east–west axis would be strengthened at the expense of north–south ties, and protectionism on both sides of the 49th parallel would ensure separate development. New provinces would be added to the Confederation as colonization and settlement spread westward in the wake of the railway, and the new nation would assume continental dimensions.

The next three decades were to prove decisive in Canadian development. In some ways, economically, they have a bad name. This was a period of world economic slow-down, once called the Great Depression. And while US expansion was still filling up the continent to the south, that giant's progress was bound to overshadow anything attainable in Canada. Nevertheless although contemporaries expressed disappointment, in perspective this period appears as one in which the foundations were firmly laid for subsequent advance.

It must be remembered that the strategy of Confederation was not exclusively based on the staple; it also envisaged the development of manufacturing in Canada and the consolidation and extension of home market activity which has already been stressed as a prominent feature of Canadian growth in the earlier part of the nineteenth century. Thus the period after 1867 saw the working out of new policies – or at least of more definite ones regarding the protection of manufacturing industry. Protective tariffs were seen in a double role. They would give Canadian manufacturers command of their own home market, albeit a relatively small one, and they would provide revenue necessary to pay for the railway system. It was accepted, more or less, that the railway could not pay its own way. Nevertheless, it should make the biggest contribution possible, and this meant increasing the volume of traffic by an expansion of the internal market – and free trade between the provinces of Canada. It is noteworthy here that industrial interests could determine tariff policy in a way impossible in a politically dependent country like India.

What ensued was the working out of the 'National Policy', the centrepiece of which was the tariff of 1879. Like other contemporary tariffs, this one was in part a depression phenomenon, but it was intended to placate the business interest and promote industrialization. There were substantial increases in the duties on textiles, iron and steel products, hardware and other manufactured goods as well as on coal, timber products and a few agricultural commodities.

The tariff wall raised in 1879 and still in existence constitutes one of the most controversial items in Canadian economic policy, and there is no intention here of examining the case for and against (mostly the latter) made with ever greater sophistication in economic literature. In practical politics, however, free trade was not a popular cause despite economists' claims that the tariff raised living costs and reduced the standard of living below what it might have been. But the policies and decisions of 1867 and 1879 were political as well as economic, they expressed an aspiration for separateness in a Canada independent not only of Britain but also of the United States. Nor was it merely a question of paying an economic price for a political aim. Canadian policy was, by and large, framed in the interest of businessmen. They thought they would benefit from the tariff, and they probably did; to gauge whether the 'nation' or consumers as a whole gained or lost is a more difficult matter. Once the tariff had become a part of Canadian economic strategy it obviously had a determining effect on many aspects of development; it helped to shape the Canadian economy of today in a quite fundamental way.

Canadian population grew relatively slowly in the last quarter of the nineteenth century, from 3.6 million in 1871 to 5.37 million in 1901; and this was one of the disappointments of the period. Canada failed to hold many of the immigrants who came to her shores, and French Canadians and others left for factory work in New England. Nevertheless, there was a steady influx of capital to finance the building of the infrastructure for the westward-moving frontier. Exports continued to grow and became more diversified. The trend towards increased manufacturing continued in Ontario and Quebec, the former tending to specialize in heavy industry while the cheap labour available in the French province was the basis for consumer goods industries such as textiles and clothing. Railway construction helped the growth of the home market, as it had done before, while Canadian capital found increasing outlets not only in manufacturing but in banking and finance and the processing of agricultural products and raw materials. Despite the failure of the economic record to come up to expectations, it was by no means discreditable and there was a sustained growth in per capita incomes.

As long as the frontier in the United States remained open and European immigrants thought that their chances of success were greater in that country, there was not much possibility of a change favourable to Canada. A basic drawback was that prairie farming, under the climatic conditions found in the Canadian region, posed serious problems for the settler and farmer. Moreover, not only railway links but a whole infrastructure of transport, storage and distribution was necessary before large-scale commercial farming became possible. The high land–labour ratio meant that machinery had to be used, so that successful farming required capital and credit. Investors and creditors had to be convinced that farmers could make a profit, and low grain prices did not encourage them. Finally, though not least important, strains of wheat had to be developed specifically to mature in the short dry growing season and to withstand early frosts. As with the railway building, the government took the responsibility for attempting to promote development. It offered land on a homestead basis; set up offices in Europe to attract immigrants; supported experimental farms; sponsored the search for an early-maturing wheat; and later intervened in the grain market with regulation and inspection of grades.

By the end of the nineteenth century a more favourable economic situation had opened up for Canada and the national policy at last came into its own. The closing of the frontier in the United States placed a new valuation on the Canadian prairie, accessible as it was by means of the expensively constructed transcontinental lines. The US wheat export surplus was declining in a world where continued industrialization and urbanization made it hungry for breadstuffs. There was, moreover, a general uplift in the economy and a shift to greater optimism in business expectations. The wheat price began to rise. The technical possibilities for large-scale wheat cultivation in Canada had improved. World demand for other Canadian staples also became more buoyant, and the country was fortunate in having a varied and seemingly inexhaustible supply of many of the basic materials of twentieth-century industrialism. Although the new boom was wheat-based, all but the most disfavoured regions and activities participated.

In the thirty years from 1901 the population of the prairie provinces, now part of the Confederation, rose from 420,000 to 2,354,000. By the latter date almost 40 per cent of all Canadian farms were in this region, and over the thirty years as a whole prairie farms accounted for 72 per cent of the investment in agriculture. This was a great process of extensive investment in which farming spread to new, virgin areas. It was made possible by the application of capital on relatively large farms and a high degree of mechanization. Of course, methods and techniques owed a great deal to the American example. The prairie farmer's outlook was similar to that of the US farmer – in fact many of the pioneers were Americans who brought with them the large amounts of capital upon which success in prairie farming depended. The farmer had a highly commercial outlook; he was in business to make money, not only from farming but also from land speculation and whatever other opportunities came his way. The amount of hired labour was relatively small, and much of it was provided by transient immigrant labour (much of it from central and Eastern Europe) paid lower wages than native Canadians expected.

The wheat boom was fuelled by a massive influx of capital, more than half as large as domestic savings in the period 1901–15. Most of this capital went into railway building, and over this same period some 17,000 miles of track were built. The railways once more provided the basis for capital accumulation by the business class. They gave employment to many immigrants and to farmers while they were getting established. The railways always played a special role in Canadian development: they created a demand for locomotives and rolling stock; their own workshops were in the vanguard of industrial advance. The railway companies were also the first examples of large-scale integrated businesses in Canada. Their revenue accounted for 11 per cent of the national income in the period 1926–30 and at that time employed 7 per cent of the labour force. But the additional lines, perhaps even more than those already built, could not be fully used. They added to the perennial Canadian problem of excess capacity, the burden of which fell ultimately on the taxpayer and consumer.

Western wheat-growing remained something of a gamble, dependent upon climatic conditions, world price movements and competition from other producers. Canadian farmers had to accept the world price, and poor crops in Canada were not offset by higher prices. The other sectors that developed rapidly in this period, in non-ferrous metals, wood and wood products, pulp and paper, were also dependent upon world demand, though in some cases Canadian producers held a stronger position than the wheat-farmer. However, all staple activity was subject to particularly sharp cyclical fluctuations, and wide swings were characteristic of the Canadian economy in the twentieth century.

With the wheat boom the Canadian economy took a giant stride forward towards maturity, but there were warning signs of the dangers of over-dependence on wheat even before 1914. The war gave a further boost to the Canadian economy as a supplier of food, raw materials and manufactured goods to the Allied war effort. Following the pattern of other countries, there was a short-lived and hectic post-war boom followed by a sharp contraction in 1920, and in the following year unemployment topped 16.5 per cent. Farm prices fell more than other prices in the slump, thus hitting the prairie provinces severely. There was improvement in the late 1920s, corresponding to the international boom, with a great increase in home investment. Canada's vulnerability as a staple-producer was soon to be demonstrated in dramatic form. The onset of the world economic depression brought Canadian export prices crashing down from 100 in 1926 to 90.2 in January 1930 and 52.4 in January 1931. Canada's exports were cut by over a half in value as the price of wheat slid from $1.05 to $0.49 a bushel. The disastrous collapse of the prairie prosperity was paralleled in most sectors of the Canadian economy and made the 1930s as dismal a decade as it was anywhere.

Industrialization proceeded fairly strongly at the turn of the century, and subsequently. Canadian industry enjoyed some of the advantages of the late-comer in that it could take over tried and tested techniques, mainly from the United States, as well as advanced forms of business organization. Increased emphasis was being placed upon capital goods production. In the 1890s, with government assistance in the shape of tariffs and subsidies, an iron and steel industry was created which turned out something like a million tons of pig iron by 1914.

While domestic builders of motorcars tended to produce for a limited, high-class market the presence of American firms soon changed that and, as in the United States, volume production for wider and growing markets was the key to success. By the early 1920s Canada was the second largest car manufacturer in the world and Canadians had begun to take to four wheels. There were 1.2 million cars on the road by 1929 when 263,000 vehicles were produced, 102,000 of which were exported.

As in the First World War, the renewed war in Europe in 1939 restored prosperity to the Canadian economy based once again on the voracious demand for primary products. Industry also experienced a forced-draught growth on an unprecedented scale. A number of entirely new industries were established and Canada's own resource-based industries received a boost. A substantial base was created for subsequent advance, spreading out existing trends and confirming the movement towards maturity.

There is no intention here to write the economic history of Canada in the twentieth century, but only to summarize some of the highlights. These can be seen, to a large extent, as the working out of trends established much earlier. With the exception of the depression period, the prevailing trend has been a high rate of growth by world standards. There seems little reason to dispute that world demand for Canada's staples has been crucial to this overall growth rate and that it would not have been possible exclusively on the basis of home market expansion. However, from the start of Canadian growth, as was pointed out, participation in the world division of labour as a primary producer has been coupled with development of manufacturing industry and the attributes of a mature capitalist economy. In other words, the internal division of labour has advanced alongside rather than in contradiction with the international division of labour.

First of all there are the overall growth trends. According to Lithwick, for the period 1926–56 actual output at 1949 prices grew at 3.89 per cent per annum, a rate second only to Japan. In the same period population grew by 20 per cent every decade*. It must be

---

* The estimates are from Lithwick, N. H., *Economic Growth in Canada: a Quantitative Analysis*, University of Toronto, 1967.

remembered that this high rate of growth has been financed largely by an influx of capital from abroad. The growth rate of capital has been about 2.2 per cent per annum for the same period. Lithwick places what he calls the 'residual' at the head of the causes of growth; factors like technical advance, productivity changes and qualitative improvement in the labour force accounts, he thinks, for more than two-thirds of the growth rate. But a shift in the economic structure has also been highly important in sustaining growth, and here another set of figures is significant. While manufacturing a large proportion of the industrial goods it consumes, Canada, like other advanced countries, has been shifting labour into the tertiary sector. This rose from 33.7 per cent of the labour force in 1931 to 50.5 per cent in 1961. Over the same period the contribution of manufacturing, with construction and transportation, rose slightly from 33.8 to 36 per cent and the employment in the primary sector (agriculture, logging, fisheries and mining) fell dramatically from 32.6 to 13.5 per cent. This corresponds to the trends in the advanced industrial countries and reflects Canada's high per capita income.

But there are two factors that appear to tilt the balance the other way. In the first place, Canada's exports are predominantly primary products, not manufactured goods – a pattern corresponding at first sight to that of an underdeveloped country. Secondly, Canada is still dependent for her growth upon a large inflow of foreign capital; much manufacturing industry as well as resource-based industry is under foreign (i.e. United States) control. This unique combination makes up the economic physiognomy of Canada today, and obviously has its origins in the past outlined here.

Certainly the great source of Canada's economic strength and its capacity for growth has lain in the fortunate possession of an abundant supply and great variety of primary products derived from agriculture, forestry and extractive industries. These have been the principal magnet for foreign capital in the past and still are to a large extent today. But the direct employment in these fields is relatively small and has been reduced by the continuous development (and mainly the import) of advanced technology. Canadian capitalists would have been unable to provide the sums required for this development, and to some extent they have preferred to see foreign capital go into staple production and new manufacturing industries while they have continued to invest in other more traditional fields.

Large-scale American investment in Canadian manufacturing industry has, on the other hand, been a comparatively recent, and perhaps avoidable, development. It has come about for a number of reasons. High among them is the existence of a high tariff on manufactured goods, the legacy of the national policy. Foreign, mainly American, manufacturers have thus 'jumped over' the tariff wall by establishing their branch plants in Canada. They have done this for reasons of cost; once their sales in Canada exceeded a certain volume they could produce more cheaply on the other side of the tariff. This meant an import of technology, machinery and managerial and supervisory personnel, but also the employment of Canadian labour – at, perhaps, slightly lower wages than in the United States. At some point as the Canadian population grew, and ten million seems to have been the crucial level, the size of the internal market dictated the setting up of branch plants or the purchase of existing facilities owned by Canadians rather than the importing of finished goods. In new industries like motorcars American ownership was predominant from an early stage, and American control is now complete or very nearly complete in a range of Canadian industries.

Meanwhile British investment, mainly of the portfolio kind, has been superseded by American investment, mainly of a direct kind. The latter has also grown at a colossal rate since 1945, giving rise to fears that Canada is losing its economic independence and becoming an economic satellite of the United States, with the suggestion, by nationalists, that this means also political subordination to Washington. In fact, the old argument between integrationists, seeing the future in (economic) union with the United States and the nationalists, wishing to preserve Canadian identity and the survival of a separate nation on the North American continent, has been given a new lease of life.

Little can be said on such a complex question at the heart of controversy in Canada today without a much wider-ranging examination of Canadian problems than can be attempted here. It is true, of course, that no nation has allowed its economic resources and production facilities to come so greatly under foreign control. On the other hand the 'foreignness' of Americans in Canada is obviously not to be compared with that of Englishmen in India. It could be said that the separateness of Canada is the result of historical accident anyhow, and that some form of integration is, in the long term, inevitable. Moreover, while many Canadian intellectuals are concerned about American domination, it seems to be less of a problem either for business or for the working class. The former have more or less passively accepted or welcomed the American capital invasion and profited from it. Workers – who include a large proportion of recent immigrants – are also not particularly concerned with the nationality of their boss, so long as they have a job and a wage negotiated by

157

trade union bargaining. In fact the trend has been, in recent years, for the wage differential with the United States to be narrowed or to disappear altogether, to the advantage of Canadian workers. Economists also seem to be mainly unmoved: growth has seemed to follow from the American involvement in the Canadian economy, and if growth is what is wanted, then further integration will take place. The nationalists recognize, generally, that any measures to restrict the American inflow or to take over American-controlled business would mean a sacrifice of real income.

The great exception to many of the generalizations about Canadian economic development was, and still is, Quebec, or French Canada. Despite, or perhaps because of, the break with France following the British conquest of North America, French Canada was petrified in the mould of the *ancien régime* and had virtually a separate economic history, although tangled with that of the rest of Canada, until the twentieth century.

French settlement, being earlier than the Anglo-Saxon and from a less developed country, retained feudal features and represented a transplantation of a backward peasant society to the new environment. It was dominated by lords and officials and particularly by the Catholic Church, which strengthened its ideological hold after the British takeover. The influence of the Catholic Church was against capitalist development and industrialization and favoured an educated élite, produced by its own schools, with a bias towards agriculture and the professions. Consequently the key positions in business and in industry when economic development took place were held by Anglo-Saxons. Thus the business élite formed a group separate and distinct from the French-educated élite leaning on the Catholic church and stressing the virtues of a predominantly agrarian society. On the other hand, French agriculture was backward and unenterprising. Forced by the very conditions of a new country to turn to the market, it did so with a chronic shortage of capital and adherence to traditional ways which placed it at a competitive disadvantage.

At the same time, under Catholic influence, population growth was rapid, so that many French Canadians had to seek paid work at least on a seasonal basis. The fact that many of the young men were away for a good part of the year, thereby increasing the role of women in the home, strengthened the influence of Catholic priests still further. In time, however, many French Canadians were forced to migrate in search of work either to other parts of Canada or south of the border. But Quebec was favourably situated for industrial development, and the overflow of the peasant population formed a large and docile labour force for the light industry developing from about the mid-nineteenth century. When local enterpreneurs emerged, they did not compete with Anglo-Saxon capital but went into other fields, such as local trade, and then into those light industries employing cheap local labour.

Consequently, then, the development of Quebec followed its own path and had its own specific features, notably the dominance of Anglophones (that section of the population which spoke English) in the economy, while the professional middle class and the workforce were French. This was a situation productive of tensions which assumed an explosive force at the time of the two world wars and more particularly since, with the rise of French Canadian nationalism and separatism. In other respects, however, Quebec, under the pressure of industrialization, has tended to move closer to the rest of Canada in material and cultural terms. In fact, much of the tension arises from the fact that French-speaking Canadians refuse any longer to accept a subordinate position; they are demanding access to the same material benefits as their English-speaking compatriots and are not satisfied with a merely formal equality. On the whole, the industrial entrepreneurs and the factory workers have had the closest connections with the English-speaking world and have been most open to its influence (witness the many French Canadians who have simply moved on and crossed the line into that world).

Although made more poignant by language and nationality and past historical associations, the problem of Quebec is only the most outstanding of Canada's regional problems. Wide differences in rates of growth and income levels have existed in the past between different provinces and regions and still exist today. The richest provinces are Ontario and British Columbia, followed by the Prairie Provinces. Although Quebec lags behind, it is the Maritime Provinces – the oldest settled Anglo-Saxon areas – that bring up the rear. In 1963, for example, per capita income in Ontario was almost twice as high as that of Prince Edward Island and New Brunswick, while Nova Scotia and Newfoundland had, respectively, a per capita income of only 74 and 60 per cent of the national average.

These disparities are the product of the way in which the different regions of Canada have developed their resources – or lack of them – and their geographical position in relation to the poles of growth. Well-endowed regions have been able to develop rapidly, while the Maritimes have tended to be left behind. Of course, average per capita income remains relatively high even in the lagging areas, though they will have also higher rates of unemployment and more poor-soil farmers. The differences do not reflect the dualism of underdeveloped countries, nor are they the product of the division of labour within Canada. The advanced agrarian provinces have a high per capita income. What is involved is the presence or absence of factors of production and their utilization – more or less successful forms of capitalist development. Capital tends to desert those areas that are less favoured, and so does labour, as the younger, more ambitious and highly qualified people tend to move off. This poses problems for the federal and provincial governments that have still to be overcome.

Despite the role of staples in the export trade and the foreign control of key sectors of the economy, Canada cannot be compared with the underdeveloped countries, nor does it seem that it is becoming a colony of the United States. It is true, however, that the east–west ties essential for the working of the Confederation have slackened. The provincial governments have assumed greater powers and control over their natural resources, and as a result north–south ties have become closer and more intricate. This has strained the Confederation and profoundly affected Canadian politics, while, at the same time it has assisted the multinational companies in their penetration of the Canadian economy. However, Canadian owner-ship and control is still manifest in railways and public utilities (like hydroelectric power), banks, trust and insurance companies, the older type of manufacturing and much of wholesale and retail distribution. Canadian investors have substantial accumulations, partly invested in concerns in these fields in Canada, partly abroad in portfolio, and to some extent in direct investment. The business class remains the dominant class in Canada; it accepts, by and large, the peculiar relationship established with its powerful southern neighbour while remaining sovereign in its own field. That does not mean to say that there is no criticism of American policy, even in business circles, for example, over the lack of interest of the multinational branch plants in exports or the fact that American investment tends to reinforce dependence upon staples. But as long as the extension of the American corporate empire into Canada brings jobs and opportunities it is not likely that a politically serious opposition to it will arise.

CHAPTER ELEVEN
Japanese industrialization: a special case?

Japan was the first case of industrialization carried out by non-Europeans. This in itself would justify an enquiry into the reasons for its success, but the rapid rates of growth achieved, and its emergence since the Second World War as the second largest industrial power in the world, make it a necessity for the understanding of contemporary international problems.

To Europeans in the mid-nineteenth century, Japan still looked like a backward and amusing Asiatic country, and the idea that its products would a century later swamp the markets of Europe would have seemed absurd. For non-Europeans Japan's economic success attracted special interest. Not only did it show that industrialization was by no means the prerogative of Europeans, but it also offered lessons to underdeveloped countries seeking a way to raise incomes and follow the path of the advanced countries. Today, following the emergence of Japan's industrial strength in the most advanced industries, Europeans now study Japanese methods to see whether there might not be some lessons to be learned by the slower-growing industrial countries, especially those now beaten by Japanese competition in many fields.

The leap made by Japan from economic backwardness to a vanguard position in the world economy within the space of a hundred years has naturally preoccupied economists and historians in Japan itself as well as in the outside world. Not surprisingly, economic history is a lively field of study in Japan, and more and more foreign scholars are turning their attention to Japanese economic history. This means a growing volume of studies; but, as usual when this happens, it also means a diversity of views and controversies over matters that at one time appeared to have been settled. For one thing, although

161

statistical data are comparatively abundant from the 1880s at least, there have been doubts about the accuracy of some vital parts of them, such as those relating to agricultural production. Thus there is not complete agreement about the rates of growth achieved during Japan's early modern economic growth, though it is certain that they were high. Moreover, there are important differences of interpretation. For example, what significance is to be attached to the military policy of Japan from the time of the war with China in 1894 to the Second World War? How much attention should be paid to the social aspects of Japan's material successes? This raises also questions about the peculiarities of the Japanese social system, such as the relative docility of the population in the face of privations, the willingness of workers to place the interests of the firm before their own and so on. Nationalism and patriotism have been powerful forces throughout Japan's history, and industrialization was itself more a response to the threat of colonization by the advanced countries than a desire to raise incomes or even to make profit for private interests. In short, while many of the processes that have contributed to Japan's growth have paralleled those in the West, there has also been, and there remains, a characteristically Japanese element, not easy to define but none the less present.

In a short treatment, and given the complexity of the subject with its controversies and open questions, no more can be done than to set the stage for more advanced study. The object, then, will be to present an outline of the early stages of Japanese industrialization down to 1914, with only brief remarks about the later period, in order to emphasize what seem to have been the main causative factors in growth. This may enable some light to be cast on the questions raised at the outset. In particular, was Japan a special case, or are there any lessons to be learned from it by the present-day developing countries – or, indeed, by those that are more advanced?

When modern economic growth began in Japan it followed the overthrow of a political system that had lasted for over 250 years and the installation of a new regime bent upon modernization. It was inspired by one major aim: to keep Japan strong and independent in a world rapidly being divided up among the advanced industrial countries. The leaders who took over in what is known as the Meiji Restoration of 1868 (that is to say, the putting back into power of the Emperor) believed that the challenge of the West, typified by the American attempt ten years or so before to force open the gates of Japan to foreign trade, could be met only by beating the foreigner at his own game, by adopting the techniques and forms of organization that had ensured his success in dominating other, weaker countries. This was the opposite policy to that pursued by the previous regime, which responded to the first appearance of a European threat in the early seventeenth century by virtually isolating the country entirely from the outside world in the seclusion policy – the same policy, indeed, that had broken down in China, leaving that country a prey to European influence and penetration.

Japan in the mid-nineteenth century was an old settled country with a long history, a high level of culture and a complex social organization. Its backwardness was the result principally of its economic basis, with the main activity being that of peasant agriculture. It could be compared with medieval Europe or with Mogul India, but there were significant differences, especially from the latter, and Japan was able to remain an independent country and to negotiate the passage to modern economic growth under the control of its own government. This was no doubt in large measure a product of geography as well as of skilful policy. Japan is made up of a number of islands separated from the Asiatic mainland, although deeply influenced in the beginning by the civilization and learning of China. In a way, therefore, Japan's relationship to mainland Asia corresponds to that of Britain's to continental Europe. Japan has also enjoyed similar advantages from its insular position, and these have become more manifest since the development of its maritime links with the outside world after 1868 in such activities as fishing, shipbuilding and ocean trade. This geographical position also meant that Japan was remote from the expanding European countries bent on colonizing the world, was, in fact at the very extremity of their empire-building, and thus was given time to contemplate its effects and guard against it, first by seclusion and then by a breakneck effort to emulate Western models.

The regime overthrown in 1868 had been set up by the Tokugawa family after defeating rival clans in 1600. It was, in fact, the most powerful of the warring feudal factions. It established its own authoritarian mode of government, the shogunate, and with its supporters from the feudal caste reduced the remainder to a kind of vassalage made particularly severe by the fear that they might be prepared to embark on renewed internecine conflict. In fact, the Tokugawa regime ensured a long period of peace (in this, for example, it was much more successful than the Moguls, no doubt because the rulers were natives of the country and were able to impose a more uniform ideology on society). The economy was not static or stagnant during the Tokugawa period; there were signs of growing

163

internal trade and of flourishing petty industry in the towns and also to some extent in the countryside, with some 'proto-industrialization' in textiles, pottery and the brewing of saki. In fact Japan may have been the most urbanized society in the world at the time of the Tokugawa regime; between 5 and 7 per cent of the population lived in towns. There were several large cities and many villages were growing into small market towns. However, the foundations of the economy did not change: it was geared primarily to producing a surplus from the land for the maintenance of the government and the ruling class. A sharp distinction existed between the *samurai*, the warrior caste making up about 7 per cent of the population, and the commoners, the majority of whom were peasants virtually bound to the land. But there was a rigid hierarchy within the ruling class, a distinction between the Tokugawa, who owned almost one-quarter of the land, and the other big feudal lords, the *daimyo*, numbering about 250. Many of these were descendants of those lords who had been defeated by the Tokugawa in their rise to power. The *daimyo* were kept under strict surveillance and had to spend part of the year in the capital, Edo (Tokyo), and to leave their families, virtually as hostages, when they returned to their domains. Many of the *samurai*, corresponding to the knights of medieval Europe, were no longer warriors: they had lost their function during a long period of peace, but they conserved their pride and arrogance even though they might be impoverished. The ideal of selfless martial service remained pervasive.

The *daimyo* collected large revenues from the peasantry in rice, or sometimes other goods, and supported large households and numerous retainers. They were constantly moving between their lands and Edo and their expenditure along the route encouraged the growth of trade and markets. It was the outlays by the feudal class and their retainers from the surplus extracted from the peasantry that provided the means for the growth of industry. But peasants also had to buy some of their requirements in the market, while a certain measure of differentiation had taken place within the peasant communities with the appearance of a richer class lending money, leasing land and engaging in trade. Indeed, Tokugawa Japan displayed the symptoms of many such economies in which money dealings are growing and creating new means for enrichment outside the feudal hierarchy. While the *samurai* and *daimyo* were a spending and consuming class, there were on the scene merchants, traders, artisans and some better-off peasants whose incomes derived from market relations and who accumulated and invested money as capital. There was already a tendency for more and more production to become geared to the market and thus to be affected by the ups and downs in prices that inevitably occur. As a result, some sections of society became richer while others, even those nominally at the top, became poorer and declined. As the latter happened, some *samurai* were forced to turn to trade, money-dealing or handicrafts or else sank into poverty despite their pretensions.

Behind the façade of stability maintained by the Tokugawa regime, therefore, deep, if still slow-moving, changes were taking place within the economy. In a way, with the advantage of hindsight, it could be said that the 'prerequisites' were being assembled, if not for industrialization at least for a development of capitalist relations which could prepare the way for it. For capitalism to triumph, however, the feudal agrarian order had to be overthrown, or substantially under-mined, and the way had to be prepared for an agrarian system based upon money rent, determined by contract, and producing for the market. There were, indeed, a few signs that this was taking place before the 1860s.

Japanese agriculture, although designed to produce a surplus for the feudal lords, was not managed by them. Husbandry was in the hands of the peasants themselves. The communal effort required in the villages where rice-growing prevailed was different from that in medieval Europe, where the peasants had to pool their animals and heavy ploughs to break up the heavy lands for sowing and to carry out the other operations of husbandry. Japanese villages were close-knit, and work had a cooperative character, but rice could be produced on small plots and each family had a certain degree of choice about how it did so. Moreover, the lords had no incentive to drive the peasants off the land but only to squeeze more surplus product out of the existing system. Although there were sporadic revolts by the peasants against their lot, they lacked allies in the towns. Money dealings did spread into the countryside. Some peasants acquired additional land (by inheritance or purchase), new land was reclaimed, and merchants acquired landed property which they leased to the cultivators. After paying their land revenue, some peasants had something left over for sale and the turn to cash crops also hastened differentiation.

It is difficult to say how advanced Japan was along the road to capitalism by the middle of the nineteenth century. There had certainly been a considerable growth of towns and inland transport, and something like a national market had come into existence for some products consumed by the upper classes. The growth of trade had enabled the merchants to accumulate capital and engage in money-lending and banking operations. The crafts had multiplied, and there was considerable division of labour between the different occupations, but there were few large-scale manufacturing enterprises and, of course, no machinery or factories of a modern type. There was little sign that Japan was moving autonomously along the road of technological advance on the lines of Europe in the eighteenth century. This may have been because of the abundance of hand labour, or it may have been that the market was still too restricted and was mainly for products not susceptible to standardized production or mechanization. The mass of peasant households was still little above the subsistence level and there was lacking perhaps the kind of middle-class consumers characteristic of Europe during the early stages of industrialization. These circumstances could have discouraged the shift of capital from trade to industry and inhibited the producers themselves from adopting new techniques and methods of organization. Traditional types of goods and traditional materials like wood, paper and bamboo prevailed, with little development of metallurgy apart from the production of weapons.

Conditions during the later part of the Tokugawa period bore witness to the breaking up of the old order. The agrarian economy was still precariously balanced and population was kept within bounds only by the practice of abortion and infanticide. Tenancy and indebtedness were increasing in the villages. The old *samurai* warrior class had disintegrated, and the *daimyo* had difficulty in maintaining their share of the surplus in the face of the challenge from the commercial classes (the urban merchants and traders, but also those landowners leasing land to the peasants). By the nineteenth century the regime had moved into a period of crisis: famines, peasant uprisings, degeneracy of the rulers and incompetence on the part of the government. There was growing interest not only in Japan's past but also in the outside world, which undermined confidence in the seclusion policy and created dissension within the ruling class. Since the beginning of the shogunate the Emperor, who was supposed to be a divine monarch, had been totally eclipsed, but there was now talk of restoring him to power as part of a national revival. The threat of foreign intrusion became more acute until the arrival of Commodore Perry in Edo Bay in July 1853 brought matters to a head. Forces may have been maturing in Japan for a change of course, but it now had to be made under external pressure. The following year the shogunate was obliged to open four ports to trade and to sign treaties with the United States and other foreign powers under humiliating conditions.

The treaties were not ratified by the Emperor, and the reaction on the part of many *samurai* and *daimyo*, especially in the south-west, was strongly antagonistic.

In a situation of growing nationalism and hostile feelings towards all foreigners, the Emperor was able to regain authority and a civil war between the clans for and against the shogunate began in 1864. In 1866 the ruling shogun died and he was followed in February 1867 by the Emperor, who was succeeded by the fifteen-year-old Mutsuhito. In October of that year the new shogun resigned and handed over power to the Emperor; in 1868, with the ending of the civil war, the Emperor, known as Meiji, assumed full power with the backing of a group of energetic reforming leaders drawn from the old ruling class, intent upon the modernization of the country.

Rather than breaking with the authoritarianism of the past, the restoration of the Emperor was intended to make it more efficient. The new leaders had their roots firmly in Japanese traditional society, but they recognized that it could not survive unless it was reformed; that the foreigner could not be kept out unless he was fought with his own methods. It was thus necessary, in the shortest possible time, to find out about, adopt and assimilate all the scientific, technological and industrial achievements of the West in order to build a stronger Japan. To that end the new regime allied itself with the modernizing elements already present, including the representatives of the indigenous capitalism emerging within the feudal framework of Tokugawa society. In the initial stages, after 1868, these business elements were the weaker party to the alliance, but the changes that were being made, whatever their motive, were such as to favour the rapid development of capitalism. The first priority, after all, was the establishment of a strong, independent state, the new leaders, although drawn from the *samurai*, represented in practice not the old feudal forces but the new emerging capitalist relations that had to be established if modernization was to be carried out.

While leaving much of the basic structure of traditional Japanese society intact, the reforms of the first part of the Meiji period none the less affected many spheres of activity in a way favourable to economic development. Within two or three decades most of the trappings of a modern state were assumed through a succession of administrative reforms. Railways, postal services, banks and modern educational establishments came on the scene. At the same time, everything was done to facilitate the movement of goods, to open up occupations to all able to carry them on and to encourage the use of money. But there were three principal spheres in which action by the

167

state opened the way for the subsequent industrialization of the economy: they were the abolition of feudalism in agriculture, the encouragement of modern industry, and the opening up of the ports to foreign trade.

The changes introduced into agriculture had the effect of achieving several aims. They introduced peasant emancipation, from above, and thus opened the way for the movement of people from the land. They gave the government a much-needed source of revenue through the land tax. They enabled the power of the former feudal lords to be ended at the same time as revenue from the land tax enabled them to be pensioned off. The way was clear for agriculture to contribute to the fund of accumulation necessary to finance industrialization.

The new regime abolished caste divisions and in their place established the predominance of contractual relations between presumed equals after the model of bourgeois Europe. The feudal rights of the *samurai* were purchased by the state in exchange for a rice allocation, then a money payment, and finally by the issue of state bonds. Peasants with a title to their land became full proprietors, subject to payment of the land tax. This was fixed at 3 per cent of the value of the land and was to be paid in cash; in the rural areas it took the place of the former tribute in rice or other forms paid over to the *daimyo*, but land tax was also levied in the cities.

It took some years for these reforms to be fully implemented, and in 1878 the rate of the land tax was reduced to 2.5 per cent. There was also a local surtax which added to the burden on the peasantry, one now having to be met in cash regardless of whether the harvest was good or bad. In times of bad harvests peasants could be driven into debt or forced to sell their land. In any case, land became a marketable commodity, and this speeded up the differentiation among the peasantry already taking place under the Tokugawa regime. The better-off peasants and landlords consolidated their position, and there was a growth in tenancy. The small-scale family-type unit of production continued to prevail; peasants who lost their land became tenants rather than labourers, but they had to pay a larger part of the product to the owner of the land. While subsistence was the main aim of the peasant family, part of the product had to be sold to meet the land tax, to pay rent or interest or to finance the purchase of inputs needed for the cultivation of the land. In any case the peasant continued to find the major part of the surplus. Instead of going to the feudal ruling class, however, this surplus now went to the state, and in the 1880s made up 70–80 per cent of its revenue. The government recognized the basic importance of agriculture and encouraged improvements. Experience showed that within the land system following the Meiji reforms this could come only by encouraging the peasants to increase their output. In that respect, the fact that the land tax was fixed in money gave an incentive to improvement, but it did not prevent 46 per cent of the land being under tenancy by 1914.

There has been considerable controversy about the contribution made by the agrarian sector to Japanese economic growth, mainly because earlier estimates of rapid growth are held to arise from defects in the figures. What seems certain is that Japanese rice yields were already high at the start of the Meiji period, being based on irrigation and intensive methods of cultivation using much labour. Steady improvement continued throughout the period to 1914, mainly owing to the use of fertilizers, improved seeds and an increase in labour productivity. The revised official figures showing an increase in output of rice of 2 per cent per annum from 1878 may not therefore be wide of the mark. This is an impressive achievement and was carried out on smallholdings without any major reconstruction of agriculture; it was primarily a response to family labour in the paddy-fields. Peasants produced more and thus had more to sell; the surplus went to the state through the land tax, to landlords, usurers or, in part, to grain dealers with a high propensity to invest. On the other hand, the peasants as a whole were buying more inputs from the modern sector both to assist husbandry (fertilizers, persticides, better farm tools) and also because they were able to purchase more goods for the household, whether of the traditional variety or factory made. Growing production enabled the non-farm population to be fed without great dependence on imported supplies. Increased efficiency meant that the farm population began to decline in absolute numbers from the mid-1880s. Peasants also increased the output of other crops, the cultivation of the mulberry for the breeding of silkworms being particularly important for Japan's economy during this period. Although there was not much scope for increasing the cultivated area in the other islands, new land was brought into cultivation in Hokkaido.

The agrarian experience of Meiji Japan contrasts sharply with that of present-day developing countries mainly because in the latter productivity gains tend to be absorbed by population increases. It was because Japan's population grew at a modest rate that it was possible to generate an agricultural surplus to support a growing urban–industrial population which at the same time furnished an increasing supply of goods to the agrarian sector. Even without an agrarian revolution, the way in which feudal relations were abolished left incentives for the peasantry to produce more. Moreover, there was considerable continuity technically between Meiji Japan and the previous system which also depended upon revenue extracted from labour-intensive agriculture. The underdeveloped countries today have to cope not only with rapid rates of population increase but also with the sequels of colonialism, which, as in the case of India, means that they have inherited an agrarian system distorted and petrified by the colonial rule which Japan was lucky not to have experienced. However, land-holding did tend to become more concentrated; many peasants were reduced to tenancy, and life in the villages was frugal and hard. Some of the accompaniments of the contemporary 'green revolution' were also visible in Japan, such as the growth in income disparities, but there was nothing like the pauperization of much of the rural population characteristic of underdeveloped countries. In fact, Meiji Japan was rapidly shedding the characteristics of underdevelopment and moving onto the path of industrialization.

It was from 1868, therefore, that Japanese development began to diverge from that of India or other countries unable to prevent foreign rule. The Meiji regime was free to take over what the advanced countries had to offer without becoming a tributary to them. It was able to encourage the innovating elements in the traditional society and to break the stranglehold of those forces opposed to change, while at the same time strengthening the power of the state. It was able to open the road to modernization in every direction while ensuring that those elements in the old society it held to be valuable were preserved. It carried through a revolution in property relations by abolishing the feudal regime, the privileges of the *daimyo* and its right to extract a surplus from the peasants without the masses making an irruption on to the scene and without the coming to power of the middle class or bourgeoisie (too weak in Japan to undertake tasks of national leadership or effect a revolution). It was, therefore, a controlled revolution, taking place from above and not fundamentally overturning the old society. At the same time, because the changes were not a direct response to market forces, there was no place for a *laissez-faire* ideology; the state had to act positively to open the way for economic growth. It took over and improved the infrastructure built up under the shogunate, and became responsible for the importation into Japan of Western techniques. The new regime did not aim at a controlled or planned economy; economic liberalism was as much an import as modern machinery. The new national state promoted the development of market forces, favoured the accumulation of capital by businessmen and encouraged them to carry through industrialization.

The Meiji regime embarked upon a policy of preparing the way for economic development by removing the barriers inherent in the feudal structure of the former regime. At the same time it took over and further developed the industrial projects it had fostered in its closing stages. Now the state very deliberately set out to modernize Japan by importing the technology of the most advanced countries and adapting it to the country's needs. It was the state that took the initiative here, not private businessmen who were reluctant to risk their capital in new and untried fields of enterprise. Japan, through state effort, thus enjoyed the advantages of the 'late-comer'; the means for industrializing the economy were available on the market, so she purchased them and hired technicians and other foreigners to train Japanese personnel. No other country was in a position to do likewise at that time outside Europe. There were, perhaps, similar possibilities for industrialization in India, and there were a number of entrepreneurs who did invest in new factories despite the odds, but India's colonial status ruled out development on Japanese lines. It should be noted that the men who controlled the state had no intention of setting up a planned economy. Their emulation of the West included the taking over of many of its institutions, including private property and free enterprise. It is true that these were curtailed where the national interest seem to warrant it, but there was without a doubt a desire on the part of the new regime to create conditions favourable to the businessmen. From 1880 many of the state factories were turned over to private capitalists.

In this way the initial investment costs of the new modern industries set up with imported machinery were met by the state from the general revenue, and they were then handed over to merchant capitalists at bargain prices when they had some chance of becoming profitable concerns. The beneficiaries were mainly commercial houses with interests in various fields who now added industries to their assets. The banking system, developed with state support, provided credit and loan capital to industry and helped to break down reluctance to invest. Except for a period in the 1880s, government financial policy was inflationary. The hot-house conditions in which modern capitalist enterprise was encouraged by the state favoured a high degree of concentration of control. Instead of many small firms growing up under competitive conditions in response to market forces, as in Britain, a number of big firms, originating from the pre-existing merchant class and assisted by government favours, extended

171

their interests into a variety of fields – industrial, banking and commercial – and not necessarily related ones. These conglomerates, to use a modern business expression, known as *zaibatsu* were specific to Japan and played an important role in its economic development.

The selling off of the factories after 1880 did not mean that the state no longer concerned itself with the economy. Not only did it keep control of strategic industries like arsenals and shipyards, but it laid down the general lines of policy and, where necessary, moderated and curtailed the operation of market forces. This was done with the object of increasing the military as well as the economic power of the nation-state. The Meiji regime had come into existence to meet a foreign threat, and it was profoundly nationalist. Important differences of interest and outlook existed between its main components: the political leaders and state bureaucracy, the businessmen and, not least, the military. Whether or not the others were reluctant partners, the latter, continuing the old *samurai* traditions, exercised a considerable influence on policy. Japan soon embarked upon a policy of military adventures for which large and powerful armed forces backed by modern armaments industries were necessary. In 1894–96 a successful war was fought against China, and in 1905 Japan staggered the world by defeating Russia, and becoming the first Asiatic country successfully to stand up to a European power. These successful wars enhanced the prestige of the military and whetted the appetite for even bigger gains. Like other aspects of Japanese development in this period, the consequences of military adventurism have given rise to conflicting interpretations. It can be argued that these wars diverted resources into unproductive outlets and that growth would have been faster had they been used to increase domestic investment and consumption. On the other hand, it cannot be gainsaid that militarism was built into the structure of Meiji Japan from the start. The defensive response to the threat of foreign aggression within a short time was superseded by a policy of carving out a Japanese sphere of influence in the Pacific area with the hope that this would ensure markets for industrial exports, raw materials and foodstuffs for domestic use and perhaps an outlet for surplus capital and population. Whether or not this was illusory, it had a powerful hold in Japan, and there was no force able to resist it, as history was to show. Only the overwhelming military defeat of 1945 reversed the tide.

Japanese growth rates from 1868 to 1914 were by no means miraculous and were far below the rates of 10 per cent or so per annum reached during the 1960s. Even so, the probable annual rate of about 1.4 per cent was comparable with that of the European countries and Japan was growing at the very time when the older industrial countries were undergoing a phase of deceleration. What was remarkable was that these rates were achieved by a previously backward Asian country; that they were sustained and later, during and after the First World War, further improved upon. Looking back, therefore, we can say that the growth of the early Meiji period was not a temporary burst but actually took Japan over the 'hump', the crucial, difficult stage beyond which a more sustained process of industrialization was possible. From the 1880s there was a continuous build-up of industry and a steady growth in production and productivity both in the traditional sectors and in the modern industrial sector. Indeed, much of the increase in output at this time came from the old-style industries and from the industrial by-employment of peasant households producing for an expanding home market. Underemployed labour was being brought into use in cottage industries, or, as in the case of many girls from peasant families, being moved into factory industries. Greater division of labour, and improved organization based on the growth of markets, both contributed to steady growth. By 1914 factory industry probably accounted for about 10 per cent of the net national product, but industrial output as a whole probably formed about 50 per cent of commodity output. Judged by the rate at which industry's share in total product was increasing up to 1914, Japan was already industrializing rapidly, but the role of factory industry must not be exaggerated.

Indeed, on the eve of the First World War – an event favouring further rapid growth for Japan – the modern sector was still modest and its output did not compare with that of the advanced countries of Europe. For example, there were 948,000 factory workers against over five million peasant households, some 1.5 million of which were engaged in some industrial by-employment. Pig iron production was only 318,000 tons, steel 283,000 and coal (rather better) twenty-two million tons; in heavy industry Japan was still lagging far behind. In 1913 there were 2.5 million cotton spindles – about as many as in France in the 1830s. Of course, Japan's spindles were by then much more efficient and her own machine-making industry was turning out spinning machines and looms to world standards. The industrial structure was quite diversified with practically every type of production represented; this was partly a result of government policy aiming to make the country self-sufficient. This did not mean, however, that Japan could be cut off from the world market; on the contrary, industrialization inevitably means growing integration. Not only had much equipment to be imported, but Japan was also short of raw materials; and a balance of payments deficit appeared which had to be met by borrowing from abroad to the extent of about $800 million by 1913. This was mostly portfolio investment; the government did not want foreign investors to obtain a stranglehold over the country's industry. To pay for import needs it was necessary to encourage exports. Exports were in any case imperative for some of the modern industries where the heavy investment had to be spread over a larger volume of output than could be absorbed by the domestic market. Japan thus appeared in the export markets, and had begun to carve out a place for herself, especially in the Pacific area, before 1914.

To summarize the position of Japan in 1914, it may be said that the economy had successfully passed through the first stage of industrialization and had established the basis for further growth. In industrial potential or in income per head, however, Japan was still far behind those European countries that had started their industrialization earlier, and, of course, she was far behind the United States. Compared with the rest of Asia and the underdeveloped countries, however, Japan had made giant strides and, above all, had remained independent – indeed, she was able to extricate herself from the unequal treaties imposed by foreign powers in the 1860s. Growth had been promoted by a reforming élite with strongly nationalist goals and the state had played a vital role in negotiating the first difficult steps along the road to economic growth and industrialization. In doing so she had fostered the development of capitalist relations, while retaining a general, overall control, and had favoured the concentration of industry and finance under the control of powerful monopolistic concerns, the *zaibatsu*. Despite the reform of the law and the administration and the adoption of a constitutional framework, however, Japan was governed autocratically; and the traditional methods of social control were used to keep the peasants and industrial workers in a position of subordination, resulting in an absence of left-wing political parties, free trade unions and costly welfare schemes. In industry there was a carry-over of the old paternalistic relations and nationalism was also appealed to as an incentive to accept labour discipline and work hard.

Around the key modern sectors, representing the advanced outpost of capitalism, there clustered a multitude of small enterprises operating more or less in the traditional way. The monetization of the economy, the growth of markets and increased purchasing power on the part of the urban population and also of sections of the peasantry was the basis for the growth of these old-style industries. But the same people now buying more of the traditional products (though not necessarily consuming more) were also customers for the factory-made goods available at relatively low prices and in increasing quantities – textiles, hardware, modern consumer goods. Peasants bought more inputs from the modern sector – fertilizers, tools, utensils. The two sectors were not necessarily in conflict – to a large extent they complemented each other.

Once on the road to growth, Japanese industry could call on the large reserve of underemployed labour in the countryside; growing agricultural output increased its availability. Wage costs were thus kept down. There was always scope for raising productivity by installing more capital-intensive plant; but there was also scope for the use of labour-intensive methods by drawing on the under-employed. For example, more industrial work could be performed by peasant families, or paid work could be found at slack times in agriculture. A similar reserve also existed in many of the handicraft industries. The surplus drawn off from agriculture found its way largely into productive investment, whether passing through the hands of the government as land tax or being skimmed off by landlords and money-lenders. The Meiji Restoration ended the parasitism of the landowning classes which holds back development in many underdeveloped countries. But, being a revolution from above, it left little of the surplus above subsistence in the hands of the majority of the peasantry, though, as has been noted, peasants were able to buy more inputs, and so may have eaten better and been able to diversify their consumption with cheap machine-made goods.

While Japanese living standards remained low and the factory towns showed the usual abuses of overcrowding, unhealthy working conditions and low wages without trade union organization, it should not be assumed that the material conditions of the masses worsened. While standards remained frugal, there was probably some improvement during the period 1868–1914, enough to prevent large-scale outbreaks of discontent once the regime had become established. Moreover, the growth of the urban population led to the steady adoption of more 'Western' styles of consumption by a new middle class of office workers, officials and professional people. Japanese development had other more objectionable features, however. There was the growing concentration of economic power in the giant concerns, and the influence of the military caste bent upon expansionism and made more menacing as Japan's industrial potential increased. Japan fought two major wars in this period and was poised to fight others in the interest of national aggrandizement and the supposed profits of colonial expansion.

The Japanese economy at this stage was able to enjoy the advantages of the 'late-comer'; in fact, she continued to enjoy them as an increasing range of new techniques offered possibilities for profitable investment making use of the country's cheap and docile labour force. Whether there are any lessons for the underdeveloped countries to be derived from Japan's experience is dubious. The special conditions of the Meiji Restoration have not been reproduced elsewhere. Either countries have experienced a revolution against landlordism and capitalism as in China, or a compromise has been made between the national bourgeoisie and the representatives of the older order as in India. These two models may be feasible alternatives; the Japanese road is not.

It is also possible that Japan's economic awakening came at a very favourable moment. Not only was it able to avoid falling under foreign domination and keep out foreign influence over the economy, but it could adopt and rapidly assimilate the advanced technology that the West had to offer in a way not possible to today's developing countries. Within the matter of a few decades, Japan could replicate the advanced economies, though on a more modest scale, because the technological gap was at that time relatively easy to bridge. Railways, textile mills, coal-mining, iron smelting and a variety of manufacturing industries could be established relatively easily in the decades after 1868, and because this was done Japan was able subsequently to follow the development of technology as it became more complex and more costly to install from its own accumulation and investment of capital. Industrialization was not an organic process to begin with; some of the prerequisites no doubt existed in Tokugawa days but the basic technical means had to be imported. Once that was done, however, and Japan was brought into intimate relationship with the world market through trade and the continuous borrowing and adaptation of the most advanced techniques, it did become an autonomous process dependent, however, both on a growing home market and, even more in later decades, on a large and growing volume of world trade. This was the Japanese path, but it is one that is no longer open because modern technology comes in a much more elaborate form. The gap between the advanced and the so-called 'developing' countries has widened enormously; it can no longer be bridged so easily, and history alone will tell whether it can be bridged at all.

CHAPTER TWELVE
South Africa: gold, white supremacy and industrialization

As countries of white settlement, South Africa and Canada had widely divergent economic histories, a product of their geographical position and climate as well as of social forces and political factors. While Canada's history was manifestly shaped by its colonial relationship to Britain and its proximity to the United States, South Africa's position made it very much more peripheral to the world economy; that, however, changed dramatically with the discovery of diamonds in the 1860s and of gold in the 1880s. Britain took over the Dutch colony in the Cape which had been founded by the Dutch East India Company in the seventeenth century as a stopping point on the long sea haul to the Far East. Dutch settlement had not been large in numbers and, by the time the British took over in 1810, it had for a long time ceased to be a country of Dutch settlement. Those already settled had put down roots in Africa and acquired a national consciousness as Afrikaners which was bound up with a sense of racial superiority over the black Africans or coloured people that they had imported as slaves. In the first part of the nineteenth century under British rule the Cape attracted relatively few immigrants. While Holland had a reputation for intensive agriculture, the Afrikaners, as they moved inland, depended more upon their flocks. Wool was virtually the only staple at this stage and, together with ostrich feathers, made up the main export. Without staple products in demand in the world market the colony had limited prospects of growth. Until the coming of the diamond boom South Africa had little to attract immigrants or investors. Meanwhile, a large part of the Afrikaner population had trekked north to escape such restrictions of British rule as the abolition of slavery, and had set up the republics of the Transvaal and the Orange Free State.

The Boer republics and the British territories of the Cape Colony and Natal were carved out in competition with the black pastoralists moving down from the north. In the contest over land, fought out in intermittent skirmishes or bloody battles, the Europeans, with their superior weapons and organization, finally won out. European concepts of landed property were imposed within the wider framework of white supremacy and black inferiority.

Under Dutch rule, slaves were imported from Africa and Asia to carry out manual and menial tasks and to overcome what the colonists perceived as a labour shortage. Intermarriage within this group, or between its members and indigenous peoples, created a labouring people of mixed race in the Cape to be known as 'coloured'. Later, to overcome a shortage of labour on the sugar plantations of Natal, indentured labourers were imported from India who formed the basis for an Indian community. From the start the racial factor played a critical role. There was not one market for labour but several, each reserved for a particular community or group.

By comparison with other areas of white settlement, in the first three-quarters of the nineteenth century the South African colonies were a disappointment. Their future seemed to be that of dependent agrarian settlements with hostile black neighbours and mistrust between Anglophones and Afrikaners. At least in the short and medium terms there would seem to have been little prospect for economic growth. The discovery of diamonds at Kimberley in 1865, followed by the gold rush to the Transvaal some twenty years later, brought a dramatic change. South Africa now reaped the fruits of its geology which had created the precious stones so coveted in civilized societies, as well as supplies of the money-stuff upon which the capitalist financial system was based. Foreign capital flowed in, enabling vastly more to be generated as mining expanded. Large numbers of people were attracted to the mining areas, first in the hope of making an overnight fortune, and then, on a more permanent basis, by the relatively high wages which could be earned in the mines. Gold-mining required heavy machinery to process the huge quantities of ore necessary to extract the precious metal as well as a large labour force made up of skilled white miners and black, unskilled labourers. The former came very largely from Europe, particularly from Britain. The great mass of Africans were recruited from the reserves, and later from neighbouring territories as well, as migrant labour. That is to say, they came from areas of subsistence agriculture, working in the mines part of the year, living in compounds, and returning to their homes for the rest of the time. This system of labour recruitment remains characteristic of mining in South Africa to this day; it was the foundation upon which the fortunes of the mine-owners was based.

While diamonds and gold-mining gave a powerful stimulus to the economy, it led to growth of a particular kind, and although it is sometimes said to mark the beginning of South African industrialization, even this needs to be qualified. Much of the plant and equipment had to be imported as did many of the consumer goods required by the population which grew up around the mines, at least at first. However, an undoubted boost was given to the domestic market, especially for food and then increasingly for locally-made consumer goods. The need for infrastructure, especially transport facilities – notably railways to the ports from the Witswatersrand – followed. However important these factors were in opening up the domestic market, the stimulus to secondary industry remained comparatively modest and subordinate to the dominant robber-economy of mining which was itself dependent upon the huge migratory army of low-paid African labour – unique in the world.

To be sure, mining became the driving force of the economy, beginning in the Transvaal where it brought the great clash between the British administration backing capitalist enterprise and the Boer republics addicted to their traditional agrarian way of life and national pride. Fuelled by such entrepreneurs as Cecil Rhodes, and others like him, the conflict finally culminated in 1899 in the Boer War, which dragged on until the final subjection of the Boers in 1902. Gold-mining, which had ceased during the war, was now free to operate and expand once more under the wing of the British Empire.

The Act of Union of 1910 brought into existence modern South Africa with a centralized government representing the white population, itself divided into two communities which had fought a bitter war. In fact power was delivered into the hands of a white oligarchy while the country became safe for the investment of British capital. One of the main tasks of the state was to preserve the interests of the white minority by excluding the black majority from any share in political power.

The opening up of the gold mines emphasized the need for improved transport facilities, particularly because of the long distances between the mines and the ports. Railway-building began in the 1860s; by 1891 over 4,000 kilometres had been built, and by 1911 there were over 11,000 kilometres in operation. Private entrepreneurs were unable or unwilling to risk the heavy outlays of capital which railway-building required. The railways were, and remained, state enterprises. Although they were a necessary complement to mining and made possible the concentration of population in the rapidly growing towns, their direct effects on industry were limited as most of the material had to be imported.

The growth of an urban market encouraged a variety of small-scale manufacturing in such fields as garments and footwear. It was characteristic, however, that although wool was produced locally the yarn and cloth required by the clothing industry were largely imported. In addition, mining created a market for intermediate goods such as explosives, from which an important industry was to stem. The spectacular and disruptive changes brought about by mining certainly resulted in the establishment of capitalist property relations in the urban conglomerations which sprang up in the mining areas, but they were extremely localized in their effects. The entrepreneurs who organized and dominated the whole process were not industrial capitalists running factories and organizing production; their fortunes were made in the fields of finance, speculation and risk-taking. These characteristics arose from the nature of the commodities – diamonds and gold – upon which their wealth was based, destined for the world market and not for domestic consumption. And, as has already been stressed, the great bulk of the labour-force consisted of low-wage migrant black Africans who did not constitute a healthy basis for the growth of the home market. There was little to attract investment in machinery for the production on a large scale of consumer goods. Although mining became increasingly mechanized the equipment it required was largely imported. There was little or nothing before the First World War in the nature of a capital goods industry. It can be said, therefore, that industrialization, as the term is used in this book, had not, properly speaking, begun in South Africa until the 1920s, although the ground had been prepared and there were perhaps some precursive signs.

Railways came to South Africa too early to play a promotional role in industrialization and were built in response to the needs of mining. In the towns small-scale industry continued to predominate, while in the rural areas white as well as black cultivators bought little in the market. Apart from some tariff protection, the state did not intervene to assist industry. Its principal form of intervention was designed to ensure a supply of cheap labour for the mines and to uphold white supremacy. A notable step was the Natives Land Act of 1913 which was intended to prohibit the black tenancy of white-owned land, other than labour-tenancy. Together with other measures, such as the application of masters-and-servants laws and control of movement by blacks, the object was to prevent the emergence of an independent peasantry farming for the market. Black landownership in white areas was prohibited. Although such laws were not always and everywhere applied in their full rigour there was no doubt that they acted in the interests of white farmers. Except as labour-tenants or workers on white lands, blacks were to be confined to reserves making up about 14 per cent of the land. It was a specific feature of the South African economy that the state not only upheld a colour bar in the labour market, but intervened in order to bring about a distribution of the labour-force in accordance with the requirements of white supremacy. This was especially so in ensuring a supply of labour for the mines and for white farmers. Its attempt to regulate the industrial labour-force was less successful. However, white workers were also concerned to maintain their monopoly of skilled and more highly paid urban jobs, and feared that the so-called civilized labour standard would be undermined if non-whites were permitted to compete on equal terms. The contradictions involved in this policy were to be revealed as urban industry expanded.

The First World War gave a certain stimulus to import-substitution industry when normal sources of overseas supply were curtailed. By this time local industry enjoyed a modest amount of tariff protection, but nothing like the Canadian National Policy. The industrial centres were widely separated but the southern Transvaal had already established itself as the main centre. It was obviously well-placed to serve the mining industry, hence a growth of engineering. Again, as was to be expected, the Johannesburg and Cape Town areas were also centres of the clothing and other light consumer goods industries, as well as being a market for their output.

After a period of upheaval among white mine-workers, which culminated in the Rand revolt of 1922 and their defeat, the Labour Party entered into an electoral pact with the Nationalist Party of General Hertzog. This represented a political alliance between Afrikaner nationalism and the reformist Labour Party which upheld the colour bar and had the support of a large part of the white working class. The pact brought Hertzog to power in 1924 with a policy of state intervention to promote economic growth. Tariffs were raised to encourage investment in manufacturing industry and to create more jobs for the unskilled 'poor whites'. The latter were mainly landless and jobless Afrikaners moving from the rural areas to the cities whose low living standards were a threat to white supremacy. Many were found jobs in the state sector at the expense of non-whites.

The main question concerning the Pact government is the extent to which it can be said to have initiated industrialization or whether the stimulus it gave to industry was an indirect result of the pursuit of other goals. Certainly it did not have a consciously worked-out policy of industrialization, nor would it be correct to see it as representative of industrial capital as opposed to mining capital. The Nationalists passed no laws inimical to the mining interests and their principal concern was to uphold white supremacy. Thus tariff protection was intended to assist those industries using mainly white labour. Government contracts were granted with the same end in view. A number of laws were passed concerned with (white) labour relations, setting up arbitration procedures for dealing with industrial disputes, and Wage Boards empowered to recommend minimum wages in industries having no collective bargaining arrangements (clearly based upon the British model).

Interventionism was carried further with the setting up in 1928 of the South African Iron and Steel Industrial Corporation. This was the first of a number of 'parastatals': industrial concerns set up under state auspices. Although shares were offered to the public, not all of them were taken up. The object was to establish a modern iron and steel industry on a scale which private capital was unable or unwilling to do at this time, despite the fact that coal and iron ore were in abundant supply.

The impact of the Great Depression of the 1930s on the South African economy was untypical. Industrial production had been rising steadily until 1931. After a temporary setback the renunciation of the gold standard and the subsequent rise in the price of gold sparked off a boom in gold-mining which boosted the whole economy. Employment in manufacturing rose following the increased demand resulting from the incomes generated from the mining boom. With the world in depression and the protectionist policy inherited from the Pact period there was a further tendency towards import-substitution industrialization. While it could be said that South Africa was now definitely on the industrialization road, most manufacturing was still on a small scale and confined to light industry in which there were many competing firms. Above all the narrowness of the home market was the major constraint. The mass of the population was able to buy few, if any, manufactured goods. Industrialization at this time was based almost exclusively upon the demand of the white minority.

The Second World War promoted further growth of metals and engineering, especially in fulfilment of military orders, while import-substitution was encouraged by the cutting off of normal sources of supply. Manufacturing in fact contributed more than mining to Gross National Product during the war. This growth was made possible by the reorganization of production and the greater use of machinery, but mainly by the setting up of many small plants, all of which were not to be viable under peacetime conditions.

It is difficult to say precisely when South Africa crossed the threshold into industrialization. By the late 1930s, and as a result of the war, there was quantitative growth and also the beginnings of structural change. The growing role of mining and foreign capital in industry has also to be noted. They were mainly responsible for technological change and the appearance of larger firms using modern machinery. As in other advanced capitalist countries, the tendency was for a smaller number of larger firms to dominate each field, but this was a very uneven process. By the early post-war period it can be said that South Africa was harvesting some of the benefits of the late-comer, notably in the import of technology and, to some extent, of capital, though much foreign investment represented a ploughing back of profits.

As industrialization advanced from the later 1930s, firms found it increasingly difficult to recruit adequate numbers of white workers, especially for the less skilled (or even semi-skilled) jobs created by mechanization. White workers tended to move up into the more highly skilled, supervisory and white-collar positions, leaving the lower-paid jobs to women, black and coloured workers.

Mining gained most from the job colour bar, as did white farmers (largely Afrikaners). In manufacturing, however, the colour bar's advantages to employers became increasingly dubious; but economic interests were apt to collide with ideology, as will be seen. This began to be apparent after the victory of the National Party in 1948, which reflected the resurgence of Afrikaner nationalism during and after the Second World War. This led to a fundamental change in policy, or more accurately the intensification of an existing one, in the shape of apartheid, an Afrikaner word which was to achieve international usage and, for opponents of racism, utter condemnation.

In its full-blown form apartheid was intended to make possible the separate development of the peoples making up the population of South Africa. The bulk of the black population was to be excluded from the towns and settled in quasi-independent 'homelands'. Massive enforced transfers of population took place and a strongly repressive state apparatus was established to enforce the laws. The apartheid regime was widely condemned abroad, sanctions were called for by the United Nations, and South Africa became something

183

of a pariah country, banned from the Olympics and other sporting events. Some foreign firms and banks withdrew from South Africa or cut back on their investments in response to pressures at home, especially after 1985.

The direct consequences of apartheid are difficult to separate from the matrix of interacting factors operating within the South African economy or resulting from its particular relationship to the world economy as a major gold-producer. To simplify somewhat, it may be said that there were three main factors: (1) the limitations of the import-substitution industrialization strategy; (2) the impact on the domestic economy of the importance of gold-mining; (3) the economic consequences of white supremacy and in particular of the post-1948 apartheid policy and, in the past decade or two, of attempts to modify or reform it. The wider political consequences and the future options for South Africa will not be dealt with here.

The import-substitution strategy, which was given its most conscious expression in Latin America, invariably runs up against limits. While it may be possible to cut down imports of consumer goods, as production increases it will be necessary to import larger amounts of intermediate and capital goods, thus reducing the saving in foreign exchange. If these items are to be produced at home further heavy investments will be required. To finance them it will be necessary to borrow from abroad or to enter into joint production agreements with foreign corporations. So the expected reduction of dependency may turn out to be an illusion.

In any case, while the composition of imports may change, their value may tend to increase. In order to pay a larger import bill there is pressure to increase exports. This raises the question of the competivity of local products in the world market and thus how to improve their quality and lower their costs of production. These problems became of growing importance.

The second question is the relationship of South Africa as a gold-producer to the world economy and its dependence upon the export of gold (as much as one-half of visible exports). The question may be asked, was industry 'parasitic' on the mines, or did mining limit the investment of capital in industry? The traditional view that gold-mining was the major driving force in the economy since the 1880s remains unquestionable. Indeed, it continued to hold a predominant position as a source of foreign exchange, a contributor to government revenue and the most powerful agent for capital accumulation in the shape of the giant mining companies. On the other hand, it may reasonably be claimed that excessive dependence on gold production has held back economic diversification and industrialization over the years. It continues to depend upon a huge migratory labour-force coming from a backward subsistence agriculture. Would South Africa have remained a dependent agrarian backwater without gold? It has after all plentiful supplies of coal and other minerals upon which a manufacturing industry might have been built. Leaving such specu-lation aside, a major factor in the economic well-being of South Africa is the world price of gold.

Consequently, when the gold price is high this will invigorate the economy, while a low or falling price will be depressive. Hence the raising of the gold price in the late 1930s helped to lift the economy out of depression. After the Second World War, and until 1971, the fixed gold price provided for by the Bretton Woods agreement was in operation. The mining companies thus sought to reduce costs of production, using, as before, the huge labour army of migrants, the major part of which now came from other parts of Southern Africa. After the ending of the fixed gold price there was a huge increase followed by oscillations at a more modest level. Hence the 1970s saw South Africa, the major gold-producer, enjoying windfall profits. Especially when prices came down the mining companies sought to reduce unit costs by introducing new techniques, opposing pressure from the miners for higher wages and opening up new mines. The total labour-force was still over half a million strong, moving to and from a background of subsistence agriculture into the mining com-pounds. The gold-mining industry faced rising costs with a more militant labour force as well as the fluctuations in the world price of gold. Despite the growth of secondary industry, gold-mining still remains a central part of the economy.

The third question is that of the economic viability of apartheid, a policy and ideology aimed to maintain white supremacy while exploiting black labour. This was to be done by the setting up of black 'homelands' based upon subsistence agriculture. At the same time, movement into the towns was to be rigidly controlled: since there was an indispensable need for cheap black labour some blacks had to be permitted to work in the industrial centres if not to live in them.

Within the apartheid system white workers, as well as coloured and Asian workers to a certain extent (although they did not have political rights), were integrated into a social welfare system. The intention was to give these workers a stake in the apartheid system, with measures which drew upon racial prejudice continuing and strengthening the traditional colour bar. On the other hand, blacks were relegated to the fringes of the system and divided into ethnically different 'nations', each with its own 'homeland' supposedly based upon historical and cultural connections. Their exclusion from political rights in the Republic thus received justification in the eyes of the architects of apartheid and their supporters.

Another factor in the policy of the National Party after 1948 was its assertion of Afrikaner nationalism against the hitherto dominant English-speaking establishment from which came the principal business leaders. Until the late 1930s there were few Afrikaners in prominent positions in business; subsequently there was a drive, supported by the state, to advance the interests of the nascent Afrikaner bourgeoisie. This was done partly through the public corporations (or 'parastatals') set up on the model of the Iron and Steel Industrial Corporation (ISCOR), partly through encouraging privately-owned Afrikaner businesses. Whether in secondary industry or in the service sector, these firms looked to the state for support through tariff protection, price supports and government contracts. New and more complex relationships between different sections of business and the state developed as the South African economy became more closely integrated with the world market and a prime investment field for multinational corporations.

All these changes and developments which accompanied or followed the adoption of apartheid policies had a contradictory character. On the one hand, the segmentation of the market meant that only the less than five million whites, making up one-sixth of the population, had the discretionary purchasing power to buy manufactured goods (especially consumer durables). Without an expansion of the market, industrial firms could not take advantage of the economies of large-scale production, as well as remaining dependent on tariff protection. On the other hand, as industrialization proceeded, so more and more blacks were needed in the labour-force, increasingly as semi-skilled or skilled workers, thus coming into collision with the principles of apartheid. This raised a further question of whether industrialization could proceed without an increase in the wages and living standards of the black workers, which would in turn raise costs of production. Also, as a result of the limitations of the import-substitution strategy, would it not be necessary for South African industry to become more export-orientated (perhaps with the newly industrializing countries of Asia as a model)? Another consideration was the type of goods that could be produced for the highly competitive world market, and indeed what part of that market South African firms could hope to target. Things were much simpler in the days when South Africa was essentially a gold-producer and exporter, and industry did not have to face such formidable competitors as Taiwan or South Korea.

Meanwhile, as apartheid was breaking down, industrialization was strenghtening the black working class. At the shop-floor level this took the form of strong trade unions which were legally recognized by the state. At the social level it was to be seen in the growth of huge squatter townships in the vicinity of the large towns housing the black labour force working in the cities or looking for work.

Finally, some of the characteristic features of South African industrialization may be noted. Firstly, it was belated by comparison, for example, with Canada. This meant that it could enjoy some of the advantages of the late-comer, such as the taking over of advanced techniques developed elsewhere or the attraction of foreign capital. However, there is some controversy about when industrialization properly began. Certainly capitalist relations were spread mainly as the result of mining, and long before there was much in the way of large-scale mechanized industry, which was a product of the period since the 1930s. Late-comer characteristics could then be seen in a number of tendencies. New industries were set up with large investment of domestic capital (as with mining) or foreign capital (as with the setting up of branch plants by forcign-owned multinational corporations). The industrial structure began to replicate, albeit on a smaller scale, that of the advanced industrial countries. A wide range of branded and packaged goods, originally American or European, were now made in South Africa for the domestic market. Because of the smallness of this market (mostly made up of some five million whites) the manufacture of the more costly items, such as durable consumer goods or motor vehicles, has been a very recent development. Thus while it could be said that Canada took to four wheels in the 1920s, this was not the case in South Africa until after the Second World War.

An important characteristic of the industrializing economy has been the role of the state. As well as providing the infrastructure – roads, bridges, transport, electric power, hospitals, oil pipelines, some housing and so on – the state has intervened directly as an agent of industrialization, notably through the Industrial Development Corporation, set up in 1960, which has sponsored and financed a series of industrial projects. Other 'parastatals' similar to ISCOR have been initiated, such as the South African Coal, Oil and Gas Corporation (SASOL) concerned with oil-refining and the making of petrol from coal, and the Electricity Supply Commission (ESCOM) in the generation of electricity. The purpose of the state sector was largely to serve the interests of private investment, financing vital sectors of the economy which private capital was unable or unwilling to undertake or to give assistance to the private sector. Most of secondary industry remains in private hands, though there are various ways in which the state, or one or another of its agencies, intervenes in promoting or financing private industry. During the 1980s, in accordance with an international tendency, state intervention has attracted increasing criticism, and more emphasis has been placed upon market forces, though this has not resulted in any significant changes.

In the meantime, the economy has become increasingly integrated into the world market, with greater dependence upon imported technology and interconnections with foreign multinationals. The severe limitations imposed by the narrowness of the home market were brought into focus. The apartheid regime had not brought stability at home and, especially from about 1986, international disapproval was expressed in United Nations sanctions and disinvestment by a number of foreign firms. These measures did not seriously harm the economy but they did slow it down and hit it at vital points, such as investment in high-tech fields. Despite heavy military expenditure, the Republic had not been able to impose itself as the dominant force in Southern Africa. It seemed that the exigencies of industrialization were undermining the bases of apartheid and it was increasingly clear that the more dynamic sectors of business had no more to gain from it, if they ever had. Social change was weakening the pro-apartheid forces: there was a decline in the weight of agriculture, more Afrikaners of the younger generation were drawn into business and were less committed to the Afrikaner ideology of which apartheid was a part. The problems (already discussed) of recruiting a labour-force for a growing manufacturing sector became more acute. More Africans had to be employed, and industry needed a more stable – and thus urbanized – labour-force. By 1970 manufacturing had become the largest employer and there was a large and growing black presence in the towns. This does not mean that apartheid was bound to disappear, but the balance of opinion was shifting. Apartheid had assumed a static society; it could not accommodate the upheavals associated with industrialization and the profound changes which had taken place since 1948. There was now a large, self-confident African nationalist movement and powerful trade unions which had obtained recognition from employers and the state.

These social and economic changes were the backcloth to the major shifts in government policy at the end of the 1980s and the early 1990s which represented the virtual abandonment of apartheid. It was recognized that there was a choice between apartheid and economic growth (and thus business profits). There was talk of the need for 'inward industrialization', offering more blacks the prospect of improving their material conditions. Import-substitution industrialization, although not entirely exhausted, had shown its inadequacies. In any case, if the South African economy was to extricate itself from the stagnation which had overcome it in the late 1980s it would have to increase its foreign earnings through a drive for 'export-orientated industrialization'. However, despite abundant reserves of low-wage black labour (with 30 per cent or more unemployment), it was difficult to conceive of South Africa competing with South Korea or Taiwan. The problem is to be able to carve out a niche in the world market under conditions of intense competition. What commodities could South Africa conceivably manufacture and sell to the advanced countries or to the less-developed African countries? Meanwhile, the portending enfranchisement of the black majority imposed further problems. In the 1980s blacks received about one-quarter of the national income while whites making up one-sixth of the population received 64 per cent (actually down from 74 per cent a decade earlier). The ratio of white to black average per capita income was eleven to one. The black majority obviously hopes that with political muscle will come an improved living standard – but how? Orthodox economists were wont to say that economic growth was favoured by the unequal distribution of income: ('White supremacy has been good for economic growth'). Whatever the outcome of the current political bargaining between the National Party and the black and other organizations, intractable economic problems will remain on the agenda for a long time to come. One thing can be said with some confidence and that is that if South Africa is going to be able to offer a reasonable standard of living to all its inhabitants in the future a great effort to industrialize will be necessary.

CHAPTER THIRTEEN
Problems and prospects

Many questions have been raised in the preceding chapters which cannot be answered from the data provided; important aspects of industrialization are not dealt with at all. This conclusion will indicate lines of approach for further study and some points of application outside the field of economic history in the narrow sense. From the examination of the industrialization process over the past 200 years, some uniformities stand out despite wide variations in detail between different countries. No later developing country could possibly reproduce Britain's experience, which took place as a spontaneous or organic process solely dependent upon the laws of the market, without the existence of precedents or a model. Possibly industrialization would have taken place somewhere else in Europe; there is evidence that much of the groundwork had been prepared, and the lag of the most developed areas behind Britain was not excessively wide. The concept of proto-industrialization suggests a move in that direction, with some areas becoming more industrial than agrarian; but it provides no inherent reason why a drive towards mechanization and the factory system should have been generated. Indeed, there were other parts of the world in which proto-industrialization could be discerned in the eighteenth and early nineteenth centuries, for example India or Japan. What has to be explained is the technological leap which came in Britain and nowhere else. As has been argued, this cannot be done without consideration of the social and economic environment favouring uniquely in Britain the application of known principles of science and technology to the mundane problem of increasing output for private profit. But although industrialization in its genesis was uniquely British, it was part of a European and worldwide transformation already going on for some centuries.

190

Industrialization was the outcome of the spread and development of the relations of production usually described as capitalist, that is to say in which the means of production are privately owned and turned towards the production of commodities for sale in the market employing free wage-labour. Slave economies, feudalism in its various forms and societies composed of small commodity producers all proved incapable of initiating a sustained process of growth on the technological basis of machine production. Moreover, industrialization has not been possible without the abolition of the old social relations and the establishment of new ones permitting the accumulation and investment of capital on an expanding scale. Wherever vestiges or leftovers from these old modes of production have survived they have tended to impede the development of the productive forces or have given industrialization a special and limited form, as for example in tsarist Russia or some colonial countries such as India. It can be said that Britain's priority in industrial development was above all a consequence of the more complete transformation of her socio-economic system on capitalist lines in the seventeenth and eighteenth centuries. It was not simply, therefore, that a certain number of factors had to be present in the right combination; there is a more complex task of investigating the genesis of industrialization in the pre-existing society in a way that is different when we consider industrialization by latecomers for whom a model was available.

This problem of the genesis of industrialization has not been dealt with systematically here; nor has it often been tackled in this way, if only because British industrialization has been considered in isolation from Europe and with inadequate reference to later experience. It is a problem concerned with the nature of pre-industrial society and the emergence of capitalist relations from the preceding feudal framework, often dealt with separately from that of industrialization. However, history is a continuum; it also imposes a search for origins and tends to push them back further into the past. In the case of Britain, for example, it may have been that feudalism, as an order imposed from outside, was different from the start to its continental forms and more subject to breakdown. A number of areas such as northern Italy and Flanders showed potentiality for industrial development long before the eighteenth century, but the transformation was cut short. This raises the problem of the false starts. Perhaps there were false starts in Britain too. Some historians claimed to have discovered an industrial revolution in the late sixteenth and early seventeenth centuries based on coal-mining and the growth of some large-scale industries. However, important as these indications of change were, they did not herald a general breakthrough but only transformed a small part of the industrial structure. It would be safe to say that industrialization required that technology should make possible a massive increase in the productivity of human labour in the production of articles of wide consumption. Attempts to promote industrial expansion artificially by state sponsorship in eighteenth-century Europe foundered on this point. Industrialization meant mass production for mass markets; an all-round transformation in the forms of labour and also in consumption. This meant the growth and constant reshaping of the internal market as new products became available; it also meant a search for foreign markets.

The role of foreign trade in industrialization can be seen from two points of view: its contribution to the initiation of the process and its contribution to the continuation. The first point arises in particular in relation to the British case, where it is sometimes asserted that the expansion of foreign trade in the eighteenth century was a vital prelude to the Industrial Revolution. Foreign trade is said to have provided markets for commodities that could not have been sold at home, raw materials necessary for industry (bar iron, timber and later cotton) and a field for capital accumulation. This sounds plausible until it is confronted with the statistical record, suggesting that not more than 9 per cent of the additional demand was accounted for by the foreign market.* Historians have tended to focus on foreign trade since customs records provided interesting material and foreign trading companies and merchants also left more evidence behind them than did businessmen whose activities were mainly confined to the home market. Indeed, statistics of home market growth must remain somewhat dubious. Even if it is accepted that in quantitative terms foreign trade was relatively less important than sometimes supposed, it could have had considerable significance in the reshaping of the economy. For example, particular industries could grow beyond the confines of the internal market and capital accumulated in foreign trade could be deployed more readily in relatively large amounts to influence industrial development. Moreover, once Britain had acquired a substantial lead, especially in cotton textiles, there is no doubt that foreign trade proved to be a pace-maker.

Furthermore, industrialization, though it went ahead first in Britain was bound to have profound international consequences and can be

* These are the calculations of Bairoch, P., in 'Commerce internationale et genèse de la révolution industrielle anglaise' in *Annales: Economies, Sociétés, Civilisations*, Vol. 28, No. 2 (1973) and not available in English

seen as a worldwide process. It brought into being an international division of labour in which industrial production was concentrated in Britain and a handful of industrializing countries in Europe and North America, later joined by Japan, while most of the rest of the world became producers of raw materials and foodstuffs for the world market they dominated. Capital accumulated in the hands of investors and capitalists in the industrial countries, while the rest of the world was opened up in a dependent relationship.

The division between the few industrial countries and the periphery of dependent primary producers became sharper still in the course of the nineteenth century. The latter carried on little trade among themselves, and their economies were geared to the production of one or a few products for export. There was no question therefore of a balanced growth of their economies. So far as a market for industrial goods existed it could be supplied mainly from external sources. The investment that took place in them was mainly foreign-controlled and had as its result the reinforcement of the dependent relationship. There was a difference, however, between the countries of white settlement with self-government and the rest of the 'colonies' inhabited by non-Europeans. Investment in the former, although mainly attracted by staple products, was not only much greater in per capita terms but also permitted a start to be made along the road to industrialization. A comparison between India and Canada, such as was made earlier, is instructive in this respect. However, the case of the Latin American countries shows that self-government did not by itself avert the danger of dependence. In fact, the ruling élites in these countries contented themselves with a position subordinate to foreign capital with little interest in promoting industrialization. Foreigners invested in railways or port facilities rather than factories and it is not difficult to see why. It enabled the resources of these countries to be opened up and imports to be distributed in the interior. Thus railways were built in South Africa to suit the needs of gold-mining. It was the First World War, and even more the Second, which led to the first attempts at import-substitution industrialization.

The uneven development of the different parts of the world economy from the time that industrialization began has given rise to two major fields of enquiry and controversy. In the first place, the irrepressible upsurge of nationalist movements in the dependent countries after the Second World War thrust firmly on to the agenda of politicians and economists the problem of 'underdevelopment' and its possible cure. This led to a new interest in economic growth and new branches of economics concerned with development. For the

193

governments of those countries now somewhat euphemistically described as 'developing', industrialization seems the way of escape from their enormous inherited problems of poverty and stagnation. In the second place, there has been a revival of interest in the historical origins and economic roots of this 'underdevelopment' under the general heading of imperialism. Although the drive for expansion by the advanced countries and the formation of colonial empires, especially at the end of the nineteenth century, was often handled under this heading by historians, the term itself, since it was elastic and was frequently used in a polemical sense, tended to fall into disrepute at least among the more conservative historians. Despite the renewed interest in recent years, the question of imperialism often finds little place in the writings of economic historians in the same way that relations with India are often left out of accounts of the British economy.

As for the approaches to these questions, two are of particular interest to the economic historian. The first, of which Rostow is one of the most powerful exponents, sees development as following a series of stages beginning with 'traditional society', with low productivity and thus a low level of income, going through a stage of preparation into rapid growth (the 'take-off') when industrialization begins and becomes self-sustaining. Theorists of this type imply that, provided certain conditions are fulfilled, most of today's 'developing' countries can proceed along the road of modernization and industrialization in much the same way as the present-day advanced countries did in the past. They see the nations of the world strung out in rising order of per capita income; but the laggards need not despair – a recipe similar to that followed by the leaders will eventually suffice to raise their incomes, if not to close the gap.

On the other hand, there are those who stress the international conditions under which successful industrialization was achieved by some countries and maintain that this was, at least in part, at the expense of those that 'underdeveloped', that is to say the sources of cheap raw materials and foodstuffs. Thus the gap between the advanced and the underdeveloped countries was a product of the world capitalist system and the political relationships of dominance and dependence to which it gave rise. As a general rule it may be said that the international economic environment does not permit most of the developing countries to follow the same path as the present-day advanced countries. The gap is now very much wider than it was when Japanese industrialization began. On the other hand, the experience of the 'newly industrializing countries', especially South

Korea, Taiwan and Hong Kong, suggests that under certain special circumstances a type of 'peripheral industrialization' may be possible, based on the export of commodities such as clothing and consumer electronics to the high-income countries. In some respects it may be said that these countries have become the workshops of the contemporary world, turning out by the million television and radio sets, video-casette recorders, hi-fi equipment and microwave ovens which have passed into the everyday consumption patterns of the advanced countries. In this process there has been a transfer of technology developed in the advanced industrial countries and often of capital as well through the setting up of branch plants by multinational corporations attracted by the existence of cheap and docile labour and stable political regimes. At the same time, a local entrepreneurial class has emerged, developing its own industries or entering into joint ventures with foreign capital. While most 'developing countries' have serious debt problems, the export-orientated newly industrializing countries have large trade surpluses. Their success has clearly depended upon the ability, and willingness, of the advanced countries to buy their exports. The newly industrializing countries of Asia are sometimes held up as examples for other developing countries. However, the fact that they have been able to insert themselves into the world market as exporters of manufactured goods, thanks largely to their principal resource, cheap and abundant labour, does not mean that the same option is open to other developing countries. In fact, by pre-empting a place in the world market they have probably made it more difficult for other countries to follow their example, especially in periods of recession. Moreover, there has long been a backlash against cheap imports from low-wage countries, especially in the case of textiles (e.g. imports into the United States are restricted). The shifting of production facilities from high-wage countries by the multinational corporations leaves unresolved social problems in older industrial areas in North America and Europe which have experienced 'de-industrialization'.

The question of industrialization and the historical experience of those countries that have industrialized are drawn very much into the front line of contemporary controversy. Indeed, the problems of the developing countries, particularly now that they are beginning to use what muscle they have as producers of scarce raw materials to drive harder bargains in the world market, are likely to become increasingly dominant in the remaining part of the twentieth century.

Reference to the policy of the ex-Soviet Union on this question is a reminder that forms of industrialization other than those taking place in response to market forces, the only kind studied in this volume, are possible. Soviet planning in the 1930s came at the end of a decade of debate on the possible methods of industrialization. Since by this time the main means of production had been nationalized and there was agreement about the need for industrialization, the debate was about the tempo of growth and the machinery through which it could best be brought about, given that there was a huge population of peasants mainly working their own plots and parting voluntarily with only a limited surplus necessary to feed a growing industrial population. Under the New Economic Policy in force from 1921, greater scope had been permitted for individual enrichment by the better-off peasants (*kulaks*) and market traders.

One tendency in the Soviet government, represented by Bukharin, thought that concessions of this type would have to be made for a considerable time and that industrialization would be slow ('at a snail's pace', he injudiciously said), dependent to a large extent on the market. The Left Opposition, whose leader was Leon Trotsky and whose chief economic spokesman was the brilliant Preobrazhensky, advocated faster rates of growth under centralized planning, the voluntary movement of peasants into collective farms and the syphoning off of part of the agrarian surplus to enable larger resources to be directed into the industrial sector. Stalin, who had strengthened his hold on the party and state apparatus after the death of Lenin in 1924, at first leant towards Bukharin's policy. The grain strike of the peasants at the end of the 1920s as well as panic at the foreign dangers facing the country brought a sudden shift in policy. This shift, a veritable 'revolution from above', comprised a campaign to drive the peasantry into hastily established collective farms, inadequately equipped with tractors, farm machinery and fertilizers, and against the stubborn resistance of a great part of the peasantry – labelled indiscriminately as '*kulaks*'. Forced-draught industrialization was begun at about the same time under the aegis of the first Five-Year Plan.

Soviet industrialization could be more accurately described as Stalinist industrialization, since it differed in crucial respects from that advocated by the main contenders in the industrialization debate as well as from economic planning as hitherto conceived of by Marxists. In the light of the subsequent vicissitudes and eventual collapse of the economy of the Soviet Union in 1991 it may be doubted whether its bureaucratic and arbitrary mismanagement deserves to be called planning at all. The system of distribution, which included a disproportionate share for the privileged 'nomenclatura', defied every socialist canon. The mass of the people had no real say in the drawing up of the plans and the ordinary consumer was always at the end of the queue. In the early stages of the self-styled planned economy it was claimed by Soviet policy-makers and theoreticians that in order to overcome the backwardness of the Soviet Union, and catch up with the capitalist world, priority would have to be accorded to the means of production industries, or Department I, as opposed to the industries producing consumer goods, or Department II. The theory behind this priority was that, until a heavy industry producing machinery and equipment had been built up, the consumer goods industries could not grow sufficiently rapidly to meet demand. Industrial development under the tsarist regime, while furthered by the state, had depended upon the market and was shaped by the interests of foreign capitalists. Thus pre-1917 Russia was weak in heavy industry and dependent upon foreign countries for much of its machinery. Stalin's policy, based on his theory of 'socialism in one country', aimed at self-sufficiency in this regard and was also influenced by the need to build up industries capable of supplying modern equipment on a large scale for the armed forces. This reached its peak during the Cold War when the huge demands of the war machine both for nuclear and conventional weapons absorbed manpower and resources which might otherwise have been available to renovate and modernize industrial plant and machinery, and improve the flow of goods to the consumer. The arms burden may well have been the factor which finally broke the back of the economy. In any case, the time when heavy industry had reached the point where it no longer had priority never seemed to arrive.

The Stalinist-type industrialization imposed enormous and perhaps unnecessary sacrifices on the Soviet working class, while forced collectivization resulted in the death of some millions of people; hardly a model to be followed. And yet, coming as it did at a time when the rest of the world was afflicted with the worst slump in history, Soviet planning and industrialization attracted considerable interest and has had an undoubted influence on economic policy even in the advanced capitalist countries. The lessons for the developing countries are still more direct, because they suggest an important difference between industrialization in such countries, if it is to have any hope of success, and industrialization in the advanced countries in the past. In the latter, the working of market forces determined the pace and nature of industrialization. As a consequence it was the consumer goods industries, or Department II, which took the lead in response to the growth of market demand, as notably for textiles.

The growth of Department I, producing the means of production, followed along in a complementary relationship: thus the growth of coal, iron and machine-making in the early nineteenth century. These industries tended to become relatively of greater importance with industrialization and to take over from textiles in governing its momentum because they were closely associated with the level of investment (and thus the ups and downs of the trade cycle). The later developing countries paid greater attention to the Department I industries from the start; German industrial strength, for example, was based upon coal and iron rather than textiles. The question is whether the developing countries should (or could) follow a pattern of industrialization in which consumer goods lead the way, or one in which capital goods lead the way. In the literature of the subject it is not surprising that Soviet theorists suggested the latter.

In the case of Indian planning since independence, the state has concentrated mainly upon building up Department I industries, such as steel and heavy engineering, power generation and machine-making, while leaving the consumer goods industries almost entirely to private enterprise. The object has been to give an impetus to industrialization and attain a greater degree of effective independence. It was assumed that private capital would be unable or unwilling to go into this sector on a sufficient scale to ensure growth, and that it was indispensable for the state to take the initiative. The fact that the bulk of the economy remained in private hands and was subject to the laws of the market, as well as the failure to carry out any fundamental structural reorganization of agriculture, distinguishes the Indian from the Soviet planning model. While taking over some of the features of Soviet planning, the development of the Indian economy overall has remained subject to the laws of the market. Whatever the growth record, boosted by state intervention and foreign aid and investment, the majority of the population has received little if any material benefit. Most of the gains have gone to a minority of landlords and wealthy farmers in the villages and to business, professional and bureaucratic middle-class people in the towns. These strata, forming between 10 and 20 per cent of the population, make up the market for most of the modern industrial products resulting from the industrialization carried out so far.

On the whole Indian experience is not a hopeful augury for the industrialization of the developing countries by trying to combine a measure of planning with the preservation of a private sector and without an agrarian revolution. These countries may thus have to choose other options as suggested, for example, by China. When this book was first written (1976–77) it was still possible to see China as offering a valid alternative for the 'developing countries'. Under Mao Tse-tung there had been a complete reorganization of agriculture with the setting up of communes. While under rigid discipline, the mass of the people appeared to be assured of a basic minimum of the necessities of life. China appeared to have avoided some of the problems of poverty, unemployed and hunger which plagued other developing countries. While industrialization was taking place in the main centres, still much influenced by the soviet model, despite the split with Moscow, more emphasis was placed upon small units of production and the harnessing of China's abundant labour to local projects. No doubt the picture was an idealized one. After the death of Mao a reaction set in against his policies, especially that of commune agriculture. His successors began to restore peasant agriculture and to appeal to material incentives. While maintaining a repressive policy against dissent, they sought closer ties with the capitalist countries, including Taiwan. Areas of China were opened up for the establishment of foreign-owned firms. China began to amass a considerable foreign debt.

The revolutionary atmosphere of the Mao era disappeared, and individuals were encouraged to pursue their own interests as long as they did not conflict with the goals of the leadership. In other words, post-Mao China began to return to the capitalist world. While industrialization continued and China was able to produce a variety of goods, including some embodying advanced technology, there was no longer a distinctive model of the sort that had existed in Mao's time. There was growing social inequality, peculation and corruption in high places, and insecurity and crime in the cities. It was very much like the old, pre-revolutionary China, with a privileged bureaucracy ruling the state as the mandarins had done in the past. The question remained as to whether the regime would be able to increase output at a sufficient rate to outstrip the rate of population increase, and so satisfy the needs of the masses.

It is natural in the light of history that people in the less-developed countries should identify progress with industrialization and seek to follow the example of the advanced countries. Whether it will be possible for them to do so remains an open question. In terms of statistical possibilities the earth's resources will not permit its expected mid twentyfirst century population of perhaps 10,000 million all to enjoy the high standard of living of the advanced countries. Indeed, the rate at which expendable resources are being used up raises doubts about the possibility of this standard being maintained anywhere into the next century. In the past industrialization really assumed an elasticity in the supply of resources that is being shown to be unrealistic. Continued industrialization on a world scale and along conventional lines assumes that science and technology will develop new sources of energy and new materials as existing ones are used up. But such an assumption may be ill-founded. A new equilibrium with the environment may have to be found, one that will necessarily limit the sheer outpouring of material goods and make necessary a corresponding adjustment of goals. The alternative may be a scramble to appropriate scarce resources by powerfully organized and equipped nations at the expense of the rest: inequality based upon brute force. However, a shift in goals is not inconceivable, and a tendency in that direction is already discernible in the advanced countries; though in most of the world it is still a question of survival. After all, industrialization did require, at its inception, a considerable shift in goals for large masses of people. The industrial entrepreneurs had to battle their way forward against a jungle of restrictions and face the disapproval of the old agrarian-based ruling classes. A new working class had to be brought into existence from a society of peasants and small independent producers. It had to be recruited and adapted to the entirely new conditions of work imposed by machinery and the factory system. The old tendency to labour until a customary standard had been reached and then to take time off had to be broken down by a new clock-governed, work discipline. Material incentives had, as it were, to be built into the psychological makeup of large masses of people, so that they responded to market forces, worked harder to buy more and thus made possible the self-expansion of the system. This was an unconscious but none the less objective process which all industrializing societies have had to undergo. There is no reason why this time as a conscious process, it should not be put into reverse, or rather why new goals and incentives should not take the place of a drive for accumulation and acquisition.

Bibliography

This bibliography is intended as a guide to the student rather than an indication of the sources of the present book, though it is that to some extent. It is confined to books and articles in English which might reasonably be found on the shelves of a university or polytechnic library or be available in the bookshops. It keeps down the number of articles to a minimum; in any case, they are usually of a specialized nature and will be picked up by using the bibliographies of the books listed. At any rate it is assumed that many readers will not need to consult all, or many, of the items. There is bound to be some overlap with the bibliographical note to *Industrialization in Nineteenth-Century Europe*, as well as with *Industrialization in the Non-Western World*, to which the reader should refer.

For reference and basic information use should be made of the *Cambridge Economic History of Europe*, now completed. The following volumes are relevant: Vol. vi, *The Industrial Revolutions and After*, Vol. vii (two parts), *The Industrial Economies: Capital, Labour and Enterprise*, and Vol. viii, *The Industrial Economies: The Development of Economic and Social Policies*. General eds, M. M. Postan, D. C. Coleman and P. Mathias (Cambridge University Press, 1965–89). *The Fontana Economic History of Europe*, ed. C. M. Cipolla (Fontana, 1973–7), has now been completed: *The Industrial Revolution*, Vol. 3, and *The Emergence of Industrial Societies*, Vol. 4 (in two parts), are the most relevant. The Cambridge volumes have some material from outside Europe, but the Fontana series tends to be strictly Euro-centred. The three volumes of *Documents of European Economic History*, ed. S. Pollard and C. Holmes (Edward Arnold, 1968, 1972 and 1973), are valuable stand-bys.

Cipolla's *Before the Industrial Revolution* (Methuen, 1976) provides an original analysis of pre-industrial society in Europe, while Fernand Braudel's *Capitalism and Material Life* (Fontana, 1975) covers much the same ground in a wide-ranging and stimulating but more descriptive survey. These books would provide a useful beginning for a comparison with pre-industrial societies in other parts of the world, such as India and Japan. The controversy sparked off among Marxist historians by the appearance of M. Dobb's *Studies in the Development of Capitalism* (Routledge, 1946) has been republished in an expanded form in *The Transition from Feudalism to Capitalism* (New Left Books, 1976) with an introduction by R. Hilton.

Students should be acquainted with W. W. Rostow's thesis as presented in *The Stages of Economic Growth* (2nd edn, Cambridge University Press, 1971) and also Alexander Gerschenkron's *Economic Backwardness in Historical Perspective* (Pall Mall Press, 1966). Rostow's model was mainly a generalization of Britain's experience; Gerschenkron's, that of Russia's and Germany's. Both have had a good deal of influence. The concept of 'proto-industrialization' referred to in the text gained currency after its use by F. Mendels, especially in the article entitled 'Proto-Industrialization: The First Phase of the Industrialization Process' in *The Journal of Economic History* (1972); see also his 'Social Mobility and Phases of Industrialization' in *Journal of Interdisciplinary History* (Autumn 1976). See also L. A. Clarkson, *Proto-industrialization: the First Phase of Industrialization* (Macmillan, 1985). M. Berg discusses proto-industrialization in relation to the industrial structure and technologies of the early period of industrialization in Britain in *The Age of Manufactures, 1700–1820* (Collins/ Fontana, 1985). On the question of why Europe was first in industrialization, see the important study by E. L. Jones, *The European Miracle* (Cambridge University Press, 1981) and his wider-ranging discussion of the causes of economic growth in *Growth Recurring* (Clarendon Press, Oxford, 1988). For other viewpoints see, for example, J. A. Hall's *Powers and Liberties* (Penguin, 1985) and *How the West Grew Rich* (I. B. Taurus, 1986) by N. Rosenberg and L. E. Birdzel.

There are a large number of reinterpretations of the Industrial Revolution. Here are some recent collections of papers and articles: J. Mokyr (ed.), *The Economics of the Industrial Revolution* (Allen and Unwin, 1985), in 'The Nature of Industrialization' series, ed. P. Mathias and J. A. Davis, also by Mathias and Davis, *The First Industrial Revolutions* (Basil Blackwell, 1989) and *Innovation and Technology in Europe* (Basil Blackwell, 1991); R. Sylla and G. Toniolo (eds), *Patterns of European Industrialization* (Routledge, 1991).

For a quantitative approach, see N. F. R. Crafts, *British Economic Growth During the Industrial Revolution* (Oxford University Press, 1985).

For advanced study of contemporary industrialization processes see H. Chenery, *Industrialization and Growth: a Comparative Study* (Oxford University Press, New York, 1986, sponsored by The World Bank).

Many of the topics that have engaged the major research interest of British economic historians in recent years are now covered in two collections: *Debates in Economic History* (Methuen), under the general editorship of P. Mathias, and *Studies in Economic History* formerly edited by M. W. Flinn (Macmillan). This series is now called *Studies in Social and Economic History* ed. T. C. Smout. The first brings together already published articles on a given theme, usually with a substantial introduction by the editor of the volume concerned. The second enables an author to sum up the present state of knowledge and the degree of controversy on a particular question. Both tend to be too advanced for the student new to the subject and reflect rather professional preoccupations; it might also be asked whether economic historians have always been pursuing the right questions.

To some extent economic history may be the victim of its own success as it gives rise to new disciplines (such as urban history), loses ground to social history or is absorbed into general history. There is still something of an insular tendency in Britain (in the choice of research topics, for example), though less than when this book was first written. International conferences have helped as well as journals such as *The Journal of European Economic History*, published (in English) by the Banco di Roma. It still seems to take a long time before important foreign works are translated into English (indeed if they ever are).

For the peasantry, see *Peasants and Peasant Societies*, ed. Teodor Sahin (Penguin, 1971), a book of readings mainly from a sociological point of view. For the economic historian the peasantry generally figures as the somewhat shadowy victim of agrarian change and as the subject of it only when it revolts, as in France in 1789. Thus it is to works on agriculture that we have to turn. See, for example, *Agrarian Change and Economic Development*, ed. E. L. Jones and S. J. Woolf (Methuen, 1969); B. H. Slicher van Barth, *The Agrarian History of Western Europe* (Edward Arnold, 1963); and M. Tracey, *Agriculture in Western Europe* (Jonathan Cape 1964). The classic studies of the French peasantry in the Revolution by Georges Lefebvre are not available in English.

For technology see the volume in the Methuen series edited by A.

E. Musson, *Science, Technology and Economic Growth in the Eighteenth Century* (Methuen, 1975), especially the Preface; also the chapter by S. Lilley, 'Technological Progress and the Industrial Revolution 1700–1914' in the *Fontana Economic History of Europe*, Vol. 3 (Fontana, 1973) and D. S. Landes, *The Unbound Prometheus* (Cambridge University Press, 1969). The views of A. P. Usher are to be found in the book of readings, *The Economics of Technological Change* (Penguin, 1971) along with other analytical treatments of the question. Marx's views are worth referring to in *Capital*, Vol. I, Chapter xv, (various editions). For a thorough recent study see I. Inkster, *Science and Technology in History* (Macmillan, 1991).

Transport is often dealt with in relation to something else or is otherwise given a dull, factual treatment. There are histories of particular forms of transport and also the attempts by the 'new economic historians' to estimate the contribution they made to economic growth. For a good summary see the chapter by L. Girard in The Cambridge Economic History of Europe, Vol. vi (Cambridge University Press, 1965). There is a more recent account which discusses the 'new economic history': S. P. Ville, *Transport and the Development of the European Economy, 1750–1918* (Macmillan, 1990).

On banking there are the two useful collections of studies of banking in different countries edited by R. C. Cameron, *Banking in the Early Stages of Industrialization* (Oxford University Press, 1967); and *Banking and Economic Development* (Oxford University Press, 1972). See also the chapter 'Banking and Industrialization in Europe, 1730–1914' in *The Fontana Economic History of Europe*, Vol 3; and C. P. Kindleberger, *The Formation of Financial Centers: a Study in Comparative Economic History* (Princeton, 1974). A collection of documents ed. B. L. Anderson and P. L. Cotterell, *Money and Banking in England* (David and Charles, 1974) sums up the present state of knowledge in brief editorial comments; there is also a good bibliography.

On the role of the state, now more controversial than ever, see P. Deane, *The State and Economic Growth* (Oxford University Press, 1986). The main points can be followed up in the different national histories; see especially Vol. viii of *The Cambridge Economic History of Europe* which also takes in Japan and the United States, and the chapter by B. Supple in *The Fontana Economic History of Europe*, Vol. 3. K. Polanyi's *The Origins of Our Time* (Gollancz, 1945) is enlightening on the background. For Britain, see A. J. Taylor, *Laissez-faire and State Intervention in Nineteenth-century Britain* (Methuen, 1972); and J. R. Hay, *the Origins of the Liberal Welfare Reforms, 1960–14* (Methuen, 1975), both in the *Studies in Economic and Social History* series. For an excellent general study see G. V. Rimlinger, *Welfare policy and Industrialization in Europe, America and Russia* (John Wiley, 1971). There is a large and growing literature on social policy.

The late nineteenth century has often been seen in terms of 'the Great Depression'. Despite the attempts by some writers to minimize it, at least as often understood, even S. B. Saul, in his *The Myth of the Great Depression* (Macmillan, 1969), does not deny that in the late nineteenth century 'Britain and several countries overseas went through unusual and worrying experiences.' The article by H. Rosenberg, 'Political and Social Consequences of the Great Depression of 1873–1896 in Central Europe' appeared in the *Economic History Review*, Vol. XIII (1943). For some of the new trends in the United States see A. D. Chandler, 'The Beginnings of "Big Business" in American Industry', which first appeared in *Business History Review* (Spring 1959); it is also to be found in various anthologies, including R. Andreano (ed.), *New Views on American Economic Development* (Schenkman, 1965). W. G. Hoffman's figures appear in *The Growth of Industrial Economies*, translated by W. O. Henderson and W. H. Chaloner (Manchester University Press, 1958).

On imperialism and associated problems there has been a considerable literary output in recent years. The best introduction is R. Owen and B. Sutcliffe, *Studies in the Theory of Imperialism* (Longman, 1972) for the economic aspects, and for its place in British political history, B. Porter, *The Lion's Share* (Longman, 1975). See also the papers in *Imperialism and After* (Allen and Unwin, 1986) edited by W. J. Mommsen and J. Osterhammel (sponsored by the German Historical Institute), for some new perspectives.

Since the first edition of this book *The Cambridge Economic History of India* (Cambridge University Press, 1985) has appeared. Vol. 2 (ed. T. Raychaudhari and I. Habib) provides a useful reference book for the period of British rule. The best introduction, however, is by a German scholar, D. Rothermund, *An Economic History of India* (Croom Helm, 1988). There is no shortage of books on Indian economic history. One of the best on the twentieth century is R. J. Roy, *Industrialization in India, 1914–1947* (Oxford University Press, New Delhi, 1979). A British introduction is B. R. Tomlinson, *The Political Economy of the Raj* (Macmillan, 1979).

The following is a selection of other works. There are some excellent articles collected in M. D. Morris et al., *The Indian Economy in the Nineteenth Century* (Indian Economic and Social History Review, 1970). A good introduction is A. Maddison, *Class Structure and Economic Growth: India and Pakistan since the Moghuls* (Allen and

Unwin, 1971). I. Habib, 'Potentialities of Capitalistic Development in the Economy of Mughal India' in *Journal of Economic History* (1969) attempts to answer some important questions about the nature of the economy prior to British rule. Among books on special topics the following may be selected: D. H. Buchanan, *The Development of Capitalistic Enterprise in India* (Cass reprint, 1966); B. Chandra, *The Rise and Growth of Economic Nationalism in India* (People's Publishing House, New Delhi, 1966); S. C. Gupta, *Agrarian Relations and Early British Rule in India* (Asia Publishing House, Bombay, 1963); K. W. Kapp, *Hindu Culture and Economic Development* (Asia Publishing House, Bombay, 1963); M. D. Morris, *The Emergence of an Industrial Labour Force in India* (University of California Press, Berkeley, 1968); B. Sen, *Evolution of Agrarian Relations in India* (People's Publishing House, New Delhi, 1962); S. K. Sen, *Studies in Industrial Policy and Development of India* (Progressive Publishers, Calcutta, 1964); D. Thorner, *Investment in Empire* (University of Pennsylvania Press, Philadelphia, 1950); D. and A. Thorner, *Land and Labour in India* (Asia Publishing House, Bombay, repr. 1965). Several studies from Moscow have appeared in English, including V. Pavlov, *The Indian Capitalist Class* (People's Publishing House, New Delhi, 1964); V. Pavlov et al., *India: Social and Economic Development (18th–20th centuries)* (Progress Publishers, Moscow, 1975); G. K. Shirokov, *Industrialisation of India* (Progress Publishers, Moscow, 1973); and A. I. Medovoy, *The Indian Economy* (Progress Publishers, 1984). An attempt at a Marxist analysis has been made by B. Davey in *The Economic Development of India* (Spokesman, 1975).

While the first edition of this book complained that 'the volume of writing on Canadian economic history in recent years has not been large' it is pleasant to record an increased amount of work. Besides the old standby, W. T. Easterbrook and H. G. J. Aitken, *Canadian Economic History* (Macmillan, 1956), heavily weighted with facts, there is a similarly large textbook, which adopts a thematic approach and tries to make the 'new economic history' palatable for students, by W. L. Marr and D. Paterson, *Canada: an Economic History* (Macmillan of Canada, 1980). A useful and concise introduction is R. Pomfret, *The Economic Development of Canada* (Methuen, 1981); critical of the staple thesis.

A number of useful essays have been brought together by W. T. Easterbrook and M. H. Watkins in *Approaches to Canadian Economic History* (Carlton Library, McClelland and Stewart, 1967). See especially the articles on the staples theory by M. H. Watkins and G. W. Bertram. The same series also contains an edition of the famous report by W. A. Mackintosh, *The Economic Background of Dominion-Provincial Relations* (Carlton Library, McClelland and Stewart, 1964). Writings of a famous economic historian who popularized the staples theory of growth are brought together in H. A. Innis, *Essays in Canadian Economic History* (University of Toronto Press, 1956). On growth, see T. N. Brewis, *Growth and the Canadian Economy* McClellan and Stewart, Toronto, 1968), and N. H. Lithwick, *Economic Growth in Canada: a Quantitative Analysis* (University of Toronto Press, 1967).

The attempt by J. Smucker to use a theoretical framework derived from Marx and Weber does not quite come off and his book does not fully live up to its title, *The Industrialization of Canada* (Prentice-Hall, 1980). For a substantial account of Canada's most industrialized province, see I. Drummond, *The Economic History of Ontario, 1867–1939* (Toronto, 1986). R. T. Naylor's *History of Canadian Business* (two volumes in one, Lorimer, 1975) puts forward a controversial thesis blaming businessmen for allowing the penetration of American capital into Canada instead of themselves investing in industry. On this question see also K. Levitt, *Silent Surrender* (Macmillan, 1970). Collections of papers include *Perspectives on Canadian Economic History* (Capp, Clark, Pitman, 1987).

Two of the standbys on Japanese industrialization have tended to date and are not enthralling reading; they are G. C. Allen, *A Short Economic History of Modern Japan* (Allen and Unwin, 1965) and W. W. Lockwood, *The Economic Development of Japan* (Oxford University Press, 1966). The earlier book by E. H. Norman (a victim of McCarthyism), *Japan's Emergence as a Modern State* (Institute of Pacific Relations, 1940) is a powerful analysis. See also *The State and Economic Enterprise in Japan*, ed. W. W. Lockwood (Princeton, 1965).

The Cambridge History of Japan Vols 4 and 5 (Cambridge University Press, 1988, 1989), ed. J. W. Hall et al. contains chapters on the economy which are useful for reference. The studies by T. C. Smith, *The Agrarian Origins of Modern Japan* (Stanford, 1959) and *Native Sources of Japanese Industrialization* (University of California, 1988) are interesting; he sees Japanese society as being similar to, but profoundly different from, that of the West. A useful, mainly statistical introduction is in A. Maddison, *Economic Growth in Japan and the USSR* (Allen and Unwin, 1969). The article by R. P. Sinha, 'Unresolved Issues in Japan's Early Economic Development' in *Scottish Journal of Political Economy* (June 1969) is very useful. See also the book of readings, *The Japan Reader I: Imperial Japan: 1800–1945*, ed. J. Livingston, Joe Moore and F. Oldfather (Penguin, 1967). A brief introduction for foreign students is M. Takahashi, *Modern Japanese Economy since the Meiji Restoration* (University of Tokyo, 1967).

Economic history is widely taught in South Africa; clearly a case where a society's development cannot be understood apart from its economic base. The considerable literature reflects wide ideological divisions as well as the contradictions arising from the very conditions of existence of a white-dominated state in Southern Africa. The books selected reflect these features. The best introduction to the history of South Africa is the classic by C. W. De Kiewiet, *A History of South Africa: Social and Economic* (Oxford University Press, 2nd. edition, 1988). The best economic history text is J. Nattrass, *The South African Economy: its Growth and Change* (Oxford University Press, 2nd. Edition, 1988). See also, F. L. Coleman (ed.) *Economic History of South Africa* (Haum, 1983). A useful account of 'The Development of South Africa's Manufacturing Industry' by G. Bloch is in *Studies in the Economic History of Southern Africa* (Frank Cass, 1991) Z. A. Konczacki et al (eds.). Also, B. Freund, 'The Social Character of Secondary Industry in South Africa' in *South African Studies*, No. 5 (Raven Press), A. Mabin (ed.). A variety of (clashing) views on the economics of apartheid are to be found in the following: M. Lipton, *Capitalism and Apartheid* (Wildwood, 1986); R. W. Bethlehem, *Economics in a Revolutionary Society* (Donker, 1988); J. W. Cell, *The Highest Stage of White Supremacy* (Cambridge University Press, 1982); M. J. Murray (ed), *South African Capitalism and Black Political Opposition* (Schenkman, 1982) and R. M. Price, *The Apartheid State in Crisis* (Oxford University Press, New York, 1991).

The economic perspective from the standpoint of neo-classical (free market) economics is discussed in D. Kantor and D. Rees, *South African Economic Issues* (Juta, 1982). For views close to the African National Congress see S. Gelb (ed.), *South Africa's Economic Crisis* (David Philip, 1991). For the history of one of South Africa's major corporations, see D. Innes, *Anglo-American and the Rise of Modern South Africa* (Heinemann, 1984). Basic facts and statistics are to be found in *South Africa; an appraisal* (2nd. ed. The Nedbank Group, 1983).

The questions raised in the concluding chapter would warrant a bibliography of their own. G. Myrdal's *magnum opus*, *Asian Drama*, 3 vols (Penguin, 1968), contains a mine of material. While the Rostow view is more or less accepted by the 'modernization' school, A. G. Frank can stand as a representative of one of the opposing schools; see for example his *On Capitalist Underdevelopment* (Oxford University Press, Delhi, 1975) and *Capitalism and Underdevelopment in Latin*

America (Monthly Review Press, 1969); for a somewhat similar view see P. A. Baran, *The Political Economy of Growth* (Penguin, 1973). The Soviet views referred to can be found in V. L. Tyagunenko et al., *Industrialization of Developing Countries* (Progress Publishers, Moscow, 1973). For an interesting 'ecological' interpretation, see R. G. Wilkinson, *Poverty and Progress* (Methuen, 1973).

On the newly industrializing countries of Asia, see, e.g., F. C. Deyo (ed.), *The Political Economy of the New Asian Industrialism* (Cornell University Press, 1987); for the less 'successful' Asian countries see B. L. C. Johnson, *Development in South Asia* (Penguin, 1983).

For a fuller bibliography of contemporary industrialization processes see *Industrialization in the Non-Western World.*

Index

accumulation of capital, 12, 17, 191
Acts of Parliament, 32
Act of Union (South Africa), 179
advanced countries, 1, 4, 8, 23, 90, 112, 176, 187, 189
advertising, 119
Africa, 177–8
Africans, 178–90
Afrikaners, 177–8, 181, 183, 186, 188
agrarian crisis, 36
agrarian individualism, 35
agrarian reforms, 18
agrarian relations, 11, 41, 131, 132, 133
agrarian sector, in Japan, 169–70
agrarian system, 7, 24, 128, 129
agriculture, 7, 20, 24, 126, 128, 129, 131, 140, 144, 165, 168, 188
  see also under peasantry and separate countries
Alpine regions, industry in, 116
aluminium, 115
America, 46, 52, 62, 67, 198
  see also United States
  American banking system, 82, 89
  American capital in Canada, 157–8
  American capitalism, 91
  American challenge, 124
  American colonies, 15
  American invasion, 124
  American ships, 69–70
  American System of Manufactures, 52
Amer-Indians, 145
ancien regime, 158
Anglo–French Treaty of Commerce (1860), 101
Anglo–Saxon countries, 104
apartheid, 171, 183–6, 188–9

Aristotelian, 75
Arkwright, R. entrepreneur, 46
armed forces, 90, 92, 197
arms spending, 103, 197
artisans, 20, 46, 52, 96, 115, 129, 130
Asia, 28, 163, 174, 178
Asiatic people, 69
Atlantic, 70
atom, 24
Australasia, 67, 104
Australia, 104
automation, 24

backward countries, 10
  see underdeveloped countries
Bairoch, P., historian, 192
balance of payments, 127, 135, 144, 174
Bank Charter Act (1844), 81, 83
Banking School, 81
Bank of England, 76–80, 83–4
Bank of France, 84
Bank Restriction period, 78
banknotes, 78
banks, banking, Ch. 6 *passim*, 6, 56, 62, 102, 117–19, 126, 160, 167, 171–2
  in America, 82
  in Canada, 82
  in France, 84–8
  in Germany, 67–9, 82
  in India, 82, 137
  in Japan, 89, 171–2, 181
  in Scotland, 79
  banques d'affaires, 8
Bavaria, 97
beaver, 145
Belgian steel, 138
Belgium, 111

210

Index

Index